"Green is a journalist by trade, and she builds *Something Must Be Done About Prince Edward County* on reams of painstaking research, interviews, and historical documents. . . . What matters is the scant but vivid voice she gives to the black citizens Prince Edward County silenced for decades, and the light the book shines on how much—and how little—has changed."

—*Entertainment Weekly*

"The decision to write the book took guts, because Green knew she would be publicly castigating not only her grandparents but other relatives and friends as well. . . . Her involvement in the shameful history of Prince Edward County provides the book with an emotional edge not easily forgotten."   —*Minneapolis Star-Tribune*

"This intimate and candid account . . . personalizes politics, jangles nerves, and opens minds."   —*Richmond Times-Dispatch*

"A vivid reminder of how things were, not so very long ago."

—*Harvard Magazine*

"Green feels compelled to stare down her past, and she does so with uncommon humanity."   —New York 1 News

"Kristen Green was born to write this book. . . . [She] deftly interweaves the personal and the historical into a compelling narrative that leaves no stone unturned. . . . [N]ot only fascinating but cinematic. . . . [A]n award-worthy book."   —*Booklist* (top pick)

"Powerful. . . . The author movingly chronicles her discovery of the truth about her background and her efforts to promote reconciliation and atonement. A potent introduction to a nearly forgotten part of the civil rights movement and a personalized reminder of what it was truly about."   —*Kirkus Reviews* (starred)

"Green's work brims with real-life detail from the journalist's eye and ear and joins the likes of Diane McWhorter's *Carry Me Home* in further developing the dimensions of the South's desegregation struggle—particularly from the perspective of white communities—for general readers and scholars of the late twentieth-century civil rights movement."   —*Library Journal*

"This book is both intimate and ambitious: Green gives the reader a far-reaching account of the political and social history of segregation and desegregation in Virginia at the same time that she tells the stories of scores of individuals, herself included, to reveal the very real human costs of this history. Moving and clear-eyed, damning and hopeful: this is an essential read."

—Jesmyn Ward, author of *Men We Reaped*

"The story of integrating American public schools has been drowned out by the much louder, dramatic, and violent history of the civil rights movement. But no struggle is as heartrending as one involving children. Return with Kristen Green to her hometown in Virginia to find out how people she loved and admired could have supported such an injustice. You'll be wiser if you do."

—Charles J. Shields, author of
Mockingbird: A Portrait of Harper Lee

"*Something Must Be Done About Prince Edward County* is an engaging and well-written book on the impact of school closures, told from a unique biographical perspective. Using her skills as a journalist to uncover the layers of history in her hometown, Green delivers a deeply moving portrayal of one of the very sad histories in American race relations. This book is difficult to put down and a must-read."

—William Julius Wilson, Lewis P. and Linda L. Geyser
University Professor, Harvard University

"Mystery wrapped in history with a touch of suspense and personal horror: Kristen Green's stunner of a book is a ride back into a past you'll wish had never happened. This is historical sleuthing at its finest."   —Chris McDougall, author of *Born to Run*

SOMETHING MUST
BE DONE ABOUT
PRINCE EDWARD COUNTY

SOMETHING MUST BE DONE ABOUT PRINCE EDWARD COUNTY

A Family, a Virginia Town, a Civil Rights Battle

KRISTEN GREEN

HARPER PERENNIAL

NEW YORK • LONDON • TORONTO • SYDNEY • NEW DELHI • AUCKLAND

HARPER ● PERENNIAL

A hardcover edition of this book was published in 2015 by HarperCollins Publishers.

P.S.™ is a trademark of HarperCollins Publishers.

HarperCollins books may be purchased for educational, business, or sales promotional use. For information, please e-mail the Special Markets Department at SPsales@harpercollins.com.

FIRST HARPER PERENNIAL EDITION PUBLISHED 2016.

Designed by Leah Carlson-Stanisic

Library of Congress Cataloging-in-Publication Data has been applied for.

ISBN 978-0-06-226868-6 (pbk.)

16 17 18 19 20   ov/rrd   10 9 8 7 6 5 4 3 2

FOR JASON, AMAYA & SELMA

"Yours is the light by which my spirit's born:
you are my sun, my moon, and all my stars."

—E. E. CUMMINGS

Contents

A Note to the Reader

This book is a hybrid of history and memoir. No names have been changed and no characters have been invented. In a limited number of instances, I have omitted an individual's name when it was not essential to the story. Anything in quotes was said to me, witnessed by me, or taken from a reputable publication. Sections of this book are written from my memory, which is, of course, fallible. I may remember events differently than other people.

I have chosen to refer to my family's longtime housekeeper, Elsie Lancaster, by her first name in this book because Elsie is what I have always called her. I refer to the students shut out of school by their first names because they are children when readers first meet them, and to avoid confusion, I chose to continue using their childhood names throughout. I use the term "black" instead of "African American" and "white" instead of "Caucasian" because this is how people refer to each other in my hometown to this day. I have included slurs, as offensive as they are, to accurately portray how people in Prince Edward spoke in the 1950s and 1960s, and how some people still talk today.

This book covers a period of more than sixty years. I have done my best to capture the key moments, both in Prince Edward's history and in America's civil rights history, but I had to leave many paths unexplored for the sake of length and focus. In addition, I did not have space to include the stories of all of the students I interviewed who were shut out of school. On their own, they could have filled a book. Their experiences were heartbreaking, inspiring, and important. I wish I could have written about every last one of them.

SOMETHING MUST
BE DONE ABOUT
PRINCE EDWARD COUNTY

Prologue

I grew up thinking of her as our Elsie, not as someone's mother. She was the black woman who had cleaned my parents' house once a week since 1975. She had worked for my grandparents for two decades before that. Until I was in high school, she was also the only black person I knew.

Every Wednesday morning at nine, Elsie Lancaster appeared at the back door of our house in Farmville, a small rural town in southern Virginia. As a young child, I listened for Elsie to be dropped off and then ran to let her in. Petite and bird-thin, she wore a neat, pressed cotton blouse with a cardigan, an A-line polyester skirt, and panty-hose with sensible leather shoes.

Her shy face, typically cast down, brightened when she saw my three younger brothers and me. She hugged us, then quickly got to work, hanging her sweater in the closet by the front door and pulling out the Electrolux cylinder vacuum. She pushed it back and forth over the dark brown living room carpet while one of my twin brothers, a toddler at the time, rode on the back. She darted up the L-shaped staircase on wiry legs, her tiny but strong arms lugging the heavy cylinder behind her.

My mom would make a quick escape to run errands, leaving Elsie to keep an eye on my brothers and me. Elsie also swept and mopped the kitchen floor, scrubbed the bathroom sinks and toilets, and dusted the furniture. She hummed and sang while she worked, and I'd trail behind her as she made her way through the house, waiting until she had silenced the vacuum for an opportunity to talk with her.

Mom returned in time to prepare sandwiches for lunch, and when I was older, I sat with Elsie and my mother around an oval oak table in our tidy kitchen. We held hands and prayed before the meal. *God is great. God is good. Let us thank Him for our food. By His hands we all are fed. Give us, Lord, our daily bread.*

My mom liked to say that Elsie was part of our family. My parents treated her better than other families who expected their housekeepers to eat separately. Mom bought Elsie birthday and Christmas presents, sent her home with vegetables from our garden, and, most important, treated her with kindness and respect. My grandmother prepared her lunch, instead of the other way around. Yet I didn't realize that Elsie's own family had been ripped apart two decades earlier, when she was working for my grandparents, and that my grandfather was partly to blame.

In 1959, faced with a federal court order to desegregate the schools, Prince Edward County's civic leaders refused to fund public education. They locked the doors of the public schools instead. It was a dramatic stance that set them apart from communities across the nation that preferred desegregated schools to closed schools. White leaders, including my grandparents, established a private school for their own children. The school was attended by both of my parents, and, years later, by my brothers and me as well. Black students like Elsie's only child—her daughter, Gwendolyn—had nowhere to go. For five years, the public schools remained closed.

During my childhood, our family rarely discussed what had happened and only in broad strokes. No one mentioned that my grandfather had opposed integration. No one explained the effects of the school closures on our loyal housekeeper, her daughter, and other black residents of our county. And Elsie never revealed that she and her husband, Melvin, had made a heartbreaking decision to ensure that their daughter received an education. I didn't know that Elsie regularly replayed that decision in her mind, wondering if she had done the right thing. That she would second-guess it forever.

I didn't know that the past lived on, a painful history hidden in plain sight.

PART ONE

Separate but Not Equal

The only places on earth not to provide free public education are communist China, North Vietnam, Sarawak, Singapore, British Honduras—and Prince Edward County, Virginia.

—US attorney general Robert F. Kennedy, March 19, 1963, Louisville, Kentucky

Chapter 1

A Perfectly Charming Southern Town

It was a crisp autumn day when I stepped off the porch of my parents' slate-blue house in Farmville and walked a block to the home of a man I had known most of my life, a man who founded the white private school I had attended. It had been fifteen years since I'd graduated and left town.

I passed through the gate in front of his brick colonial, stepped onto his porch, and rang the doorbell. A black nurse answered the door. She escorted me through a formal living room, decorated with Oriental rugs and ornate lamps, to a dark den in the back of the house where Robert E. Taylor was sitting in a recliner, his feet elevated.

Taylor had always been a rotund man with a hearty laugh and a booming voice, a boisterous Southern storyteller who paused only long enough to take a puff of his pipe or to sip a cocktail. On this day, in November 2006, I found a different person. At eighty-seven, Taylor was a tamer, thinner version of himself, breathing with the help of oxygen.

"I got pieces of both kidneys cut out and half a lung removed," he told me, and he was still hanging on.

For several years, I had wanted to learn more about what had happened in Farmville before I was born, events in which Taylor had played a key role. His daughter-in-law warned me that his health was failing and suggested that if I planned to interview him, I should do it soon. I wanted to talk about his life's greatest work: the establishment of a whites-only academy, founded under the auspices of the Prince Edward School Foundation, which he oversaw for decades.

Taylor told me he supported the decision to close the public schools rather than integrate them. As a young businessman, he joined forces with other white town leaders, offering to use his contacts as a contractor to build a permanent location for the white school, Prince Edward Academy. "I've been on the board from the first day we talked about it," he said.

He expected me to know the details of the school's history, a history I was never taught. When I asked why he became involved, he answered as if the question didn't deserve a response.

"Because I had three little children and the schools were closed," he snapped, briefly forgetting his Southern manners. "Do you know any better reason to form a school?"

I had flown home to Virginia from Massachusetts, where my husband, Jason Hamilton, was attending graduate school and I was working as a correspondent for the *Boston Globe*. I'd come to talk with Taylor about what had inspired him to establish a school that excluded half of the community's kids. I wanted to know why he and other white leaders had preserved this segregated academy for decades, a relic of the past.

I had known Taylor since I was toddling around in diapers. I grew up babysitting his grandchildren and later asking them to join the girls club I had founded. After we all went off to college, when a couple of years' age difference didn't mean much, we drank beer together in smoky bars at Thanksgiving and Christmas. Taylor's daughter-in-law was a close friend of my mother's. His daughter had been a childhood friend of my aunt's. My maternal grandparents, Samuel Cecil and Emma Lee Patteson, had known him for decades, too. Papa, my grandfather, had served on the academy's board with Taylor for twenty-five years and rarely missed a meeting.

Papa died while I was in college and now Mimi, my grandmother, was sick, and we didn't expect her to live much longer. I wanted Taylor to tell me what Papa couldn't and Mimi wouldn't. I needed to know why white county leaders had believed so adamantly that black and white children shouldn't go to school together.

I was struggling to come to terms with my community's history and my own grandparents' beliefs. When I tried to talk to Mimi about how dramatic—and unique—the county's stance had been, she responded, "It didn't seem like a big deal at the time." That was all she would say.

Knowing my hometown's history seemed particularly compelling after I married a multiracial man of American Indian descent. Jason and I wanted to start a family—a family that would represent what Taylor, my grandfather, and other white town leaders had tried to prevent: the mixing of the races.

I sank into Taylor's sofa, listening as he described life in small-town Virginia when the schools closed.

"Betty," he yelled out to his petite, gray-haired wife in the next room. "Betty, where's that picture of the school board?"

"It's right over there on the table."

I hopped up from the sofa and grabbed two enormous three-ring binders. I lugged them over to his recliner, and he flipped through the laminated pages, pointing to people I had known my whole life—many of them already dead. My beloved Papa's face smiled back at me from the pages.

The scrapbook was filled with newspaper profiles of a younger Robert Taylor. As I examined the photographs and skimmed the headlines, he boasted that he and his friends used public school resources to establish the white school. "We never did let the children miss a year," he said.

When he didn't mention the black students who were left out, I asked if he ever regretted that they were denied an education. "Do you feel you have anything to atone for?" I asked.

"Not a damn thing, as far as I'm concerned," he said. "We were taking care of our children."

He heard something he didn't like in my line of questioning. He paused and looked at me as if I were a stranger, someone who had betrayed his Southern sensibilities. "Living around Northerners has changed you," he said with disdain.

He was right. I had changed. By then, I had lived outside the South for nearly a decade and traveled extensively. After college I moved to Oregon, then California, before crisscrossing the country again, bound for Massachusetts. I had watched a friend get married in Peru, spent four months traveling mostly alone through Central America, and flown to India. I had worked as a reporter since graduating from college, focusing my efforts on people of color and the poor, those that newspapers tend to overlook.

I asked Taylor if, here at the end of his life, he still considered himself a segregationist. He found the question ridiculous. "Of course," he said. "Always have been."

His black nurse was in the next room as Taylor told me he was accustomed to spending time around blacks. He described how another black nurse had raised him from birth and how he had regularly played with black children. Growing up in Prospect, a little railroad community ten miles west of Farmville, he noticed there were twice as many black residents as there were whites.

But he believed that black and white people were different, he told me. "The morality in the black school"—the black public schools—"was so low that our white children wouldn't be able to understand," Taylor said. He cited tired stereotypes of how black men behave. "You'll see high school graduates in legal problems or else they're living off some black woman—or several black women. They don't work, but they have money and nice automobiles and all that," he said. "If I offered seven of 'em jobs, I couldn't find one who would take one."

I sat in his den, spellbound, rapidly taking notes as his oxygen machine hummed. This was just the kind of conversation the journalist in me found scintillating. I wondered how these black men he described would have fared if they, or perhaps their parents, had gotten an education. On a personal level, his words stung. I was sad that at the end of his life his beliefs seemed not to have changed since he'd founded the academy nearly fifty years earlier. He had wanted his children to get a quality education. But he had also wanted to maintain the purity of the white race, he told me.

"It doesn't sound good," he confessed. "It's going to make a lot of folks mad. But it's true."

I asked why separating black and white children in schools had been important to him. "Do you know how many white girls got pregnant by black guys?" he responded.

During the sixteen years I lived in Farmville and the subsequent four years that I came home during college breaks, I had only one white friend who dated a black teenager. I couldn't think of anyone who'd gotten pregnant, let alone pregnant with a mixed-race baby. And I didn't remember seeing mixed-race children in town. It didn't seem to be an issue. I shook my head.

Taylor didn't buy it. "You don't?" he asked again, glaring at me.

"I've never heard anybody talk about it," I told him.

"You've never heard anyone talk about it?" Now he sounded incredulous.

White girls aren't used to "the pressure," he told me. He meant the pressure to have sex, as if white girls didn't get that from white boys. Black boys impregnate white girls, he explained, and the girls' parents end up raising half-black, half-white babies: "pinto" babies that nobody wants. The children are socially ostracized, he said, marked by "a cross to their very soul."

I'd never heard the term "pinto" applied to a person before, but the minute he said it, I understood what he meant.

Taylor knew my husband was not white. Taylor's son and daughter-in-law had been guests at our wedding, witnesses to the vows Jason and I had exchanged under an enormous oak tree on a farm at the edge of town. The next day they hosted brunch for our wedding guests at their lakeside cottage.

It dawned on me that Taylor wasn't talking simply about the mixing of the black and white races anymore. He was talking about my husband, and about the children Jason and I wanted to have. Multiracial babies that Taylor both pitied and reviled.

Disgusted, I wanted to get up and leave, to put this whole interaction behind me. But as I sat across from him, frozen, maintaining my Southern civility, I thought about having this conversation with my own grandfather and what it might have revealed about his beliefs. I wondered if Papa had shared Taylor's feelings about mixed-race children. And I realized that Taylor believed that I had betrayed them both in some fundamental way by embracing what they had tried to protect me from, what they most feared.

My face flushed in anger as Taylor talked. I wanted to dismiss him as the last of his kind—a closed-minded old man whose time had nearly come. But weeks before his death, he was giving voice to what I knew many whites in my hometown, perhaps even my own dying grandmother, still believed, more than fifty years after the *Brown v. Board of Education* decision: blacks and whites don't belong together.

SIX MONTHS LATER, I SAT in the front of Farmville Baptist Church, staring at the sanctuary's lavender walls, tall ceilings, and enormous brass chandeliers as an uncle delivered my grandmother's eulogy. He told stories about how Mimi had loved her church, and what a good mother and grandmother she had been. He mentioned her devotion to her mother and to Papa as their health declined. He talked about how generous she was, replacing a needy family's refrigerator and helping a nurse make rent.

As the minister led the congregation in a series of prayers, I considered that my grandmother would never meet the baby growing in my belly. My mind wandered back to my childhood in Farmville, a childhood Mimi had filled with love, the kind of childhood I wanted for my child.

I remembered sitting in this sanctuary, on these pews, twenty-five years earlier, as Mimi removed peppermint candies from crackling wrappers and handed them to me. Papa, a church deacon, slid down the velvet-cushioned pew to sit next to us after he passed the collection plate. During the hymns and the prayers and the long sermon, I daydreamed about the lunch we would eat together at Cedar Brook Restaurant after the service, the fried chicken that would be my reward for accompanying my grandparents and sitting still during church.

Mimi and Papa were numbers three and four in my life, right behind my parents. To my younger brothers and me, they were perfect—silver helmet hair, boat-sized Bonneville and all. They were generous participants in our lives. They rooted for us on the basketball court and cheered our flips off the diving board. Mimi planned elaborate Easter egg hunts, summer cookouts, and family trips to the beach. After a day at work as a dentist, Papa took us fishing at his farm in neighboring Buckingham County, where he tended a herd of Hereford cattle. We regularly visited their pretty colonial-style brick home on Oak Street, less than a mile away from our house. Decades earlier, they had built the house along a little country road that was later expanded to a four-lane highway. While Mimi gardened, we climbed the hill in the backyard. At dinner, she served us seconds of meatloaf without asking if we cared for more and stuffed us full of hot rolls.

Mimi and Papa had both grown up on farms in Buckingham. Papa's mother's family had lived in the county for generations. According to a family history, his great-great-grandfather Colonel Jesse B. Holman had owned "a great many slaves," and his great-grandfather Samuel Daniel Holman had instructed his children to care for the family's black employees who lived on the 1,400-acre family homestead when he died in 1905. The family of Papa's father had arrived in Buckingham County in the eighteenth century and at the time was considered to be among the wealthiest families in Virginia. His father had attended medical school and become a doctor, and Papa, the second of eight children, went on house calls with his dad and helped on the family farm. Papa attended the University of Richmond, then dental school at the Medical College of Virginia. He and Mimi, who met on a double date, married in 1943, and then Papa was sent to China and India, serving as a captain in the US Army Dental Corps. Mimi, whose parents were farmers, had attended Pan American Business School and worked as a teller in a Richmond bank. When Papa returned, they briefly lived with her parents while he established a dental practice. Soon, they built their brick home in Farmville, where Papa moved his business and became active in local civic groups. They had three children, and my mom was the middle child.

Mimi and Papa are the foundation of many of my childhood memories. In 1978, my parents dropped my brother Chaz and me at their house, across from Southside Community Hospital, when my mom went into labor with a third child. I was making construction-paper cards for my soon-to-arrive sibling—one in case it was a girl, and one if it was a boy—when Dad surprised us with the news that Mom had delivered twin boys.

Months later, when I underwent testing for high blood pressure at the University of Virginia hospital, Mimi and Papa appeared in the intensive care unit with a tic-tac-toe game for me. Later that year, when I had surgery to replace a blocked artery to my kidney at Vanderbilt University Medical Center, my grandparents drove to Nashville to visit.

No matter the time of year, we saw them a couple of times a week, usually more. During the winter, Mimi dropped off a pot of beef stew for our dinner. In the summer, she sat in the shade of our backyard in a yellow sundress, watching us play in the pool, rarely wading in. Her coifed hair, styled weekly at the salon, wasn't meant to get wet. On warm evenings, she drove by the house to find us still playing in the front yard, chasing fireflies and finishing off popsicles, and we ran out to her car in bare feet.

Mom regularly loaded the four of us into her tan 1972 Volkswagen Squareback station wagon and drove to Mimi and Papa's house, where my brothers and I paraded around the circular driveway ringing their home, twirling bright umbrellas from Mimi's collection. We counted passing cars, making our own games. We sipped lemonade while rocking in iron chairs on the breezeway—the porch between the back door and garage.

Mimi made a big deal of holidays and birthdays. She hosted two dozen family members at Thanksgiving, seating us all around an oversized table in the dining room, added on to the house for precisely those occasions. For my birthday, she took me to dinner at the Golden Corral, where she told me to select a dessert from dishes of green Jell-O and sliced chocolate cake on the cafeteria line and place it on my plastic tray. While I filled my plate at the salad bar, she slipped away to find the restaurant manager and ask him to wish me a happy birthday over the loudspeaker. When I turned ten, Mimi threw a birthday luncheon for me in the same dining room where we ate our holiday meals, serving chicken tetrazzini on dainty porcelain plates. It was too formal for a kid's birthday, but I loved it. As a child, I thought my grandparents could do no wrong.

Nothing was better than having their attention all to myself, and I waited to be invited to sleep over. During the day, I would play with paper dolls on the cold cement floors of the basement while Mimi sewed. While she tended her irises, I rode my bike around the driveway. When she applied lipstick to her plump lips or rouge to her rounded cheeks, I dressed up in her jewelry and tried on her clothes. At night, I worked puzzles on the floor of the dark wood-paneled den, where the back wall was plastered with dozens of framed family photographs. Papa stretched out on his brown recliner beside me, unwinding. Mimi prepared dinner, slapping pile after pile of buttery mashed potatoes on my plate, until I complained that my belly ached. The next day, she took me shopping for a new outfit at a discount store before dropping me at home. As I climbed out of the car, she would reach into her purse and slip a crisp five-dollar bill into my hand.

Papa, a tall man with large ears, a long nose, and a warm, friendly smile, sometimes took my brother Chaz and me on excursions to his four-hundred-acre farm. We rode on the bench seat of his covered GMC pickup truck while he drove his property line, checking on his cattle and looking for breaks in the barbed wire fence. Several dogs trailed behind, including my aunt's three-legged collie, Lucky. Papa jumped out of the truck to unlock the heavy metal gates, leaving us in the toasty warmth of the cab, where his hunting rifles hung over our heads. On other outings, we played in the barn while he baled hay or helped him pluck potatoes from the fields. When he took us fishing, Chaz and I ran along the lakeshore while Papa sat patiently waiting for a nibble. Later, we grilled hot dogs and roasted marshmallows on a fire he had built.

Now, in 2007, fourteen years after his death, I sit listening to the preacher talk about my grandmother, glancing a few pews in front of me, where my mom is seated next to Elsie. For decades Elsie had avoided my grandparents' church, where in 1963 twenty-three people, including Elsie's daughter, Gwen, were arrested for disrupting the service after they were refused entry. The police arrived as the group of black students and their leaders were kneeling on the church steps and singing. Today Elsie was in the church sanctuary for my grandmother's funeral, sitting with my mom and her sister and their children, in the ultimate display of loyalty to our family.

I had this sinking feeling that we hadn't been nearly as loyal. We had ignored the impact of the school closures on Elsie and other black residents. Whenever I asked about the reason the white school existed, my mom said that her parents had been looking out for their children. But who had been looking out for the black children? And what had been the cost to them? What was the story I hadn't been told?

Prince Edward Academy hadn't been established, as I long believed, in reaction to the public schools' closing. Instead, it had been dreamed up five years earlier as a way for the county to avoid integration. And my grandfather had been in on it from the beginning.

FARMVILLE IS CALLED THE "HEART of Virginia" for its location at the geographic center of the state. It is, as its name implies, a small town surrounded by lush farmland and gently rolling hills.

It's also a place you don't just happen upon. Rather, you have to make a point of getting there. It's a college town, population 8,079—including about 3,500 students of the state-funded Longwood University. Farmville couldn't be more different from the Virginia suburbs of Washington, DC, 170 miles to the north. On a drive south on Interstate 95, through the traffic of northern Virginia, past Richmond and onto local roads, row after row of identical suburban houses and strip malls full of Bed Bath & Beyonds finally give way to farms dotted with cows, hay bales, and faded red barns. Here, on the edge of the Black Belt, the South's agricultural heartland named in part for its large black population, farmers set up roadside stands to sell just-picked vegetables, fresh eggs, handmade soap, and wildflowers straight from the fields.

At the Prince Edward County line, an enormous farm unfolds, its bright green fields and pair of grain silos reminders of the county's agricultural base. In this county of twenty-three thousand, rural roads weave through 354 square miles of countryside, passing chicken coops and dairy farms. They wind around a patchwork quilt of tobacco fields and an assortment of historic homesteads, decrepit mobile homes, and tidy brick ranchers.

This is the country's piedmont region, where the Blue Ridge Mountains of western Virginia meet southern Virginia's rolling hills. It is sometimes referred to as "God's country" for its scenic landscape of wooded forestland, slightly sloping terrain, and grassy fields that stretch as far as the eye can see. It's a part of the world where things don't just look different, they are. Relaxed and slow. Nobody is in any particular hurry, and nothing seems to change, not very quickly anyway. Even conversation comes slow. Words get strung out like laundry on a clothesline, "stairs" becomes *stay-urs* and "past" is pronounced *pay-ist*. My dad likes to say that the signs at the entrance to town should read, "Welcome to Farmville: Set Your Clock Back Twenty Years."

It is the Virginia of my childhood, where summers are sultry and the house cooled with noisy box fans, the air always thick. Where plump, juicy tomatoes are plucked from backyard gardens and washed down with jugs of sweet tea. Where the roads are full of mud-caked Ford pickups, where children skip school at the start of hunting season and the region's twice-weekly paper, the *Farmville Herald*, runs photos of them holding the prized bucks they score. Where nobody is a stranger for long. Where the back door is always unlocked and where neighbors are glad to lend a cup of sugar, where handwritten thank-you notes are expected, where people bring over a casserole or a plate of ham biscuits when a family member passes. Where the police seize stills of moonshine and cows escape their farms, blocking country roads. Where locals stare as if they're mapping your face, trying to identify your kin. Where roots go back generations, where people never leave.

Now a Hampton Inn sits at one entrance to town across the street from an eightplex theater, enormous brick buildings incongruously perched on formerly wide-open fields. A development of new condominiums has also popped up, seemingly out of nowhere, like a crop of corn. A smattering of auto body shops, tractor parts stores, and humble brick office buildings line this stretch of blacktop leading to town. Just down the road, the streets of downtown Farmville feel more cheerful, even quaint. Three blocks of brick buildings that date as far back as the 1800s have been mostly restored to preserve the town's original character. With welcoming signs hanging from handsome lanterns and young trees planted in the medians, the quiet Main Street is charming. The gracious campus of the now coed Longwood, founded in 1839 as Farmville Female Seminary Association, sits blocks away.

Many Virginians know Farmville for one thing: not its tragic history, but Green Front Furniture. Wealthy homeowners from up and down the Eastern Seaboard flock to the town to fill their houses with Oriental rugs and fine wooden furniture at bargain prices. In the 1960s, Richard "Dickie" Cralle, a graduate of Prince Edward Academy and Hampden-Sydney College, helped his grocer father grow the business from a discount furniture store to one that would gross sixty million dollars a year at its peak. For decades, he has traveled the globe collecting furnishings, paying cash to buy up warehouses full of hand-stitched rugs, carved treasures, and traditional furniture. In his original store on Main Street, Oriental rugs hang on two-story racks, like dresses in a department store. Over time, the famously cranky Green Front owner bought at a considerable discount a handful of abandoned tobacco warehouses. He also purchased the Craddock-Terry Shoe Corporation plant and Baldwin's Department Store, eventually amassing more than a dozen buildings and renovating them into imposing showrooms. The smell of tobacco, which once permeated the buildings, has grown faint.

By resuscitating old warehouses, Cralle breathed new life into the town. He lured a restaurant, Charley's Waterfront Café, into one of the tobacco warehouses. He also donated land along the Appomattox River to the town, and the property has been converted to a park where free summer concerts are held. His stores attract tens of thousands of visitors each year who wouldn't otherwise come to Farmville, providing customers for other downtown businesses. Across the street from his first building sits the historic—and, now, bright yellow—Walker's Diner. A European bakery, a modern art gallery, and several antiques shops have sprung up, too. The single-screen theater, the only place to see a movie during my childhood, was transformed into an outdoor amphitheater after its roof caved in, while a former Roses department store became an art museum. The town converted yet another former tobacco warehouse into a market where farmers sell produce year-round. Near the original Green Front store, the state opened a thirty-one-mile crushed limestone trail that weaves through three counties on old railroad tracks, crossing over the historic 125-foot High Bridge that sits in Prince Edward County.

The south end of Main Street provides a glimpse of how downtown Farmville might look were it not for Cralle—nearly deserted, like many small-town centers. There are a few locally owned stores that have been around for decades, including the athletic goods store Pairet's, Key Office Supply, and Red Front Trading Company, a clothing store that sells work overalls. But most of the retail spaces are empty or boarded-up. Gone is the First National Bank that once anchored downtown and over which my grandfather's dentistry practice was located. The old bakery, where my parents bought me cinnamon twists when I was a child, gone. Martin the Jeweler, the family-owned store that repaired a ring given to me by my grandparents, also gone. Vital businesses have long since relocated to shopping centers on the outskirts of town or closed for good.

Farther south, on the same block as First Baptist Church, the historic black church Elsie has long attended, Longwood has built a brick village of apartments for college students. It offers ground-floor stores such as a college bookstore operated by Barnes & Noble and a Chick-fil-A. The rest of the university's handsome campus sits across Main

Street on the edge of downtown, and it features a street-turned-brick-walkway that links its academic buildings with dorms, a library, and the athletic complexes. Across High Street from the campus, a statue of a Confederate soldier stands upright, a reminder of the allegiances of this town and the whole South during the Civil War.

Farmville once had several grocery stores, but only a Food Lion and a Walmart Supercenter remain. The sole department store is a sad little Belk in a mostly deserted shopping center. A few years ago, a Lowe's home improvement store arrived just outside town. The shopping center where I walked as a child is now mostly empty—Kroger, Dairy Queen, Country Cookin, and a discount store have all left. The company that operates the town hospital is converting some of the vacant buildings into medical offices.

The rural county is majority white—about 63 percent—and not particularly segregated outside of town. White and black farmers are neighbors, sharing tools as well as the crops they grow. In one community, blacks and whites experimented with combining their churches but ultimately decided against it. But the town of Farmville itself remains segregated, though not as dramatically as when I was a child. Back then, it was unusual, even suspicious, to see blacks walking down streets stocked with elegant, century-old houses. A black family that moved onto my parents' block a few years ago reported feeling accepted.

East of First Avenue, blacks occupy house after house. The homes range from small wooden structures in need of repair to well-maintained brick ranchers with short-cropped lawns. Longwood students have encroached on this historically black neighborhood that sits on the edge of the college's campus. Black businesses such as barber shops and funeral homes, along with a black church and a Masonic hall, are still located there. Some of the businesses date back to the late 1950s and early 1960s, when a larger black neighborhood was dispersed after the state used eminent domain to take homes—many of them black—and a black church to allow Longwood to expand. Heading east across Main Street, another predominantly black neighborhood sits at the foot of the hill below Fuqua School, and a road winds around to a subsidized housing complex with eighty units, primarily occupied by blacks.

In Prince Edward, a portion of the population can afford groceries only after welfare checks are issued. The county has a nearly 20 percent poverty rate, almost double the state's, with a per capita income of $17,500. Yet college professors and other professionals stop by the European bakery on Main Street to buy fresh baguettes, gourmet cheeses, and bottles of French wine. Walmart is the common ground, the place where the two worlds collide: the desperately poor and the professionals both shop here, though some higher income residents prefer to drive to Richmond for groceries, carrying coolers to store perishables.

Farmville is still the quiet community where I spent long summer afternoons floating in my parents' pool. On the surface, it is a perfectly charming Southern place to grow up, a seemingly wholesome town to raise a family.

That is, until you dive in.

CHAPTER 2

Homecoming in Black and White

On our wedding night, after Jason and I recited the vows we had written to each other, the ground soggy under our feet, we kissed on my parents' front porch swing as a photographer documented the moment.

Being with Jason was easy. We met and wanted to be together, and that was it. I never worried about how my parents would react to my having a boyfriend who wasn't white, and I didn't care what people in my hometown thought. I was deep in love, and Farmville was 2,500 miles away from San Diego, where I worked as a newspaper reporter.

Maybe I would have been more worried had Jason been black. In that case, the residents of my town likely would have expressed overt disapproval. I figured that a boyfriend with mixed racial heritage—difficult for most to identify—was easier for Southern whites to accept. With skin the color of raw pecans and shiny black hair tucked behind his ears, Jason appears South Asian to some.

Still, when I wanted to take him home to Virginia for the first time in 2001, a few months after we met in San Francisco, I asked Mom to make sure that my grandmother knew that he wasn't white. It was Jason I was thinking of, not Mimi. I was trying to avoid an encounter like my friend, Crissy Pascual, had with a white boyfriend's mother when they were introduced: the woman refused to shake her hand. My grandmother was old-fashioned—she still referred to blacks as "colored" and Papa had used the word "nigger." I had a strong sense that she would be less than thrilled with my bringing home a brown boyfriend. By making sure Mimi knew what to expect, I was hoping to protect Jason from the humiliation my friend had experienced. I never asked my mom how my grandmother responded. I didn't want Mom to give voice to Mimi's disapproval. I saw it as Mimi's problem, not mine. It was easier not to care what other people thought if I didn't know.

After Jason proposed, we decided to get married in California, where we had met three years earlier. Our lives were there and so were most of our friends. Plus, it would be easiest for us to plan a wedding where we lived.

I first noticed Jason on the dance floor of a nightclub when Crissy and I were visiting San Francisco for a weekend. I watched him dancing across the room, carefree, caught up in the music. When our eyes met, I flashed a bright smile, and I looked up a moment later to find him standing in front of me. We danced and talked the rest of the evening. He called me in San Diego the next week, just after I had returned home from work at the newspaper. I slipped off my flats and walked barefoot across the smooth hardwood floors as we talked about our experiences growing up in the South—he was from Fort Worth, Texas—and about newspapers, books, and travel. He told me about moving to California to attend Stanford University. I talked about my job as a reporter. He had a quiet confidence, different from other guys I had dated. Seven months later, after a long-distance romance, he moved to San Diego to be with me.

It made sense to get married in the place where we began our life together. Although Farmville was my hometown, it didn't connect to our life as a couple. But as I scouted wedding venues in San Diego, none of them felt right. I thought about how expensive attending our wedding would be for my parents, brothers, aunts and uncles and cousins, and for Jason's mom and stepfather, who lived in Maryland.

If we married in California, our relatives would have to travel across the country, rent cars, and reserve hotel rooms. Mimi wouldn't be able to make the trip. The wedding would cost significantly more in California, and Mom couldn't help with planning.

My mind wandered to Virginia, to its lovely historic homes, to its enormous magnolia trees and fragrant flowers, to the farms that stretched into the horizon, to my quaint Southern town. I pictured the food we could serve, from steaming shrimp and grits to country ham tucked inside delicate rolls, food that would echo our Southern upbringings. When my dad asked us to consider a Farmville wedding, he sealed the deal. Getting married in my hometown was the most natural thing to do. I could envision the ceremony on an estate that family friends owned on the outskirts of town. I could see us reciting our vows under a tree next to the house, which dates to the 1800s, surrounded by fields of flowing yellow grass where horses graze. We could move the reception one-and-a-half miles to my parents' intimate backyard, which contained my family's history. The party would take place under tents in my mom's gardens, bursting with zinnias. In my mind, I could picture the whole event unfolding.

But then my thoughts turned to Jason, to his father and brother, and to the Asian, Latino, and black guests we planned to invite. I remembered Farmville's history, still vague in my mind. What would it be like for Jason and his family and our many friends of color to walk into a community that was still segregated—geographically, economically, and socially?

I thought of them streaming into my little town, bringing their different religions, cultures, and accents. I wanted them to see the beauty of the South, particularly my little neck of the woods, to admire the homes with wraparound porches, the extravagant gardens, and the rural landscape. But I worried about them encountering its ugliness, too. It would only take one slur uttered by a drunk guest to make me regret the decision.

We moved forward with a Farmville wedding, despite these doubts. I joked that it could be the most diverse event ever held in my hometown, a bad attempt at humor to distract from an uncomfortable truth. Deep down, I knew some residents of my hometown would object to my marrying someone of a different race, and this was a sad reality I didn't want to confront.

But I had to. My grandmother never warmed to Jason. Our friends noticed how segregated the town is. Most of the waitstaff at our wedding was black while our neighborhood was white. The *Farmville Herald* declined to run a picture of Jason and me in its free wedding announcements, citing a policy to run only brides' photographs. My mom canceled her subscription in protest, informing the publisher, whose grandfather had publicly opposed race mixing in the 1950s, that the policy had racist undertones. Worst of all, the judge who wed us would later tell Jason, at a Christmas Eve party in his home, to "ride that Indian pony," implying that Jason had been accepted to business school at MIT only because of his American Indian heritage.

THE FIRST TIME I NOTICED an interracial couple I couldn't stop staring. My parents had driven my brothers and me to Virginia Beach for a long weekend. I was sitting on a blanket next to my mom, reading a book while my brothers played on the beach, tossing a Frisbee with my dad. I was eleven, maybe twelve.

I glanced over at another young family spreading out their blanket next to ours. I had never seen a family like this one. Black dad, white mom. The three kids looked different from any children I had encountered: creamy brown skin and curly brown hair. Neither black nor white, but both. Finally, I asked my mom about these children.

"It must be hard for them," she told me.

She said little more, but the message was clear. There was something impractical, maybe even abnormal, about people of different races marrying.

Many Virginians viewed race mixing in a harsher light. After all, the state had spawned the landmark civil rights case *Loving v. Virginia*. Eighteen-year-old Mildred Jeter, a part-black, part–American Indian woman, and her neighbor and childhood sweetheart, Richard P. Loving, who was white, were living in Virginia when they married in June 1958 in Washington, DC—an act then considered a crime in two dozen states, including Virginia. The commonwealth's antimiscegenation laws, adopted in 1662, said that any marriage between a white and a nonwhite person was void, even if the couple had wed in a place where the marriage was legal. The Lovings had hoped to go unnoticed when they returned to live in rural Central Point in Caroline County, ninety-five miles south of the nation's capital, home to a large mixed-race community. Instead, the following month, the county sheriff and two deputies raided their home early in the morning, shining flashlights in their faces.

One of them asked Richard Loving, "Who is this woman you're sleeping with?" Mildred Loving answered, "I'm his wife." Richard Loving pointed to the couple's marriage certificate, but the sheriff told the couple, "That's no good here." The Lovings were charged with felony unlawful cohabitation and jailed, and they faced a punishment of up to five years in prison.

The judge in the case, Leon M. Bazile, told the court that "Almighty God created the races white, black, yellow, Malay, and red, and he placed them on separate continents. . . . The fact that he separated the races shows that he did not intend for the races to mix." The Lovings accepted a plea bargain that called for a one-year prison sentence to be suspended if the couple left Virginia for twenty-five years.

They moved to Washington, DC, and had three children, traveling back to visit family separately. But in 1963, Mildred Loving had had enough. She decided she wanted to live with her family in Virginia, and, after watching the civil rights movement unfold, she was willing to fight for that right. She reached out to Attorney General Robert F. Kennedy, who referred her to the American Civil Liberties Union. The ACLU took her case to the Virginia Supreme Court of Appeals and then to the United States Supreme Court. In its unanimous 1967 decision, the high court found that state bans on interracial marriage—the country's only remaining segregation laws—were unconstitutional.

But perched on the sand, my eyes fixed on the three mixed-race children, I didn't know any of that. Nor did I know that I had just glimpsed my future.

I AM SITTING IN MY newborn daughter's tiny nursery in Somerville, Massachusetts, staring at the pale pink walls as I rock her to sleep in my arms.

The October Sunday she arrived was crisp and cold, the night the Red Sox clinched the 2007 World Series. My mom caught a last-minute flight after my water broke Saturday morning, and she accompanied Jason and me to the hospital when we checked in Sunday, supporting me in the delivery room, rubbing my back, feeding me sips of Gatorade from a straw. Moments after our baby was born, she snapped a photo of Jason and me, glowing, holding our tiny daughter, whom we named Amaya.

Now, in December, I am waking every three hours to feed her, giving more of myself to another human being than I had ever considered possible. I am physically depleted and sleep-deprived, yet utterly and completely in love, content to be her mother. Holding Amaya on my lap, I caress her chocolate-malt skin. I stare into her almond eyes, with their hint of green, and I tease her smattering of cinnamon hair. I hold her little hands in mine and admire her feet and her impossibly small toenails. I rub her cleft chin, identical to Jason's, and her

generous lips and wide nose that resemble mine. Taking in all her miniature features, I feel a rush of gratitude and love. I would do anything
to protect our daughter.

In the weeks after her birth, after my mother flew back to Virginia
and Jason's mother came and went, I have spent most of each day
alone with Amaya. Jason is busy in his final year of graduate school,
trying to complete two degrees. He hunches over his computer writing
papers and works with other students to wrap up group projects. Se-
cluded in our old house, I bundle up Amaya and head outside, meeting
with other new moms, stopping by the market, anything to interact
with adults. The days are impossibly long.

Jason comes back from school and, taking Amaya from my arms,
encourages me to escape the house. He tidies the mess I've made of the
kitchen and living room and asks about our day, keeping me company
until bedtime. But then, during 3:00 a.m. feedings, I am alone again.
Other than a few rowdy college kids who stumble down our street,
Amaya and I are the only people awake. In these hours of profound
isolation, my thoughts turn to my own childhood.

Home is the house where I grew up, the six of us eating dinner together every night around the oval wood table tucked into the kitchen.
It is Mom making dinner, and Dad lounging in his green leather chair,
describing a story he read in the *New Yorker*. It's my brothers laughing, playing basketball on the street, skateboarding down the sidewalk, sneaking out of the house at night. Home is my high school, the
pretty downtown streets, the beautiful tobacco and dairy farms that
have long sustained my community.

Even during this sleep-deprived new-baby haze, I know I will want
to share the story of my hometown with Amaya. My history is her
history. It is a part of her family narrative, like the story of her birth, a
story I already know how to tell. I imagine myself sharing how excited
I was to learn I was pregnant, nudging Jason awake one Saturday
morning holding a positive pregnancy test. I will describe feeling her

move inside my belly and explain how she arrived two weeks early, before we had installed her car seat.

But telling her about my hometown's place in history will be more challenging. I already know she will love her grandparents the way I loved mine. I can picture her sitting on my dad's lap as he reads her a story or playing in the garden with Mom. This part of the story is easy. But I want my daughter to know the whole story, including the town's tragic past—the one I didn't know growing up, the one so many of my classmates, friends, and relatives still have not learned. The one that has haunted me for years. Now that I have my own child, I feel an urgency to dig deeper, to unearth the details I have hesitated to uncover.

Since my conversation with Robert Taylor, I have avoided thinking about Farmville's past. It has become a painful topic for me, a source of shame and guilt. I feel torn between my love for my grandparents and embarrassed by their prejudices. I want to be loyal to them and protective of their legacy. Yet I believe that this story is worth exploring. My discomfort, and others' discomfort, is all the evidence I need.

THREE YEARS LATER, IN 2010, I am unpacking boxes in our new home in Richmond, the capital of Virginia, already second-guessing our decision to move back to the South. I was tired of being isolated at home in Massachusetts during the excruciatingly long winters, a feeling exacerbated by the birth of our second daughter, Selma, the previous year. We didn't belong in the North, I decided. Most of our friends from graduate school had left Boston for new jobs. We didn't have any family nearby. I felt especially cut off from the story I wanted to research and tell about Virginia. I missed home.

The idea of raising our girls in the South, in the part of the world where we both grew up, appealed to us. They too would grow up passionate about barbecue and pickles and tomatoes fresh from the garden. They would learn Southern manners and speak with a Southern accent. We were intrigued by the thought of going back to the part of the country that, for all its problems, for all its racial animosity, contained our roots. Maybe our daughters could be part of a new generation of diverse Southerners that would right some of the past's wrongs.

Most important, we would be closer to our families. I wanted to be near my parents and my brothers, who were starting families of their own. I imagined having dinner with them and still going home to my own bed at night. I could go back to work as a reporter with the support of my close-knit family, calling on Mom to help when Jason was traveling for work or when one of the children got sick at school.

But leaving our home in Boston hadn't been easy. As the movers arrived to pack up the Victorian we had lovingly renovated—the house where we went from husband and wife to a family of three, then four—regret swept over me. Our girls had learned to crawl on the living room rug, and they had taken their first steps on the hardwood floors. It was the only house they had ever known. Boston, with its own legacy of segregation and racism, had embraced us. I hoped we would be able to say the same about southern Virginia.

But as we stroll Monument Avenue in our new neighborhood, statues of Confederate generals such as Robert E. Lee and Stonewall Jackson greeting us every few blocks, all my reservations and fears about being back in the South surface. I worry about how my interracial family will be received here in the capital of the Confederacy, where rebel flags flutter in the wind. I'm afraid that Jason won't feel comfortable and that people will stare at the girls.

I know any discrimination and racism they might face will not resemble what blacks endured in Prince Edward County. I see the numerous ways blacks are still discriminated against in America, particularly the South, and Jason and our children will not face the same kind of treatment. Yet Jason is distinctly not white. He experiences life as "the other," from being called a "wetback" to being routinely asked, "Where are you from?" We expect our daughters may have similar experiences as brown-skinned children.

Because we want to be closer to family, Jason and I agree that it's worth giving Richmond a chance. It is the city I grew up visiting. My parents drove the hour and fifteen minutes from Farmville to Richmond to put us on Santa's lap at the Miller & Rhoads downtown department store at Christmastime. In high school, I rode school buses to tennis tournaments and public speaking competitions. In college, I dated guys who lived here, whiling away winter breaks drinking beer in dark bars. And because a number of my college and high school friends moved here after graduation, I already have a network of friends and acquaintances.

The Fan District neighborhood where we've moved is perfectly quaint, a thriving historic district on the edge of the Virginia Commonwealth University campus. Named for streets that radiate, or fan, westward, it is bursting with restaurants and Victorian homes. Jason accepted a job with an Internet start-up in a suburb of Richmond, but we aren't ready to move to a cul-de-sac just yet. Since we met, Jason and I have preferred to live in more urban areas, first in San Diego, then Somerville.

Richmond is a segregated city—majority black, though just barely— and the Fan is a historically white neighborhood, isolated for the most part from the violence that is routine in other neighborhoods. However, its proximity to one of the most racially diverse universities in the country brings a wide array of people to the area. The Fan reminds us of other communities where we've lived—walkable, with a park, a grocery store, restaurants, bars, and a coffee shop blocks away.

Some friends in Farmville consider Richmond unsafe and warn us against moving into the city. But Richmond has changed since I left. It's not the same city of the 1990s, when the crack cocaine epidemic peaked, the city's murder rate soared, and residents fled.

It is not the same place where, in 1995, some whites told a mostly black city council that they objected to a statue of the black tennis star Arthur Ashe being placed alongside Confederate heroes on Monument Avenue, claiming it would threaten the avenue's historic integrity. The city is finally recognizing its black history, and the mayor has even called for public discussion of the historic oppression of blacks. "We must be comfortable in making each other uncomfortable," Mayor Dwight C. Jones has said. In 2007, a fifteen-foot Reconciliation Statue of two bronze figures embracing was installed to acknowledge Richmond's role in the slave trade. A slave trail has been established, a slave jail site excavated, a slave burial ground preserved.

Richmond is being revitalized, too, and Jason and I see potential. Old tobacco warehouses have been renovated into lofts, and microbreweries are opening, one after another, in formerly abandoned buildings. New restaurants pop up like weeds. The city is embracing biking and other outdoor activities, particularly along the James River. Residents are arriving from other states, even other countries, to work for one of the universities, a downtown advertising agency, or Capital One, the region's largest employer, bringing new energy and out-of-town perspectives.

Still, its legacy of racial discrimination concerns me. I worry that it will be like Farmville. What if it hasn't changed enough or in the right ways? Richmond long buried its slave-market history, and segregation is still a profound problem. I worry about what my husband's life will be like, if our daughters will feel any effects. I want them to have all the opportunities I had and to be accepted. And I want to protect them from the racial hostility for which the South has long been known.

As I rip the tape off a box of glassware, Jason arrives home from his new job and envelops me in a warm hug. He's trying to adapt to this place, too, and I know it's more difficult for him. He doesn't have the familiarity with the city I do or the network of friends and former classmates. But he wants to make it work, too.

Jason and I imagine raising our kids with all we love about the South, minus the hardship, but we don't know if that's possible.

NOW THAT I LIVE AN easy drive from Farmville, I can finally, wholeheartedly, pursue the story of my hometown.

After college, I spent fifteen years reporting and writing stories for daily newspapers, large and small, from tiny Winchester, Virginia, to the capital of Oregon, from the coast of California to the heart of New England. I covered murder trials and deadly fires, legislative sessions and speeches by presidential candidates. I sat through hundreds of county meetings and studied zoning ordinances. I wrote about a neighborhood built on a toxic waste dump and the challenges Sudanese refugees face building new lives in America. Front-page news stories, business profiles, features, I have written them all. But the story of Prince Edward County is my most complicated yet. It is also the one I am most passionate about, the one I moved south to pursue. Exploring Farmville's past, though, is agonizing. Yet the story of my hometown keeps calling me back.

For years, I have been chipping away at it, conducting interviews, researching, and writing. But now that I am closer to home, I plan to investigate Prince Edward County's past the way I investigate corrupt politicians. I will visit dusty libraries and dig through stuffy archives. I will interview my family members and friends, leaders of the white academy, black students who had been shut out of school. I will talk with experts who spent their careers studying this little-known piece of Virginia—and American—history. I will read scores of books about Southern politicians, about the *Brown v. Board of Education* decision and its impact, about the civil rights movement. I will work to paint a more complete picture of what happened here, to tell the difficult truths, to make sense of what happened in my hometown.

It's important to me to be as honest and as forthright as possible in the telling. This, of course, is taboo in the South, where uncomfortable subjects are shelved. "Virginians are allergic to the truth," a journalist friend gently informs me, pointing out that the state's history of slavery has never been adequately addressed.

Setting out on this journey of discovery and peeling back the layers of my town's history will mean questioning the explanations I have been given about what happened in Prince Edward. It will require acknowledging that I come to the story from a place of privilege, in large part because of the color of my skin. I attended college financed by my parents, who also attended college, while generations of black children were denied educations, their lives and bright futures forever altered by the school closures.

It will mean moving beyond the story I grew up believing and finding my own truth. It will mean trying to answer the question always in the back of my mind: What is wrong with my hometown?

CHAPTER 3

Prince Edward Joins *Brown v. Board of Education*

To understand the full story of the school closings, I have to go back to the beginning, to 1951. The building where it all started sits less than a mile from the house where I grew up. Before I was born, Robert Russa Moton High School had been a public black high school, named for the Prince Edward resident who had succeeded Booker T. Washington as president of the Tuskegee Institute. A historically black college founded in Alabama in 1881, Tuskegee gained fame in 1941 for creating the country's first all-black flight squadron, the Tuskegee Airmen. The Moton school building was used as an elementary school during my childhood, yet I never learned its significance.

In 1939, Prince Edward County built this one-story brick high school with hardwood floors and giant windows on a triangular parcel of land south of downtown Farmville at the intersection of Main Street and Griffin Boulevard. The county's first stand-alone public black high school, it was constructed for forty thousand dollars nearly seventy years after the county established a public school system. Before it opened, black elementary and high school students were educated in private schools established in homes or across the street at Mary E. Branch Elementary School, which had added high school years through eleventh grade.

At the time, schools were completely segregated. It wasn't just lunch counters, water fountains, and city buses. Like communities across the nation, Prince Edward operated two school systems—one for white children and a clearly inferior one for black children.

Moton High School reached capacity almost immediately after it opened, in part because, in the early 1940s, the county finally offered bus service for black students. By 1950, a school that was originally constructed for 180 students was squeezing 477 into its eight classrooms. The black community was well aware of the overcrowding and had formed a parent-teacher association in the early 1940s to address it.

Elsie's minister, the Reverend L. Francis Griffin, stepped in. Since the feisty, thirty-two-year-old minister had returned to Farmville in 1949 to help preach in his ailing father's downtown church, he had been raising the issue of school overcrowding at school board meetings. Eventually Griffin, who also chaired the black parent-teacher association, was asked not to return. The board would let him know when it was time to build a school. But Griffin, restless and rebellious, wouldn't be silenced easily. He organized and coordinated a chapter of the National Association for the Advancement of Colored People.

Moton's black principal, M. Boyd Jones, also had repeatedly asked School Superintendent T. J. McIlwaine, who oversaw both the white and black schools, to address the overcrowding. The request seemed to fall on deaf ears, though McIlwaine bragged to visitors that Moton was one of only twelve black high schools in rural Virginia. Parents of black students attended the school board meetings to demand a new high school. Still, nothing happened.

The Prince Edward County School Board, consisting of only white members and appointed by the School Trustee Electoral Board, discussed building an addition to Moton High School. The state appropriated fifty thousand dollars in 1947 but the county board of supervisors would not match the allocation with local funds.

The school board's chair, Maurice Large, didn't think residents were ready to support the bond measure he believed would be necessary to build a high-quality school—unless they could tie it to constructing a white school or two. Large, who headed a construction firm in town, said a bond measure for "a 'nigger' school" would have been rejected. Finally, after years of neglect, the board of supervisors agreed in 1948 to pay up to twenty-five thousand dollars for a quick fix, funding the construction of two additional classrooms behind the school and one in front.

The new classrooms looked like chicken coops. Flimsy, wood-framed tar paper shacks that reeked of petroleum and leaked when it rained. Wind whipped through the thin plywood walls. In the winter, cracked potbelly stoves spewed hot coal. Students seated in the back of the classrooms, bundled in heavy coats, shivered and rubbed their hands together to stay warm. Those with desks next to the stoves roasted, no matter how many layers of clothing they peeled off. Children sniffled and sneezed through the winter, perpetually fighting off colds.

The overcrowding at Moton forced teachers to hold classes in the auditorium—and up on its stage—and, on sunny days, outside on the school grounds. They even led classes in parked school buses. The black high school was inadequate in other ways, too. It didn't have a gym, a cafeteria, a science laboratory, or locker rooms. Football players had to change into their uniforms in the classrooms. Many of the black high school's resources were hand-me-downs. Black children were picked up on dilapidated buses that had once belonged to the white schools. Since all the black students couldn't fit on one school bus, some children routinely missed their first class while they waited for the bus to make a second run. When they were finally dropped off at school, they sat in cast-off desks, reading secondhand books that were missing pages.

Six blocks away from Moton High School, over four hundred white high school students, including my great uncles, arrived on brand-new buses to their handsome two-and-a-half-story school, originally constructed in 1912 and rebuilt after a 1936 fire. The brick colonial revival–style school was located at First Avenue and School Street, tucked into the neighborhood of stately homes on tree-lined streets. Students at Farmville High School studied from new books and enjoyed amenities such as a gymnasium with locker rooms, an infirmary, even a machine shop. Classrooms in the school's interior overlooked an elegant, open-air courtyard in the center of the brick school.

This was what separate but equal looked like in southern Virginia in 1951. And it seemed as though nothing could be done about it. But then along came Barbara Rose Johns.

BARBARA WAS A JUNIOR AT Moton High School, quiet and reserved, but with a fiery temper. She had big brown eyes and a smile that sparkled. Born in New York City, she had spent most of her childhood in Prince Edward. When she was one, she and her family moved to her maternal grandmother's farm in the community of Darlington Heights, sixteen miles west of Farmville, where she was expected to do chores.

Barbara later moved to the home of her paternal grandmother, and she spent her spare time roaming the woods, looking for a quiet place to curl up with a book. Her uncle, the civil rights leader Reverend Vernon Johns, taught her to play chess and encouraged her to study black history. A friend of Griffin's, he kept an enormous library at her grandma Sally's house, and he ordered Barbara to read the encyclopedia volumes in order, from A to Z. Sometimes, in an act of rebellion, she hid Archie comic books between the pages. But she became a voracious reader and a deep thinker, just as Johns was, burying herself in Booker T. Washington's *Up from Slavery* and Richard Wright's *Native Son*.

After her parents built a home, Barbara often retreated to the attic bedroom she shared with her sister Joan to read. When her mother took a job in Washington, DC, Barbara became a second mother to her younger siblings, preparing the family's meals and readying her brothers for school. At Moton High School, she joined the debate team, the student council, and the chorus, and she traveled to better-furnished high schools. She was embarrassed when students visiting from other high schools laughed at Moton's chicken shacks, snapping photographs to show friends and family at home. She began to think of Moton High School as a blemish on her community.

Barbara wondered why public officials hadn't responded to complaints about the school's conditions from students, parents, teachers, and the principal. She had become close to her music teacher, Inez Davenport, and mentioned how dissatisfied she was. Davenport, who was dating the principal, paused for a few moments before responding, "Why don't you do something about it?"

"What one could do about such a situation, I had no idea," Barbara wrote in her diary. "But I spent many days in my favorite hangout in the woods on my favorite stump contemplating it all."

For months, she thought about her teacher's words and about how differently black and white students were treated. "Their classes were not held in the auditorium, they were not cold . . . their buses weren't overcrowded," she wrote. Their teachers and bus drivers didn't have to stoke the fire before classes could begin.

The turning point came one morning when Barbara ran home to grab the lunch she'd forgotten and missed the school bus. An hour later, she was still considering how she could get to school when a half-empty school bus en route to the white high school passed by and left her standing on the side of the road. She was furious. "Right then and there, I decided indeed something had to be done about this inequality," she wrote.

She wanted to walk out of Moton and refuse to attend classes until a new school was under construction. Over several weeks, she worked quietly to assemble a team of twenty students who held positions of authority at the school and whose parents were respected in the community, students who would be willing to help her and could keep a secret. She approached John Stokes, the president of the senior class, and his twin sister, Carrie. Since his freshman year, John had said the tar paper shacks weren't fit for animals. The cows he had milked growing up were better sheltered than the Moton students, he said.

Barbara passed John notes until he finally agreed to meet her on the football field's bleachers to listen to her plan. She told him and Carrie that their parents' attempts to pressure the school board to build a new school had failed. She thought a student-led strike would draw more attention to the school's abysmal facilities. In this case, she said, "a little child shall lead them."

John was impressed. Barbara seemed determined and driven, even fearless. He believed if anyone could pull off a strike, Barbara could. She was a natural leader, he thought, and she had a way of talking that made people listen. He and Carrie signed on to help. Barbara also recruited John Watson, a senior who served as editor of the school newspaper. For years, he and his family had been concerned about the conditions at Moton. He wanted to do anything he could to keep the students out of the tar paper shacks.

At John Stokes's suggestion, the students named their secret plan the Manhattan Project, after the code name for the effort by the Allies to develop nuclear weapons during World War II. This was the students' own personal war. For six months they schemed, telling no one of their plan. They swore not to mention it to their families. Barbara didn't even tell her sister.

On Monday, April 23, 1951, they were ready. Midmorning, John Watson walked to his house six blocks from the school to make a phone call to the principal that would lure him away from the high school campus.

Holding a cloth over the phone to muffle his voice, John Watson pretended to be a white business owner. He told Jones that a pair of students had skipped school and were causing trouble downtown. Other students watched for Jones's departure, and then ran back to school to tell the strike organizers. The mood was quiet. Notes were sent to all the classrooms announcing an emergency meeting. Barbara had signed the notes with her initials, "BJ"—the same as Principal Jones's.

Teachers and students entered the tiny auditorium, where Barbara, John and Carrie Stokes, and other student organizers were hidden behind a thick curtain onstage. When everyone had been seated, the curtain parted and Barbara stood at the lectern. The principal was not present.

Barbara announced that the meeting was for students only—not teachers. The strike's leaders wanted to get the student body on board before the administration learned about the strike. Barbara removed her shoe and smacked it on the side of the rostrum. "I want you all out of here!" she yelled. Most of the teachers complied. They were just as fed up with the wretched conditions as the students. Barbara called on one teacher by name, asking him to leave. Two football players escorted out another teacher. A couple of other teachers pretended to leave and then snuck back in.

As students sat packed into the stuffy, hot auditorium on folding chairs, they listened as Barbara told them that they shouldn't have to endure Moton High School. In spite of their parents' urging and black community leaders' pleas, the school board had not acted to improve the miserable conditions. Nothing would change, she told her classmates, unless they banded together and demanded a new school.

Barbara's younger sister Joan cringed and slid down in her chair, shocked by the protest her sister was suggesting. "All I was thinking about was the consequences of our actions in this white county," Joan said later.

Cheers of support rolled through the auditorium like a summer thunderstorm, building to a roar. Students shouted and chanted. In the middle of the assembly, Principal Jones rushed into the auditorium, begging students to return to classes. Barbara suggested he go back to his office—students didn't want him to get in trouble. After a few minutes, he relented and left.

Barbara called on her classmates to stay out of school until Moton High School was improved. She told them that the Farmville jail wasn't big enough to hold all of them. As she marched out of the auditorium and out of the overcrowded school, 450 students followed. Some held signs that read: "We Want a New School or None at All" and "Down with the Tar Paper Shacks." Others went home to their parents to explain what had happened.

Word of the strike quickly spread around town. Griffin, the black preacher who chaired the local chapter of the NAACP, rushed to the school to offer the students assistance. He spent the evening driving the back roads of the county, knocking on doors to talk with parents and building support for the students' cause.

The strike Barbara led that day would forever change the lives of black children, not just in Prince Edward but across the nation. But no one knew that yet.

FOR NEARLY TWO DECADES, OLIVER W. Hill Sr., a forty-three-year-old black lawyer from Richmond, had been working to end segregation. He had won his first civil rights case as a young attorney in Norfolk in 1940, when the school system was ordered to provide equal pay for black teachers. He and his cocounsel at the NAACP's Richmond office, Spottswood W. Robinson III, were fighting segregation laws county by county, and at one point, they had seventy-five cases pending before the courts.

After the Moton strike, Griffin urged the students to call the Richmond NAACP. When Barbara and Carrie Stokes, the president of the student body, dialed Hill's office, he was already familiar with their situation. He had appeared before the Prince Edward County School Board several times in the previous decade to ask that the board respond to complaints about the conditions of the black schools.

At the time, Hill, thin and balding, was busy drafting a motion for a case in southwestern Virginia on behalf of a black student forced to ride sixty miles to attend the only school that served black students in the region. Hill listened to the young women, but dismissed them. "You don't need representation," he recalled telling Barbara. "You made your point," he advised her. "Go on back to school."

But Barbara, an especially precocious teenager who took after her uncle Vernon Johns, would not be swayed. Determined to get the attorneys' attention, she and Carrie typed them a letter. "We hate to impose as we are doing," the young women wrote, "but under the circumstances that we are facing, we have to ask for your help."

The next day, a Tuesday, the student organizers arranged to meet with Superintendent McIlwaine. As they marched downtown to his office in the county courthouse, white businessmen came out to watch. Instead of meeting the students in his office, the superintendent directed them inside an empty courtroom.

He insisted that the black students' school was equivalent to the white school and suggested that the decision to build a new school for black students wasn't his to make. County residents would have to vote on it. When he saw the students weren't persuaded, the superintendent tried intimidation. Disgusted by what he thought was an adult conspiracy, he hinted that they might be expelled.

They stomped out of the meeting, unsatisfied. The superintendent wouldn't even look them in the eye. Besides, they had seen what happened when they took what was handed to them.

That day, the students were alerted by the Richmond NAACP office that Hill and Robinson had decided to stop in Farmville the next day to talk with the strike's leaders and their parents. The attorneys were passing through town on their way to Pulaski County for a meeting about a federal desegregation suit they were preparing to file.

The previous year, the national organization had decided to change direction and was no longer seeking equal facilities. The attorneys had realized that even if they won case after case, black schools would remain inherently unequal. Instead, the NAACP would focus on the wider fight for desegregation—"the whole hog"—arguing that even if they were equal, segregated schools were unconstitutional. The NAACP's chief counsel, Thurgood Marshall, a close friend of Hill's from Howard University Law School, saw schools as the entry point for ending all segregation and was looking for a case to take to the Supreme Court. He wanted to challenge the 1896 *Plessy v. Ferguson* ruling, which had found that separate facilities for blacks and whites were constitutional as long as they were equal. But it had become clear that whites would never grant equality.

The path ahead was daunting. The NAACP had filed numerous lawsuits in eleven Southern states and the District of Columbia seeking equal facilities. The strategy called for challenging racial segregation head-on in an attempt to have it declared unconstitutional in public schools. Marshall's mentor, Charles Hamilton Houston, a vice dean at Howard University Law School and the NAACP's first special counsel, believed that if the organization could build up enough small victories in the courts, precedents would be established for the Supreme Court to eventually declare all forms of segregation in education to be unconstitutional.

The NAACP had its first major Supreme Court victory in 1938, when the court found that a black student, Lloyd Gaines, was improperly denied admission to the University of Missouri School of Law. The court ruled in *Missouri ex rel. Gaines v. Canada* that states that provided schooling for white students must give the same opportunity to blacks. Marshall planned to use the precedent to file similar cases and ask for integration.

In 1950, the NAACP won two important Supreme Court cases. In the first, *Sweatt v. Painter*, the court ordered Heman Marion Sweatt, a black mailman, to be admitted to the all-white University of Texas School of Law. The school had rejected him on the basis of race and suggested he attend a "law school" for blacks in the basement. The court also intervened on behalf of George McLaurin, a sixty-eight-year-old black teacher who had been admitted to the University of Oklahoma, where he was pursuing a doctorate in education, but had been segregated in classrooms, the library, and the cafeteria. *Mc-Laurin v. Oklahoma State Regents* had established that the rights of blacks to receive a graduate-level education were the same as whites'.

The NAACP still had not made much progress in opening up secondary education, though its lawyers had already tried several cases that had advanced to the Fourth Circuit Court of Appeals, a federal court in Richmond. Hill, the first black man elected to the Richmond City Council after Reconstruction, was on the lookout for a strong case in Virginia.

OLIVER HILL SR. DIDN'T PICK the Prince Edward County case. It picked him.

"Oliver Hill was in great demand for the whole state. He was the lawyer who was leading the forces for change," said Virginia state senator Henry L. Marsh III, who became Hill's law partner in 1961. "He had a full plate of things to do, and he managed to talk to these children on his way to Southwest Virginia."

The NAACP's strategy for getting to the Supreme Court was to choose the right cases—cases that were well documented and clearly showed the impact of segregation on black students. In 1950, the organization had filed a lawsuit in Clarendon County, South Carolina, challenging the constitutionality of separate schools.

On the drive to Prince Edward County, Hill told Robinson he would listen patiently to the Moton students' story, and then he'd advise them to go back to school. The attorneys met the student strike organizers and their parents in the dank basement of Griffin's First Baptist Church on Main Street. They changed his mind. "He was so impressed with their situation and their determination that he agreed to take the case," Marsh told me. "You had to be impressed with those kids."

Barbara told the attorneys that the students refused to return to class in tar paper shacks. The attorneys were pleasantly surprised, and they offered to represent the children if they could get their parents' support. "We didn't have the heart to break their spirit," Hill said later.

There was a catch: the NAACP was interested only in suing for desegregation. This fight wouldn't be about getting a new school, as the students had sought. It would be about enrolling black students in the white Farmville High School. The attorneys also warned the students and their parents that the fight would be a long, difficult one. It would take years, and Barbara and the other students would never enjoy the rewards. The case would have to be taken through the federal courts before it eventually landed in the Supreme Court.

The students hesitated. They hadn't intended this kind of fight. They had simply wanted real classrooms instead of tar paper shacks. Did they really want to take it this far? When the organizing committee held a vote, the decision to pursue the legal fight won by only a single vote.

On Thursday night, nearly one thousand parents and students packed into Moton High School for a mass meeting. The NAACP's attorneys couldn't make it—they were in Pulaski as planned—but the state NAACP secretary, W. Lester Banks, attended, signaling the organization's interest in a case. A new school would not bring equality "if it were built brick for brick, cement for cement," Banks told the crowd. "There is no such thing as separate but equal."

Parents knew what happened to blacks who challenged racial segregation. Their white employers could fire them or cut their hours at will. The bank loans on their farms were at risk. Most of all they feared violence. Across the South, blacks were regularly attacked or beaten, even lynched, although less so in Virginia. Still, many black parents felt they had no choice but to support their determined children. The case was moving forward.

Two weeks after the strike began, students headed back to classes, as Hill had instructed them. On May 3, Hill, Martin, and Robinson petitioned the school board to end segregation at Prince Edward's schools, claiming that the board was denying equal educational opportunities to black students. When the school board rejected the petition, the NAACP filed a desegregation suit. *Davis et al. v. County School Board of Prince Edward County*—named for the ninth-grader Dorothy Davis, the first name to appear in the list of students—was filed in federal court with the signatures of parents for 117 Moton students and their families.

Attorney General J. Lindsay Almond Jr. promised that the state would intervene and use its resources to defend separate schools. In Prince Edward, white leaders immediately offered to build a new black school in exchange for the lawsuit being dropped. Black leaders refused the offer. They didn't believe the promises and supported the new mission to fully integrate the schools. The school board moved ahead anyway. The board directed McIlwaine to apply for a $600,000 loan from the state literacy fund to add to a $275,000 grant the county had been awarded to construct the school, and in July, the board approved the acquisition of land. The $875,000 allocation was more than twenty times the cost of the original school. As the *Davis* case wound through the court system, county and state officials hoped the new school building would show a history of concern for black education. A state-of-the-art facility for seven hundred students just outside of Farmville, it opened in 1953, two years after the student strike. This new school was also called Moton High School but would later be renamed Prince Edward County High School. When the case went to the Supreme Court, county leaders would argue that the new school had been planned all along.

Barbara never had the opportunity to attend. Concerned about her safety after her life was threatened, her parents sent her to live with her uncle Vernon Johns in Montgomery, Alabama. Accused of mishandling the strike, Principal Jones was dismissed. He and his new wife, Inez Davenport, who was pregnant, also moved to Montgomery, where he joined Johns's church.

Black students could finally attend a quality high school that compared to the white high school. Some black parents were satisfied. But many were fueled by this win and had set their sights higher, on integration. Yet they couldn't know the sacrifices it would require of their community for years to come.

In 1952, the Prince Edward case became part of something much bigger. The Supreme Court agreed to hear *Davis* with four similar cases being appealed to the court. The other cases from across the country—Delaware; Washington, DC; South Carolina; and Kansas—questioned the constitutionality of state-sponsored segregation in public schools.

The five cases were combined under *Brown v. Board of Education of Topeka, Kansas*, to avoid the appearance of addressing a specifically Southern problem. The larger case was named for Oliver Brown, a railroad welder and assistant pastor whose seven-year-old daughter, Linda, attended a black school one mile from her house instead of the white school seven blocks away.

The Topeka chapter of the NAACP challenged the "separate but equal" doctrine governing public education, asking Topeka Public Schools to integrate. When that didn't work, the NAACP in February

1951 filed suit in federal district court against the board of education of Topeka Public Schools on behalf of Brown and nineteen other plaintiffs. The district court ruled in favor of the school board and the case was appealed to the US Supreme Court.

The first of the cases, *Briggs v. R. W. Elliott*, was filed in 1950 by twenty black residents of Clarendon County, South Carolina, against school officials on behalf of their children. The parents were seeking school buildings, teacher salaries, and transportation equal to that provided white children, but the case was later amended to challenge segregation. For three years black parents had asked for buses for their children, some of whom walked five miles to school. One school lacked running water, and some schools had outhouses instead of toilets. The US District Court in June 1951 found that the black schools were inferior to white schools, and the lower court ordered the defendants to promptly give black students equal facilities. But the black children were denied admission to the white schools, the request for abolishing segregation in South Carolina's schools shot down.

In Delaware, two cases, *Belton v. Gebhart* and *Bulah v. Gebhart*, filed in 1951 and combined, involved two black schools with similar issues. The first was the overcrowded Howard High School in Wilmington, which black students traveled fifty minutes each way to attend. The state board of education would not permit them to enroll in the new white school in Claymont, where they lived. The second was a one-room elementary school in the rural community of Hockessin, where black students were not provided bus service. Sarah Bulah thought it was only fair that her daughter, Shirley Barbara, be able to ride a bus to school the way white children in her community could. The cases were filed in US District Court in Wilmington.

The state requested that the Delaware Court of Chancery hear the cases, where Judge Collins J. Seitz addressed the doctrine underlying racial segregation in the schools, something the other cases hadn't done in such a direct way. Children were being denied equal protection of the law by being forced to attend inferior schools. "The cold, hard fact is the state in this situation discriminates against Negro children," he wrote.

"I conclude from the testimony," Judge Seitz wrote, "that in our Delaware society, a state-imposed segregation itself results in the Negro children, as a class, receiving educational opportunities which are substantially inferior to those available to white children otherwise similarly situated."

He ruled that the "separate but equal" doctrine had been violated and that Shirley Barbara Bulah in Hockessin and Ethel Louise Belton and nine other plaintiffs in Claymont should be admitted to the white school in their communities—the first time a court had ordered a white public school to admit black children. The state supreme court upheld his ruling, which the Delaware Board of Education appealed.

The *Bolling et al. v. C. Melvine Sharpe et al. (District of Columbia)* case was filed on behalf of eleven black students, including Spottswood Thomas Bolling Jr., a twelve-year-old whose request to attend a modern white junior high school in southeast Washington was denied. Instead he had to attend a ragged black high school. His attorney, James Nabrit Jr., rejected the idea of seeking equal facilities and instead challenged the constitutionality of segregation per se. The case was filed in 1951 in US District Court, which in turn justified segregated schools in Washington, DC, by citing *Plessy*.

The Prince Edward County case, filed in 1951, was the only one spurred by a student strike. Hill argued that blacks want the ability to develop their talents, but that in the segregated school system, black children do not have that opportunity. The three-judge US District Court panel concurred in March 1952 that racial separation rested "neither upon prejudice nor caprice nor upon any other measureless foundation" but had become part of the values of the people. The court even suggested that segregation had given blacks great opportunities. The judges said that, in Prince Edward, "We have found no hurt or harm to either race." The NAACP lawyers appealed the ruling.

Brown v. Board was the culmination of twenty-five years of work by Houston, Marshall, and the Richmond attorneys to end the exclusion of blacks from every level of education. Marsh, the first black mayor of Richmond and a long-serving state senator, always thought *Brown* should have been named for the Prince Edward case. "The revolution . . . took wings in Prince Edward County. The spirit of blacks in Prince Edward is the spirit that fired the civil rights movement to overturn *Plessy v. Ferguson*," he told me. "It started right there."

The case was first argued before the nation's highest court over three days in December 1952, as three hundred people—about half of them black—packed into the hearing room and four hundred more lined the hallways. Robinson argued that Virginia's segregation laws were "intended to limit the educational opportunities of the Negro," citing evidence that for every dollar the government had spent on schools for white children, it had spent sixty-one cents for black children.

The deeply divided court had been expected to rule in June 1953. Instead, the court scheduled *Brown* to be reargued in the fall, inviting the attorney general of the new president, Dwight D. Eisenhower, who had been sworn into office in January, to present a brief. The court put off a decision, in part, because the justices believed the "political upheaval" would cause an outbreak of violence.

Before the case could be heard again, Chief Justice Fred Vinson died of a heart attack at sixty-three. Eisenhower nominated as his replacement the popular three-term California governor Earl Warren, who had helped Eisenhower win the Republican presidential nomination by securing the California delegation's votes. He had also called for anti-lynching and anti–poll tax legislation. Taking the bench in October 1953, Warren, sixty-two, would have more impact on civil rights during his sixteen-year tenure than any other judicial appointment in history. Eisenhower, uncomfortable with the outcome of *Brown* and with other high court decisions he considered liberal, would come to regret the appointment, terming it "the biggest damn fool mistake I ever made."

His Department of Justice opted not to argue against desegregation in the *Brown* case. Attorney General Herbert Brownell Jr. submitted a brief to the Supreme Court in November 1953 that supported overturning *Plessy v. Ferguson* but couched his stance, suggesting that desegregation would take as long as a decade to implement.

When the case was reargued in December 1953, spectators lined up outside the court before the sun came up to ensure they could get a seat for the one o'clock arguments, which would last three days. To keep schools segregated, Marshall told the court, was "to find that for some reason Negroes are inferior to all other human beings" and to attempt to keep blacks in a form of slavery.

"Now is the time, we submit, that this Court should make it clear that that is not what our Constitution stands for," Marshall argued.

When the court met to discuss the case, Warren quickly informed his colleagues that he thought de jure school segregation—segregation imposed by law—was unconstitutional. For him, the issues were moral. He wanted to work toward a unanimous decision to discourage resistance in the South.

The justices spent months discussing the case, and in order to reach unanimity, Warren compromised, agreeing to a "bare-bones" decision that did not stipulate how the ruling should be implemented, giving the South time to adapt. The cases could be reargued later, Warren believed, and the court could consider then how the decision should be implemented.

On May 17, 1954—three years after the Moton walkout—the Supreme Court issued a unanimous ruling that racial segregation in public education was unconstitutional. Warren, delivering his first major opinion, wrote that separating children "solely because of their race generates a feeling of inferiority as to their status in the community that may affect their hearts and minds in a way unlikely to ever be undone." The detrimental impact, the court found, was more profound when the law sanctioned segregation.

The court's decision directly addressed segregation—not inequality in school facilities—and found that even if schools were equal, black children's separation from whites was "inherently unequal." The court ruled that the separation constituted a violation of the equal protection clause of the Fourteenth Amendment. The justices also found that receiving a quality education is critical for all children and that the state is responsible for ensuring educational equality.

"In these days, it is doubtful that any child may reasonably be expected to succeed in life if he is denied the opportunity of an education," Warren wrote. "Such an opportunity, where the state has undertaken to provide it, is a right that must be made available on equal terms."

The verdict was reached, in part, by the attorneys' use of social science rather than legal precedent. Kenneth B. Clark, a New York social psychologist and assistant professor, and his wife, Mamie, a psychologist, had developed a study that showed the harmful effects of segregation on black children. They used dolls placed in front of black children that differed only in skin color—two were pink and two were brown. They found that the majority of children preferred the white doll and referred to the black doll as "bad." Kenneth Clark, who wrote a brief explaining the psychological harm to black children from living in what was essentially a caste system, suggested that segregation creates a feeling of inferiority and humiliation that leads to self-hatred and the rejection of their own race. He argued that segregation harmed white children, too, feeding distrust and hostility and producing a distorted social reality. He suggested that there was no reason for segregation to continue, arguing that most differences between racial groups are environmental and rejecting segregationists' claim that there was a scientific need for separation.

By overturning *Plessy v. Ferguson*, the Supreme Court put an end to more than fifty years of legal racial segregation and paved the way for school integration. When the verdict was handed down, Marshall was "so happy" that he felt "numb." He ran from the court and bound into the NAACP offices, wearing "a grin as wide as Fifth Avenue." He walked over to Roy Wilkins, the NAACP's executive secretary, and kissed him. A long night of celebration followed, but a cautious Marshall warned his friends that "we ain't begun to work yet." The next day, he was quoted in the *New York Times* predicting that school segregation would be wiped out in five years. Hill, too, believed whites would accept the ruling and integrate the schools. He rejoiced that the long battle was over.

But in Prince Edward County, it was just beginning.

CHAPTER 4

My Family's Part

I'm at my desk at the *Richmond Times-Dispatch*, frantically wrapping up work on an article before I dash out of the newsroom, drive across town, and retrieve my daughters from day care.

The days are a blur. I am reporting a story about how black activists are disappointed that a recently preserved African burial ground near downtown Richmond is being used for dog walking and Frisbee tossing instead of quiet reflection. At the same time, I am working on a piece about the white owners of a million-dollar riverfront property who are worried that a rezoning decision could block their pristine view. This is the yin and the yang of Richmond, the black and the white, the haves and the have-nots.

Working for the paper a year and a half, I have seen how the legacy of the slave trade and segregation have made their marks on Richmond. A huge swath of the black population lives in crushing poverty, isolated from whites—and from opportunities for a better life. Too many black children grow up in this city's concentrated public housing and some never leave. Driving the neighborhoods, I begin to grasp how segregated Richmond still is, how much inequality still exists. This city, and the whole South, projects an image of friendliness and hospitality yet is built on a rarely acknowledged history of racial oppression.

The transition to life here has been challenging at times. New acquaintances warn us against walking two blocks to the "ghetto" grocery store—ghetto, I surmise, because some shoppers are black and poor. Others joke about hearing gunshots across Broad Street, but I don't get the joke. At social gatherings, Jason and the girls are often the only people of color. When I mention my project to a friend from high school, she denies the reason for the academy's founding. My aggressive reporting style and my interest in covering race and poverty seem misplaced in a setting where Southern manners are valued and uncomfortable topics best avoided. I spend a lot of time thinking about whether this is the right place to raise our children.

And then, one April morning, my focus changes in an instant, and those concerns fade into the background. In a peach-colored waiting room in a suburban medical building, a doctor surprises me with a diagnosis of early stage breast cancer. The best kind of cancer to have, I'm told, but still cancer. I escape out a side door of the building to call Jason, sobbing into the phone as he quietly comforts me.

After meeting with doctors, I opt for surgery and radiation. I change my schedule to spend more time with my daughters, now three and five, and fewer hours working as I recover and heal. But these minor alterations to my routine are not enough. I view my family and my future differently now. Nothing is guaranteed. I need to reprioritize so that I can do the work I value most and also pick the girls up from school.

After I finish my treatment, I walk into my boss's cubicle at the newspaper and tell her I am resigning. I am free, empowered even, to pursue this story that has nagged at me for so long.

BLACK ADULTS WEPT WITH JOY when the *Brown* decision was handed down, telling their children it was a great and important day. The *Washington Post* optimistically announced that the verdict was "a new birth of freedom" for black Americans. White leadership in the stunned South reacted with absolute outrage.

How dare the federal government tell the states that blacks and whites had to attend schools together? How dare it exert that kind of authority?

On the floor of Congress, Representative John Bell Williams, a Democrat from Mississippi, branded the day "Black Monday." In South Carolina, the distraught governor, James F. Byrnes, said that "ending segregation would mark the beginning of the end of civilization in the South as we have known it." Georgia's governor, Herman Talmadge, said that the decision had reduced the Constitution to "a mere scrap of paper" and announced that "there will never be mixed schools while I am governor." His successor, Marvin Griffin, referred to the decision as a "bitter pill of tyranny," and said "the South will not swallow it." In Mississippi, US senator James Eastland announced, "The South will not abide by or obey this legislative decision."

Virginia joined in, and ultimately led this pushback. "The greatest resistance to *Brown* anywhere occurred in Virginia," Henry L. Marsh told me.

The most powerful politician in Virginia, US senator Harry Flood Byrd Sr., the son of a wealthy apple grower and newspaper publisher, considered the *Brown* ruling to be an unconstitutional infringement on states' rights, calling it "the most serious blow."

When the ruling was first handed down in May 1954, Virginia's governor, Thomas B. Stanley, announced hours later that he would go along with the decision, which he said warranted "cool heads, calm study, and sound judgment." He promised to consult with leaders of both races to pursue a policy "acceptable to our citizens and in keeping with the edict of the court." But he would not follow the course he suggested.

In response to his calls for moderation, "the top blew off the US Capitol," Stanley later said. Byrd, a former governor himself who had a firm hold on Stanley, warned that the *Brown* decision would bring "dangers of the greatest consequence." What kind of dangers, he didn't say. Byrd's regime, which controlled Virginia politics, would use its influence in the general assembly to prevent integration.

The governor was berated by legislators such as State Senator Garland Gray, who believed that school integration would lead to intermarriage and the destruction of white culture. Gray called together a group of white legislators and community leaders from Southside Virginia—the part of the state south of the James River, which includes Prince Edward County. The group met at a Petersburg fire station in June 1954 and declared that they were opposed to integration. Gray believed the high concentration of blacks in Southside, where he grew up, made integration impossible, and he suggested ways to circumvent the decision.

Governor Stanley changed his tune about consulting leaders of both races, and he later announced, "I shall use every legal means at my command to continue segregated schools in Virginia." He added that, if he failed, "careful thought" should be given to repealing the section of the state constitution that required the Virginia General Assembly to maintain free public schools. At Byrd's urging, Stanley appointed a group of white men in September 1954 to consider the state's response to the *Brown* decision. Gray was asked to chair the commission that would be named for him.

In his quest to avoid desegregated schools, Byrd would coin the phrase "massive resistance"—becoming the face of the South's defiance of *Brown*—and extend his reach beyond Virginia's borders. He believed that if the Southern states could organize against the court's decision, it would be only a matter of time before the rest of the country realized that the South would not accept integration.

IN PRINCE EDWARD COUNTY, OUT of sight of the state capitol, the *Farmville Herald* declared that white community leaders were "in a state of shock." Residents already harbored a deep distrust of the federal government that went all the way back to the Civil War. Nearly a century after the war ended, they were still smarting. The final battles were fought—and lost—on the county's productive farmland, its rolling hills.

Prince Edward County was founded in 1754 from land in adjacent Amelia County and named for a young prince, Edward Augustus, Duke of York and Albany. He was the second son of Frederick, the Prince of Wales, and the younger brother of the future king of England, George III. First inhabited by whites in the early 1700s, the county had been the hunting ground of the Appomattox Indians and other tribes. Numerous arrowheads and spearheads, along with pottery, have been found along the Little Buffalo Creek. But there is no evidence American Indians were living in the county when two groups of settlers arrived in the area that became Prince Edward. The first group came from eastern Virginia, and most were English, although some were Scotch and Welsh. The second group—Scotch Irish migrants from Pennsylvania—arrived in 1735.

The county was an agricultural oasis, two-thirds of it covered with oak and yellow Virginia pine forests ideal for lumber. There were fields of corn and wheat and hay as well as apple and peach orchards. The land also proved perfectly suited for raising tobacco, which quickly became the prized crop in colonial Virginia.

Slaves provided labor for the first farms in the county, and, along with other property, they were sold at public auction on court days and at special sales, sometimes at the county courthouse. Some of the slaves had been transported directly from Africa, while others were billed as "Virginia-born slaves." The numbers of slaves in the county steadily grew as planting of the labor-intensive dark-leaf tobacco increased, but indentured servants and convict servants also provided labor, along with family members of the farm owners.

Farmville was founded after the American Revolution in 1798 along the Appomattox River on land owned by Judith Randolph, the widow of Thomas Jefferson's cousin Richard Randolph. The town was one of a select few locations authorized to inspect tobacco, and by 1845 it was the fourth-largest tobacco market in Virginia, with two warehouses and ten factories. Farmers from surrounding counties brought their crop to town by wagon or canoe, and after inspection, the dark-fired tobacco was shipped by wagon or by flat-bottomed boats known as bateaux to eastern river ports in large wooden barrels, or hogsheads. The Appomattox River, which flows into the James River, connected central Virginia with commercial ports in Petersburg and Williamsburg, from which tobacco could be shipped to Europe. Trains arrived in 1854 when the South Side Railroad opened a line from Petersburg to Lynchburg, passing through Farmville as well as two other towns in the county. The route, which required a steep crossing of the Appomattox River known as High Bridge, brought an end to the commercial navigation of the river around Farmville.

Even prior to the Civil War, a significant portion of Prince Edward's black population was independent. A community known as Israel Hill consisting of ninety free blacks was settled in 1810 and 1811 after Judith Randolph complied with her husband's will years after his death, freeing his slaves and giving them land. The Israelites worked as farmers, bateauxmen, and skilled tradesmen, and they bought and developed real estate in Farmville. Although state laws restricted free blacks, such as one law passed in 1806 by the assembly that required free slaves to leave the state within a year unless granted special exemption, Prince Edward did not enforce these laws.

In 1861, the county's representative to the Virginia Convention voted to support Virginia's secession from the Union. Over the course of the war, Prince Edward County sent enough men to fill eight military companies for the Confederacy, among them blacks and students at the all-male Hampden-Sydney College. A general hospital of the Confederacy opened in Farmville in 1862 with a capacity of 1,500 beds, and those who died were buried at a Confederate soldiers' cemetery in town.

But only at the war's bitter end was a single battle fought in Prince Edward County. In April 1865, as the Confederates retreated from Richmond and Petersburg, General Robert E. Lee directed his soldiers to Farmville, where rations were waiting for the hungry men. As his troops pulled wagons of supplies across Little Sailor's Creek, the advancing Union troops attacked. Nearly a quarter of Lee's remaining men—7,700 soldiers, including eight generals—were killed or captured.

After the devastating battle, Lee ordered a portion of his troops to march to Farmville over the 2,400-foot-long High Bridge and set it on fire to keep the Union troops from advancing. On April 6 and 7, both Union and Confederate forces tried to burn the railroad trestle, which towered 60 to 125 feet above the Appomattox River valley, along with its lower wagon bridge. The Confederate cavalry took eight hundred Union troops prisoner there, then burned one end of High Bridge and set fire to the wagon bridge before retreating. But the bridge didn't catch fire fast enough, and Union troops extinguished the fire on the wagon bridge and crossed into Cumberland County.

It was from the Randolph House's porch in Farmville that Union general Ulysses S. Grant sent a note to Lee, who had fled town, suggesting surrender. Two days later, Lee agreed to do so in Appomattox, and, as the war ended, thousands of hungry, thirsty Confederate and Union soldiers took over farmhouses in Prince Edward and elsewhere in Virginia, confiscating livestock and pillaging dried goods, canned fruits, and vegetables.

Residents lost much, or everything. One man applied for food for his family and for the wounded soldiers who had been left at his home. Union troops set up camp, converting the Confederate hospital into a distribution center to supply the county's black residents with food. Union troops remained in the county for weeks, but it would be years before the farmers recovered their losses. And residents would not soon forgive these unwelcome guests.

AFTER THE *BROWN* DECISION, PRINCE Edward's leaders didn't wait for the commonwealth to rush to their defense. Many believed the county's schools would be among the first in the nation required to integrate because one of the *Brown* lawsuits had originated in the community. They figured that the sleepy, rural county would be held up as an example to the rest of the country, and they were not willing to stand by and let that happen. They would fight desegregation.

The person at the helm was the white-haired editor and publisher of the *Farmville Herald*, J. Barrye Wall, who managed his family's twice-weekly newspaper. He led the community's criticism of—and resistance to—the *Brown* decision, which he viewed as a threat to its way of life. In the pages of the community newspaper, the *Brown* decision never had a chance. Four days after *Brown* was handed down, the *Herald* announced its opposition to integration in an effort to shape public opinion.

"This newspaper continues its firm belief in the principles of segregation in the public schools in Southside Virginia, and hopes that a plan can be formulated to continue development [*sic*] the schools on a segregated basis within the framework of the decision," read an editorial written the month of the *Brown* decision. "We believe it is in the best interest of all our people."

The paper portrayed desegregation as a threat to the heart of the community and called for the county to formulate a plan to keep blacks and whites separate in schools. "The segregated races formed a citizenship, and a way of living together, which has brought phenomenal developments into the South, particularly industrial progress," the editorial read. "This is now being changed. The opening wedge is public education on an integrated basis."

The paper believed that blacks wanted not just "token" integration, but "total" integration, in all facets of life, "a little at a time."

In a November op-ed, the newspaper claimed that blacks were a year to eighteen months behind whites in their ability to learn and were more mature physically, which the paper reasoned would result in a two-to-three-year differential between black and white children of the same age. The newspaper also argued that a segregated public school system had been developed because of a "difference in the background, the ability, and the desire among the races in Virginia to seek an education," implying that blacks didn't want to attend school or be educated and that they weren't as smart. Black children would be demoralized in a classroom with white children, the newspaper insinuated.

And the paper repeatedly made the unsubstantiated claim that the majority of both blacks and whites in Prince Edward County wanted to maintain their own schools. "We cannot understand why so much furor has been raised in regard to the 'rights' of a small minority, and the rights of an overwhelming majority be completely overlooked," a July editorial read.

Segregation was "in the best interest of all our people," the *Herald* stated matter-of-factly. Integration, it wrote, was a "far-reaching concept."

The paper raised fears that the *Brown* decision would contribute to the spread of communism by dividing the country, and it suggested that other regions of the United States—the North was often mentioned—were attempting to slow progress in the South. "Certainly the best way to curb [the South's] prosperity is to foment rifts in its churches and schools," one editorial read.

But most of the blame for the *Brown* decision was reserved for the NAACP, which the paper accused of conspiring against Prince Edward County, giving credence to a notion popular in the white community—one that Robert E. Taylor repeated to me more than fifty years later—that the student strike had not been organic. Editorials suggested that "forces from the outside" had selected the community for a desegregation experiment and had chosen Prince Edward to see what would happen if one community pushed back. Naive black parents had been played. "Those who had but little interest in our happiness or welfare carried far afield the original intention of the unsuspecting," the paper editorialized. It was a claim Hill repeatedly denied, adding that he would have chosen a more metropolitan location to file a suit if it had been an option.

Six months after the *Brown* decision, the *Herald* warned that there would be repercussions for desegregating schools. "Any attempt to integrate," a November op-ed read, "will multiply present problems to an extent as to threaten the very existence of public education." Signing off on the editorials, Wall urged his readers to stay the course against integration, adding that many looked to the county for a national solution: "Stand steady, Prince Edward!"

As I tried to understand what led to the school closings, I sat in Longwood University's Greenwood Library reading through dozens of the *Farmville Herald*'s editorials from the 1950s, studying how the white publisher used his newspaper to advance his personal agenda—and the agenda of other powerful whites.

It was a typical move by a newspaper leader in his era. The editor of the *Richmond News Leader*, James Jackson Kilpatrick, took a similar stance on a bigger stage. In a series of editorials, he laid a framework for Southern politicians to push back against the *Brown* decision. He popularized the now-discredited doctrine of "interposition," once championed by Senator John C. Calhoun of South Carolina, which suggested that states had the authority to ignore federal rulings and to nullify them. Kilpatrick laid out his beliefs in a book, *The Southern Case for School Segregation*. "It is a way of life that has to be experienced," he wrote, trying to explain the relationship between blacks and whites in the South.

The competing daily newspaper, the *Richmond Times-Dispatch*, praised Prince Edward's leaders on its editorial page. "Your firm determination not to have mixed schools in your county is understood and supported throughout Virginia," the paper opined. "Do not let yourselves be pushed around."

And yet the perspective of black children and their parents rarely appeared in the newspapers. The *Herald* hadn't covered the school board meetings when the conditions at Moton were discussed, and it termed the walkout organized by Barbara Johns "mass hookie." Many of the newspapers appeared to have only whites' interests at heart. "Wall has not felt a newspaperman's curiosity with regard to the Negro," Bob Smith, an editor at the Norfolk *Virginian-Pilot* wrote in his 1965 book, *They Closed Their Schools*.

I had assumed that the decision to close the schools was made spontaneously by white leaders after a court ordered the county to desegregate its schools. But as I read through newspapers from the days and weeks after the *Brown* decision was announced, a different story emerged. J. Barrye Wall, a native of Prince Edward who was proud that his newspaper was locally owned, staked out his public position immediately after the decision was handed down. He used his newspaper to send a forceful message directly into his readers' homes that integration would not be tolerated. He even addressed many whites' deepest fears: once black and white kids sat together in school, they would date, marry, and give birth to mixed-race children. He wrote that integration would result in the "destruction of two great races" and would make "the people of America a mongrel nation."

Letters to the editor from his readers addressed concerns about miscegenation even more frankly. J. Guy Lancaster, a Farmville resident, suggested in an October letter that integrating schools would force blacks and whites "to associate closely together against the will of either race" and lead to "interracial breeding." "Until we are sure that a greater race is produced by interracial mixing," Lancaster concluded, "let us try to keep our races as pure as possible."

Wall's editorials frequently cloaked segregationist beliefs in intellectual arguments about constitutional rights and state sovereignty, notions the South had clung to during the Civil War. He mentioned the interference of communists. But he did not discuss the motivation whites had to keep blacks uneducated so that they could preserve cheap labor for their businesses and maintain the existing social hierarchy that benefited whites.

Wall's exertion of authority didn't end on the pages of his newspaper. He imagined an organization that would advocate for whites the way the NAACP represented blacks. Within months of the Supreme Court decision, Wall, one of his sons, and other white leaders quickly convened meetings in Prince Edward to draw up their battle plan. They also organized gatherings in Petersburg, twenty miles south of Richmond. They established a statewide organization known as the Defenders of State Sovereignty and Individual Liberties. The name closely mirrors the words inscribed on the Confederate monument built in Farmville in 1900—"Defenders of State Sovereignty"— a monument that served as a reminder of exactly how much had been sacrificed during the Civil War.

The Defenders drew two thousand members from thirteen counties in Southside Virginia. In counties with a racial makeup similar to Prince Edward's—nearly half of the sixteen thousand residents were black—whites may have feared an uprising. Nat Turner's 1831 slave revolt, which occurred one hundred miles away in Southampton County, was still on their minds. Fifty-five whites had been killed in the uprising, including Turner's master and family, before the slave leader was kidnapped and executed.

The Defenders' directors included state legislators, a county treasurer, a county commonwealth attorney, and members of the various county boards of supervisors. In October 1954, the Defenders secured a statewide charter, and a Farmville man became the organization's first president. Robert Crawford, who owned a dry cleaning business, had sat on the Prince Edward County School Board for fifteen years and bragged that "the Negroes counted me as one of the champions for the cause of their schools." Yet the organization he now headed had been formed to ensure that schools operated "on a separate basis," he said. The organization also pledged to maintain states' rights and individual rights, and to give voice to "an unorganized majority." Its members devised a "Plan for Virginia": deny state funds for schools forced to desegregate and close public schools as a last resort.

"The organization will act with determination and firmness to retain, by all honorable and legal means, segregated schools," William B. Cocke Jr., the secretary of the organization and clerk of the court of Sussex County, told the *Farmville Herald*. "We are unalterably opposed to integration in the schools."

Any applicant for membership—at an annual fee of ten dollars a person—had to agree that he was a "white law abiding citizen" of Virginia. Members were expected to believe that "the segregation of the races is a right of the state government, in the sovereignty of the several states and in the freedom of the individual from government controls." They should not belong to "any organization detrimental to the peace and welfare of the USA."

A Farmville chapter also formed. Within a year, the organization would have more than two dozen chapters and twelve thousand members from across the state. But its base of power was firmly situated in Southside.

SEATED AT OUR DINING ROOM table in Somerville, Massachusetts, in 2008, I'm reading a book published in 1965 about Prince Edward County's reaction to *Brown*. I'm doing research for a graduate school paper I'm writing at Harvard Kennedy School while Amaya, now a one-year-old toddler, is napping upstairs.

Flipping through *They Closed Their Schools*, I come across a familiar name. My grandfather's. S. C. Patteson. Papa. I reread the paragraph:

> The list of officers and directors of the local Defender chapter included tobacco manufacturer J. W. Dunnington, Mayor W. C. Fitzpatrick of Farmville, Dr. S. C. Patteson, J. G. Bruce of the Board of Supervisors, former school board chairman Large, and of course, publisher Wall. There could be little doubt at this point that the Defenders had control of the organs of government in Prince Edward County.

The words leap off the page. I sit in stunned silence. Since I was a child, I have known that Papa helped establish and oversee the operations of the private school for white children. He served as a board member for at least twenty-five years. But I had pictured my grandfather traveling down a path chosen by other white community leaders, helping out, doing what was asked of him in that effort to build a new school. I thought of him as a loyal supporter, nothing more. I figured that, like other white parents, he realized that once the schools were closed, he needed to ensure his children could be educated. I had adopted my mother's words: He was just doing what was best for his kids.

But reading this book, I realize that his role was something altogether different. My grandfather had been a Defender. And he wasn't some anonymous member, I would later learn. He was a founding member and an officer of the organization. The book said:

> The Defenders' organizers in Prince Edward combed the ranks of the county's staunchest segregationists to find officers of unquestioned propriety and standing in the community.

Papa had sided with other white leaders in the community, the state, and the South who impulsively announced that they would prevent integration at any cost. Papa had been willing to stand as one of the earliest advocates of this logic. And he had joined with other men who not only opposed desegregation in Prince Edward County, but, as I would later understand, actively lobbied for the county to close its schools.

I am trying to wrap my head around the new information when I hear Amaya stirring in her crib upstairs. As I pluck her from bed, I think about what I have just learned. My grandfather wasn't simply a follower in this movement. He was a leader. I have a sinking feeling, a burning disappointment in the pit of my stomach. Helping to found a school and serving on its board was one thing. Being a Defender was quite another.

Ashamed and sad, I can no longer put all the blame on my town for the tragic school closings. My own family is at fault, too.

CHAPTER 5

Locked Out

School districts around the South deliberately flouted the *Brown* decision. The ruling had not stipulated how schools should be desegregated or on what time line, and the vague wording of the decision allowed school leaders to avoid making any changes.

President Eisenhower hadn't helped matters either. Although he had called for the desegregation of Washington, DC, schools, he had not articulated what the states should do, and he never publicly endorsed *Brown*. He was reportedly unhappy with the decision but knew, as president, that he had to accept it. "The Supreme Court has spoken," he said, "and I am sworn to uphold their—the constitutional processes in this country, and I am trying. I will obey."

Some interpreted this remark as the president distancing himself from the decision. "It makes no difference whether or not I endorse it," he said. Later, he would tell an aide that the decision had slowed progress in the South by fifteen years.

Soon after the *Brown* decision was handed down, Prince Edward's leaders began formulating ideas about how to keep the federal government from interfering with the schools. They were concerned that the county would be ordered to integrate as an example to the rest of the country. In response, the Defenders devised a drastic but simple plan: to withhold funds from the public schools. Wall, the short, plump newspaper owner and founder of the Defenders, raised the idea of abandoning public education on the opinion page in November 1954. If Prince Edward's schools weren't open, they couldn't be desegregated.

Five months later, in April 1955, a group of Defenders asked the board of supervisors not to fund public schools. At the meeting that night, the supervisors delayed a decision, but the issue came up again a month later, on May 31—the same day the Supreme Court handed down a follow-up decision to *Brown*. A year earlier, the court had asked the attorneys general of all states with laws permitting segregation in public schools to submit plans for how they would proceed with desegregation. The new decision, which became known as *Brown II*, gave the task of carrying out school desegregation to district courts and suggested it be done "with all deliberate speed."

The Supreme Court had still refused to set a deadline, rejecting Thurgood Marshall's call for segregation to be quickly dismantled. The justices believed that great social change comes slowly. With the new decision, members of the Prince Edward County Board of Supervisors expected a district court to order the county's schools to be desegregated by September. School board chair B. Calvin Bass told the supervisors that he and McIlwaine, the superintendent, had met with the school board's attorneys in Richmond that day, and they'd been advised that the county would be permitted to operate segregated schools for at least another year.

"That's not good enough for me," one man in the audience responded, and his comment was met with applause.

Standing in a crowd of Defenders, Bass urged the board of supervisors to allocate adequate money for the schools, warning that the school district's teachers might find jobs outside Prince Edward if the schools were not funded. But the Defenders stood up one after another to ask the supervisors not to finance the schools. Ultimately, the board voted unanimously to support a proposal by Supervisor John G. Bruce, also a Defender, that called for allocating the schools the minimum amount allowed by the state—$150,000 for the year. It was far less than the proposed $686,000 school budget, which supervisors feared might be used to support integrated schools.

The board did exactly as the Defenders had asked. The supervisors' vote to underfund the schools—hours after the Supreme Court's *Brown II* decision was issued—made news across the country. The decision signaled that Prince Edward County would continue to fight desegregation, and it was a powerful foreshadowing of the more dramatic steps the county would take. The supervisors would flout the law. They did not believe the courts could force them to pay for desegregated schools.

"We shall use every legal and honorable means to continue the high type of education we proposed to give the children of both races in Prince Edward County," Edward A. Carter, chairman of the board of supervisors, wrote in a statement, adding, "I don't believe integration will serve to elevate or make better citizens of either race."

DAYS LATER, FORTY-FIVE COMMUNITY LEADERS—among them Defenders and presidents of the white public schools' parent-teacher associations—formed the Prince Edward School Foundation. They began making plans to establish a private school for white children, the academy that would, in some ways, define my family. My grandfather, like other white parents in town, would help establish the school and sit on its board. Both my parents would attend, and later they would enroll my three brothers and me. My aunt and uncles and some of my cousins would go to school there, too. My father would chair the parent-teacher association and sit on the school's board of directors. My mother would spend twenty-five years working as a guidance counselor at the school, and my youngest brother would teach and coach there, too.

The Defenders called a public meeting to rally white residents around their concept for a separate all-white school system on June 7. More than 1,500 people—nearly all of them white, with the exception of a handful of blacks—packed into Longwood's Jarman Hall auditorium. Maurice Large, the former chairman of the school board, warned the crowd that "unless there is some change of position on the part of the Board of Supervisors, there will be no schools operated in this county in 1955–56." Large, also a Defender, gave voice to an idea that had been touted in the *Farmville Herald*. On the stage, he was surrounded by PTA presidents from each of the county's white schools.

After J. Barrye Wall presented the Defenders' proposal to close the schools if the county was ordered to desegregate, the PTA representatives, who also happened to be Defenders, expressed support for starting a private school. The county appeared to have already united around the idea, making parents and community members who disagreed with this approach nervous about expressing themselves.

The outgoing president of Longwood College, Dabney S. Lancaster, stood to speak, warning that integration would "set public education back half a century." Yet Lancaster, a former state superintendent of instruction, believed that the community "could not afford to close the schools." After his remarks, a Longwood professor and the Reverend James R. Kennedy, the pastor of the Farmville Presbyterian Church, called for shelving plans to immediately close schools.

James Bash, the principal of Farmville High School, was surprised by the unified stance of the PTA presidents just weeks after the Farmville district PTA had issued a statement opposing private schools. He thought the Defenders had manipulated the meeting to present the appearance of consensus. He raised questions about the logistics of closing the public schools and opening a private school system in its place. Where would classes be held? Who would pay the teachers? Would they lose their retirement funds? "I am a public school man and I cannot take any salary from any organization designed to circumvent the ruling of the Supreme Court," he told the crowd.

The Farmville High football coach, Robert C. Gilmer III, who would become a legendary figure at the private school, shouted out, "I don't feel that way. You pay my salary and I will teach your children." His response was cheered. When another Longwood professor got up to protest the idea of closing the schools, he was booed.

The crowd in attendance voted to establish a nonprofit Prince Edward School Foundation to solicit donations to cover the white public school teachers' salaries. They hoped this would keep the teachers from looking for jobs outside the county. That night, the Defenders collected $46,000 in pledges. Two days after the meeting, a charter had been set up for the foundation. By midsummer, $180,000 had been pledged. In a July editorial, the *Farmville Herald* praised the efforts as necessary.

But funds for the private school wouldn't be needed right away. The Supreme Court's use of the phrase "all deliberate speed" to stipulate how it expected schools to be desegregated proved to be more ambiguous than the wording in the original decision. The NAACP's Marshall said the term "all deliberate speed" was code for "S-L-O-W." *Brown II* provided legal justification for school districts, including Prince Edward's, to delay or avoid desegregating for years. On July 18, 1955, a federal court panel ruled that Prince Edward County would not have to desegregate its schools for the new school year and did not set a deadline. For now, the county's public schools would stay open and segregated.

The newly formed nonprofit held on to its pledge cards should the landscape change. The Defenders knew the threat of desegregation had not disappeared, and they wanted to be ready to launch a white school at a moment's notice.

The Prince Edward County Board of Supervisors continued to allocate money to the schools on a month-to-month basis rather than at the start of the fiscal year. By doing so, *The Farmville Herald* explained, the county could simply go "out of the public school business."

In May 1956, after the NAACP asked the court to order Prince Edward's schools desegregated, white parents went back to the supervisors to make their position clear. They presented a petition signed by more than four thousand county residents—half the county's white population. It read:

> We, the undersigned citizens of Prince Edward County, Virginia, hereby affirm our conviction that the separation of the races in the public schools of this county is absolutely necessary and do affirm that we prefer to abandon public schools and educate our children in some other way if that be necessary to preserve separation of the races in the schools of this county. We pledge our support of the Board of Supervisors of Prince Edward County in their firm maintenance of this policy.

Virginia's leaders were also working to support the county. Governor Stanley's Gray Commission, which consisted exclusively of white male legislators, many of whom represented Southside, concluded in a November 1955 report that segregation was best for both races and that "compulsory integration should be resisted by all proper means in our power." Blacks would be humiliated sharing a classroom with whites, they determined.

The commission recommended that the state's school attendance laws be amended to ensure that children were not required to attend integrated schools, that state funds be allocated for tuition grants to families who opposed integrated schools, and that local school boards be authorized to assign white and black children to schools on a student-by-student basis. Later that year, Governor Stanley called the general assembly into special session, seeking a statewide referendum to amend the state constitution in order to allow public funds to go to private schools. In January 1956, voters backed the initiative.

As desegregation suits were filed in other Virginia localities, Harry F. Byrd continued to protest integration, promoting a "Southern Manifesto" that denounced the Supreme Court's decision as "a clear abuse of judicial power" and discouraged the state from implementing the decision, which he said was "contrary to the Constitution." He secured the signatures of nearly a hundred Southern congressmen who agreed with him. "I think that in time the rest of the country will realize that racial integration is not going to be accepted in the South," Byrd said.

In Virginia, he was preparing to do even more. With recommendations from the governor's commission in hand, Byrd crafted a "massive resistance" strategy that became the battle cry of the South, and he met with Stanley and Gray to discuss thirteen proposed bills. The package of laws was approved in August by a narrow margin in a special session of the state assembly. Most extreme was the law that enabled the state to cut off funding and order the closure of any public school that prepared to integrate.

FOR FOUR YEARS FOLLOWING THE *Brown* decision, Prince Edward County and other localities in the state of Virginia managed to avoid desegregating schools because of the Supreme Court's failure to address enforcement and the slow pace of the lower courts. Groups like the Defenders had gained traction, in part, because Eisenhower did not publicly support *Brown*.

However, his administration had not argued against desegregation and had quietly integrated the schools that military children attended. The president also believed that preserving public order was his obligation, prompting him to act in Arkansas in 1957.

In 1955, the local school board in Little Rock had adopted a plan to integrate Central High School. When nine black students prepared to enroll in the all-white high school two years later, Arkansas's governor, Orval Eugene Faubus, a segregationist, ordered the National Guard to surround the high school, saying "blood will run in the streets" if black students attempted to enter the school. A mob of white people shouted, "Niggers, go home!" as the black students arrived on September 4, and National Guard troops would not allow the black students to pass. As one of the students, Melba Pattillo, tried to flee with her mother, a group of white men, one of them carrying a rope, chased after the pair. Another man swung at the girl with a tree branch.

Eisenhower didn't want to pick sides, but after the situation had dragged on for days and Little Rock's mayor, Woodrow Mann, asked for assistance from the White House, the president federalized the National Guard and sent more than one thousand US Army soldiers armed with billy clubs to the school. He went on television to tell the public that he believed it was his "inescapable" responsibility to uphold the *Brown* ruling and to prevent "mob rule." The next day, September 25, nine black children walked through the school's front doors.

Less than a year later, on August 20, 1958, Eisenhower declared it was "the solemn duty" of Americans to comply with the Supreme Court's order to end racial discrimination in public schools, and he implied he would again use force to integrate the schools if necessary. But when Governor Faubus closed Little Rock's public schools to prevent their integration a month after Eisenhower's August speech, the president did not intervene.

Yet Eisenhower's talk stirred the new governor of Virginia, J. Lindsay Almond Jr., who in his inaugural address in January 1958 had suggested Virginia would fight back. "Against these massive attacks, we must marshal a massive resistance," he announced. A day after the president's August comments, Almond called a press conference and told reporters that he would close schools if federal troops were sent in. "There will be no enforced integration in Virginia," he said.

The Virginia General Assembly had authorized the governor to close any school that came under the protection of the federal troops and to close the rest of the district's schools, too. As district courts in Virginia began to order desegregation, Almond warned Prince Edward, as well as Charlottesville, Norfolk, and Arlington on September 4 that he would close white schools if blacks were assigned to attend, and he was ready to keep his promise.

On September 15, the governor shut down Warren County High School in Front Royal, located seventy miles west of Washington, DC, and attended by one thousand white students. It became the first school closed under the state's massive resistance laws after a federal district court judge ordered the admission of twenty-two black students to the school—the county had no black high school—and the judge at the Fourth Circuit Court of Appeals denied a stay. On September 19, Almond closed a high school and an elementary school in Charlottesville that were preparing to desegregate, shutting out 1,700 children. And on September 27, Almond shut six white schools in the military community of Norfolk, locking out ten thousand children, after a federal judge ordered the schools to be desegregated. When the Norfolk School Board announced that it had assigned seventeen black children to its schools, Almond issued a proclamation within minutes, declaring the Norfolk schools under his control. The governor made use of rights that had been granted to him by the state assembly years earlier in anticipation of this moment.

In the three communities, nearly thirteen thousand students were locked out of school at the end of September, and the response in Virginia was "stunned silence," the reporter Benjamin Muse reflected later. Some white parents banded together, forming the Virginia Committees for Public Schools to demand that the schools be reopened, and ministerial associations in Norfolk and Front Royal chimed in. The editor of Norfolk's *Virginian-Pilot* newspaper, Lenoir Chambers, one of the few Virginia newspaper leaders who publicly opposed the school closures, criticized the decision that locked out or threatened 5,500 children of navy families from all over the country. More than two dozen business leaders pressured the governor to reopen the schools. At the start of the New Year, 1,800 blacks gathered in Richmond to protest the school closings in an eighteen-block march.

Two court decisions on January 19—one from a federal court, the other from the state supreme court—found the massive resistance laws to be unconstitutional and demanded that the schools be reopened. Almond reacted angrily in a radio address on January 20, declaring, "We have just begun to fight." He said new tools would be sought in legislative session to replace the massive resistance laws that had been struck down.

Addressing "those whose purpose and design is to blend and amalgamate the white and Negro race and destroy the integrity of both races," "those who don't care what happens to the children of Virginia," and "those who defend or close their eyes to the livid stench of sadism, sex, immorality, and juvenile pregnancy infesting the mixed schools of the District of Columbia and elsewhere," he said, "I will not yield to that which I know to be wrong and will destroy every semblance of education for thousands of the children of Virginia."

Almond, who once vowed to "cut off my right arm" before allowing a black child to enroll in a white school, later regretted the harsh rhetoric he had directed at blacks. His options had run out, and some saw the speech as his last stand. He quickly realized the futility of his stance and asked the general assembly to repeal the massive resistance legislation, to the bitter disappointment of Byrd and others who did not accept the decision. In February, black students enrolled in white schools in Norfolk and Arlington, just miles from the nation's capital, without drama or disturbances. This ugly chapter of Virginia's history seemed to be coming to a close.

Still, Prince Edward remained resolute. The Defenders' Robert

Crawford proclaimed that the whites of the county "are standing just where they were five years ago," adding "they're just as firm in their opposition to integration." As other communities chose to integrate their schools—or at least desegregate classrooms in some schools— rather than sacrifice public education, Prince Edward's leaders were determined not to give in to the federal government.

After years of avoiding desegregation, Prince Edward's day of reckoning finally came in May 1959. "The U.S. Fourth Circuit Court of Appeals dropped a bombshell on Prince Edward County," the *Farmville Herald* proclaimed in a front-page headline. An appellate court reversed a lower court's decision that the district had until 1965 to desegregate and ordered the schools to take immediate steps to admit qualified black students, noting that the county had not taken a single step toward desegregation. The court set the deadline for September 1959.

What happened next had been foreshadowed years earlier. The county's white leaders responded exactly as they had warned. Defying the new court order, the Prince Edward County Board of Supervisors announced it would eliminate the county's entire education budget, thereby closing all twenty-one white and black public schools. The operating principle of ethical governments—"do no harm"—was roundly ignored. It was better to abandon schools, county leaders decided, than for white children to sit in a classroom next to black classmates.

"It is with the most profound regret that we have been compelled to take this action," the board said in a statement. The board suggested that it "should not bring about conditions which would most certainly result in further racial tension and which might result in violence." The board added that the schools had been closed "in accord with the will of the people of the county."

Gordon Moss, an associate dean at Longwood, denounced the decision as "unchristian" and an act of "unintentional evil." The

Ministerial Alliance of Farmville and Vicinity urged the supervisors to rescind it, saying it was "contrary to the simple laws of decency, the American ideal of democracy, the Christian concept of justice, and the moral law of God."

A Prospect man, J. V. Lewis, had no sympathy. "The condition that has been brought about here is due to the colored people themselves," he declared, "and they'll just have to suffer it."

"We have reached the point of no return," Farmville's mayor, William F. Watkins Jr., said.

The doors were chained and signs were posted:

SCHOOL PROPERTY
NO TRESPASSING
UNDER PENALTY OF LAW
PRINCE EDWARD CO. SCHOOL BOARD

The county's three thousand students were locked out.

Governor Almond offered his support for the county's leaders, saying, "What Prince Edward has done is in conformity with Virginia's law. . . . The locality is under no legal compulsion to appropriate money for public education. Those who object to the action of Prince Edward have only to thank the NAACP and the courts which do their bidding."

The NAACP promised to vigorously fight the closings. "The people of Prince Edward will not be abandoned by this organization in their quest for their constitutional and human rights," said W. Lester Banks, the secretary of Virginia's NAACP branch. Oliver W. Hill also promised to defend the black residents. "We believe that public education is the cornerstone of American democracy," he said, "and we propose to pursue every legal and constitutional means to preserve it in Prince Edward and everywhere else in Virginia."

Prince Edward's leaders had followed through on threats made five years earlier, making a once inconceivable response to a Supreme Court decision a reality. It would forever change the county and affect black families in heartbreaking ways, halting—and sometimes ending—black children's educations and breaking up families who would send their children away to school.

Ultimately, the county's youngest residents would pay the steepest price.

PART TWO

The Lost Generation

Our school was not the first one
To be built of hopes and dreams
With walls of high convictions
And with faith for her beams.

First to leave the old ways,
The first to dare to try;
Fought for with such assurance,
How could they think she'd die?

Prince Edward stepped a new way,
Made history at her start;
She's first in strength and courage,
And the first in our hearts.

—PRINCE EDWARD ACADEMY ALMA MATER

CHAPTER 6

The Segregation Academy

I left for college thinking that my grade school experience—and my community—was normal. I didn't realize how sheltered I had been. The white academy I attended didn't admit black students until I entered eighth grade. By the time I graduated, my circle had barely expanded. I was still isolated from blacks and other people of color.

A boy at my school called me "nigger lips," and I spent middle and high school thinking they were something to be ashamed of. When police accused a black teenager of taking the cassette player from my banged-up Hyundai Excel, he reinstalled it and my parents agreed not to press charges. After that, the radio never worked properly, and I had a personal reason to associate black men with crime.

Mary Washington College, an hour south of Washington, DC, wasn't particularly diverse, but I made my first Latina friend within hours of my arrival. I was immediately drawn to Flavia Jimenez, but I didn't know what to make of her. She spoke Spanish on the phone to her parents, who grew up in Argentina and Peru, and she had traveled the world. Her life was endlessly different from mine, and that appealed to me.

Studying Spanish in high school hadn't made sense to me, because I had never left the country. It had never even occurred to me. My parents didn't have passports either. I was a small-town girl, still dressed in preppy cable-knit sweaters, a satin bow tied around my curly blonde ponytail. I was loud, hyper, and overly enthusiastic. It was the only way I knew how to be.

A whole new world opened up to me in that first semester of college when I enrolled in a journalism class. I introduced myself to the professor, Steve Watkins, and I followed him to his office. He asked me where I was from, and I tried to compose the story of my hometown. But I had never learned the full history and I muddled the explanation, confusing segregation and desegregation. I was embarrassingly uninformed.

Still, something clicked. From that day forward, I was a reporter. I learned to think for myself, to question authority. Watkins instructed his journalism students to fact-check even our most basic assumptions. Repeating a journalistic mantra, he told our class, "If your mother says she loves you, check it out."

I worked for the college paper, the *Bullet*, writing stories about black students' complaints that they had been forced to walk through a metal detector before a concert at the Underground pub. I reported a story on public funds set aside for tutoring black students that weren't available to whites. For the first time in my life, I was considering issues of race.

In my naïveté, I assumed that the school's administrators were always truthful, if not forthcoming. One afternoon in the *Bullet*'s dingy offices, as I hung up the phone after an interview, I declared a college vice president to be "nice." Watkins exploded, visibly irritated that I had just been worked over. "The hell with nice!" Watkins snapped. "Nice doesn't mean good!"

He was responding to my childlike sense of the way the world worked, in which civility was valued above all else. "People will nice your story right out of your hands," he told me. "Don't be a sucker like that."

Watkins's lesson would still resonate twenty years later. Prince

Edward County's leaders were well-mannered Southern gentlemen. They had also closed the schools. Nice doesn't mean good.

AFTER COLLEGE, I LEFT VIRGINIA, which for all its beauty felt oppressive. I headed west, breaking free of the traditions and expectations under which I had been raised. I landed a reporting job with an Oregon newspaper.

My move across the country surprised my parents. In Farmville, people tend to stay put. They might attend college in western Virginia or live in Richmond in their twenties. But move anywhere else and no one back home can understand why. One of my mom's classmates, a former member of the county board of supervisors, bragged that he had only left the state twice. Life in this small town insulates and protects its residents, making them forget there is a world beyond southern Virginia. But I couldn't wait to get out of Farmville and figure out who I was supposed to be.

Although a Southerner in a strange land, I made friends quickly, and the new surroundings opened my mind to different ways of looking at the world. I took an interest in Oregon's growing Latino population. A Spanish-speaking neighbor explained the discrimination they faced. He translated for me so I could interview the parents of a teenage boy killed in burgeoning gang violence. Two years later, I moved to San Diego, one of the most diverse places in America, to work as a reporter for the *San Diego Union-Tribune*. My closest girlfriends were Asian and Latina, and I also made black and gay friends. I dated guys who weren't white. My life in Virginia seemed far behind me.

Yet the learning curve was steep. My Filipina friend, Crissy, gently informed me that although rugs are Oriental, people are Asian. She was allowed to mock Asian drivers but I was not. One night when we were dancing in a mostly black crowd at a downtown club, I told her I felt awkward. Imagine how I feel always being the only brown person in the room, she responded. Another time, when I described my brother's tall, athletic girlfriend as all-American, she questioned the term. What made her all-American, she asked. Her blonde hair and light eyes?

With Crissy's gentle nudging, I regularly confronted how much I still had to learn. Having friends of color, gay friends, and immigrant friends that faced various forms of discrimination opened my eyes to the ways that I benefitted from white privilege. The growing awareness changed my focus at work, too. I was curious about the experiences of those people the newspapers overlooked. I teamed up with Crissy, a photographer at the paper, to produce stories about people of color, the poor, and the disenfranchised. We wanted to show readers the world that existed beyond their front doors, to inspire them and invite them to engage with their neighbors. I wrote stories about diverse communities in which people of different cultures interacted. But my attention wasn't always well received. When I covered San Diego's black community, many interviews were rife with tension, my journalistic focus unwelcome.

Living in a county with a large Spanish-speaking population, minutes from the Mexican border, I began to believe that learning the language was essential. I realized how many doors would open, how many stories I would be able to report and write, if I could communicate in Spanish. I signed up for night classes and started planning an extended trip to study in Latin America. Soon after, Crissy and I took a weekend trip to San Francisco, and I met Jason.

I couldn't have predicted that ten years later we would move back to the South, together.

By the late spring of 1959, Prince Edward County's public schools were officially closed, and white leaders were suddenly facing a three-month deadline to ready their private school for the coming academic year. Classrooms had to be prepared for more than 1,500 white children countywide, and money needed to be raised to pull it off. It seemed like an enormous feat.

The first step was bringing in money, Robert T. Redd, the longtime headmaster of Prince Edward Academy, told me. The white academy had already raised about $11,000 before the board of supervisors' historic vote to end public education in 1959, and its directors wanted to secure an additional $200,000 that had been pledged years earlier. The private school foundation would also be supported by tuition grants from the state and tax credits from the county. The board of supervisors in 1960 would adopt a tuition grant law that provided one hundred dollars for each child from county funds and allowed taxpayers to donate up to 25 percent of their real and personal property taxes to a private school. After one year, a federal judge found this aid for segregated schools to be illegal.

It was also time to appoint the school's leadership. The Prince Edward School Foundation's president, B. Blanton Hanbury, who had served as president of the Farmville Elementary PTA, approached Redd, who worked as a shop teacher at Worsham Elementary, a white public school south of Farmville, and asked him to come on board. Redd had already met many of the school's leaders, but more important, he was willing to do whatever it took to get the school open.

On July 1, Redd and the Worsham principal, J. Boyd Bagby, became the school's first two employees. The pair didn't know the first thing about starting a school from scratch, and Redd wanted to get advice from others who had already accomplished what they were about to do. He and Bagby drove north to Warren County to spend a day at another school formed to avoid integration, the John S. Mosby Academy, which had more than four hundred students attending classes in a converted restaurant and a new four-room building. The school was among the South's first segregation academies.

In Warren County, administrators explained to Redd and Bagby the task they were about to undertake, walking them through each step. They should create an organizational schedule. They needed to determine an annual cost per student, set salary scales, and hire a bus service. They would have to line up facilities that could provide classroom space, and they'd have to furnish the rooms with desks and blackboards. They needed to secure schoolbooks and purchase paper and bathroom supplies. Redd and Bagby returned to Farmville overwhelmed and nervous. But at least they had a better understanding of the daunting task before them, and they spent three hours briefing the school's governing committee.

In mid-July the board appointed a retired oil executive, Roy Pearson, to lead the school initiative. A businessman who had worked for years with Standard Oil, establishing offices abroad, Pearson was an answer to the board's prayers. He treated the school like a business start-up.

Robert Taylor offered the third floor of a building he owned downtown at the corner of North and Third Streets, near the Farmville Herald building, as office space for the school. Redd crossed the street to ask neighboring businesses for donations of surplus furniture to fill the empty floor. He partitioned off the space to create three distinct offices and arranged for the telephone company to install lines. Then he hired a secretary.

Redd figured that since churches weren't in use on weekdays, they would be the most appropriate hosts for the new school, though it meant all the classrooms wouldn't be under one roof. Redd, Bagby, and Pearson fanned out across the community, asking leaders of the many churches to borrow their Sunday school rooms.

The foundation secured insurance policies for each of the buildings and signed rental agreements with the owners. The Farmville Presbyterian Church offered its basement and first floor, which gave the school space for an office and a guidance counselor. The school also planned to house students at the United Methodist Church, Farmville Baptist Church, Farmville Moose Lodge, the Farmville

Woman's Club House, and a vacant phone company building. The owner of the town's white movie theater, State Theater, agreed to let the school hold assemblies there. The foundation also planned to have one school in each of the county's five magisterial districts outside the town of Farmville, and churches such as Pisgah Baptist Church offered space.

Redd drew up a floor plan for each of the buildings and worked to furnish them. The churches agreed to let the school use their metal folding chairs, but students needed flat surfaces to write on, so Redd put his shop skills to use. He asked Smitty Brothers Electric Company for help making desk attachments for the chairs. Working in the company's storage room, the men bent metal conduit pipe and screwed the pieces to blocks of Masonite to create writing tablets. Then Redd organized assembly lines of volunteers to complete the daunting task of attaching legs to donated doors to make tables for classrooms. "We worked day and night," Redd told me.

The white community was solidly behind them.

EVEN AS THE PRINCE EDWARD School Foundation's officials worked to establish a school from scratch, they were trying to figure out exactly how to pay to operate it. They needed money for teachers' salaries and to purchase supplies. They would have to pay for operational costs such as heating and water and basics like toilet paper and paper towels. Even with commitments from years earlier, "we didn't know where we were going to get money," Redd told me.

But their worries soon dissolved. Donations came in from all over the country from "people who sympathized with what we were attempting to do," Redd said. The gifts ranged from five-dollar bills to checks for several thousand dollars. Virginia localities launched fundraising drives, and neighboring Nottoway County raised $8,500 in a month. The academy was able to operate exclusively off donations for the first year. Still, Redd remembers gently nudging parents and local business owners to donate to the foundation. You seem to be making pretty good money, he would say to a business owner or a professional. Don't you think you can give a little more?

The school's administrators had reached out to textbook suppliers, who agreed to donate books. School districts around the country sent surplus materials. Even buses were donated. The United Daughters of the Confederacy ran a book drive for the academy, which needed three thousand volumes to be accredited. School officials also raided public school resources, which had essentially been abandoned. They helped themselves to whatever they needed from the locked public schools—books, desks, even goalposts for a new football field the Jaycees were building for the school. "Everything but the clocks," Taylor told me.

Redd wouldn't admit to this. When I asked him if what Taylor had told me was true, he smiled but wouldn't say more.

PRINCE EDWARD ACADEMY IS ONE of a handful of private schools that opened before 1960 in the South that were formed specifically in response to threats of integration. It would be another five years before South Carolina opened its first segregation academy and the White Citizens' Council, based in Mississippi, opened the first of a chain of schools. By 1965, thirteen private schools attended by more than 5,600 white pupils were operating in Virginia.

For a quiet farming community, Prince Edward was ahead of its time in the segregation academy movement. It threatened to be a model of defiance for other localities around the South, as New Orleans and Atlanta both considered whether to integrate or to close their schools. Roy Pearson, who led the establishment of Prince Edward Academy, visited both communities. He told New Orleans residents in 1960 that private schools were the only way to maintain segregation, and he described the benefits of a private school system to the Georgia legis-lature. He suggested that neither of these cities would have any more difficulty than tiny Prince Edward County in setting up a network of private schools. When delegations from other localities in the South visited Prince Edward, Pearson encouraged them to follow the same course, saying it simply took "determination." He even wrote and pub-lished a handbook explaining how to do it.

Many Southern communities developed two school systems: an underfunded public system mostly attended by black students, and private schools set up for white children. Within a decade, these seg-regation academies would be an accepted part of the Southern land-scape. By 1969, three hundred thousand students were enrolled in all-white schools across eleven Southern states. And twenty years after *Brown*, in 1974, 10 percent of the South's white school-age children were attending private schools, only a fraction of which had been open before *Brown*. The region's 3,500 academies enrolled 750,000 white children, a number that reflected a migration from public to private schools that was linked to the movement of black children into formerly all-white public schools. In Jackson, Mississippi, white en-rollment in the public schools fell by twelve thousand students, from more than half of the student body in 1969 to less than a third eight years later. The proliferation of segregation academies threatened to create all-black public school systems in the rural South, particularly in counties with majority black populations.

The effect of these private schools would be felt decades later.

WHEN I CALL REDD, WHO served as the headmaster at Prince Edward Academy when I was a student, he seems to be expecting to hear from me. Even the tiniest tidbit of news zips through Farmville, and he had talked to Taylor about our interview years earlier. Redd suggests we meet at the new Central Virginia Regional Library in Farmville.

I would have recognized him anywhere. But the once portly head-master is now a slight man in his eighties. He moves cautiously, and his breathing is labored. At home, he uses oxygen. He talks more slowly, too. But he appears happy to see me, and we embrace. I think about how he cheerfully greeted me when I climbed off the bus as a first grader.

When Redd asks about my project, I tell him that part of my mo-tivation is learning more about my grandfather's role in the school. I tell him that I have been studying what happened in Prince Edward County, and I am struggling with the decisions that white leaders like Papa made so many years ago.

"Don't blame yourself," he tells me. "They weren't wrong. Not at that time."

Redd explains that white leaders established the school only after careful consideration. He compares Prince Edward County's decision to close the schools to the stance the South took leading up to the Civil War, reminding me that in 1861, leaders of Southern states thought they were doing exactly the right thing to secede from the Union. My heart sinks.

I believe the Civil War was fought over slavery, over a desire to keep blacks subservient and pay them low wages. Now Redd is con-necting Prince Edward's fight against desegregation to another South-ern cause I consider immoral.

Of course, I know that many Southerners claim the Civil War wasn't about slavery. They argue it was fought to protect states' rights and maintain a certain, cherished way of life. But now this rationale sounds eerily similar to the reasons the Defenders gave for not want-ing the schools to be desegregated. I see other parallels, too. Prince Edward's white leaders could benefit from keeping blacks uneducated the same way they benefitted from slavery.

Redd tells me the white residents of Farmville didn't want to be taxed for something they didn't believe in. They took pride in their efforts to start a school from scratch. "We thought it was monumental that we were maintaining lifestyle, culture, style, so important through the South," he tells me.

Redd is trying to make me feel better about the positions my grandfather and other white leaders staked out more than fifty years earlier. It's easy to look back and judge actions taken by others in the past, he tells me.

Like Robert Taylor, Redd senses disapproval in my line of questioning. "Whether you like it or not," he finally tells me, "your grandfather was a staunch supporter of PEA. He didn't give an inch."

The way Redd saw it—and perhaps my grandfather, too—desegregation would have happened gradually if it hadn't been forced down people's throats. The community would have accepted the change if it could have happened slowly, over time. "It could not happen en masse," Redd explains. This idea was one that had been regularly espoused by the *Farmville Herald* as well. There was too much difference in culture and ability between white and black students to suddenly combine the public schools, Redd believes.

Redd explains that the white leaders were doing what they thought was best for the community and that the negative coverage of his beloved academy still stings. "People say, 'Oh, look what they did down there,'" he tells me. "The reason they did is because they loved their children as your grandfather did you. We're not bad people," he says, locking eyes with me.

"I would do it again, probably," he adds. He wants to make sure I know I'm not any smarter than my grandfather and the other white leaders who made the decision to found the academy a half century earlier. "They made it on the basis of what they thought at that time was in the best interest of our country and our dearest possession—our children. That was what it was all about," he tells me. "You would have voted for it, too."

I can't help but wonder if what he says is true.

CHAPTER 7

Waiting and Seeing

Black parents had no plan. For years they'd heard the threats to close the public schools, but they figured that's all they were. Threats. No one wanted to believe that white leaders would actually refuse to provide public education. Even if white townspeople tried, surely the courts would not let them get away with it.

Parents kept their children out of the discussion in order to protect them—the same way white parents such as Mimi and Papa protected their children. The first time black students caught wind of the possibility of the schools' closing was in May 1959, as the school year was winding down. The Moton High School girls' basketball coach told the players to clean out their lockers, but the students paid little attention. Even after the supervisors' historic, well-publicized vote to cut off funding, many students still had trouble believing that white leaders would let the schools close.

"When you're seventeen, that's not real," said Marie Walton, who was going into the twelfth grade. "You can't conceive of the schools not opening." Other rising seniors felt the same. "It just didn't seem practical," said Bob Hamlin, a tall, shy teenager. "Why would they not want us to go to school?" "We thought they were just bluffing," said Ronnie Ward, the quarterback of the Moton football team.

Ronnie, compact and fit, kept right on practicing football with his teammates on the field at Moton, in spite of the news. "Aw, it's not going to close," he and his friends told each other. "We're going to be there another year."

Walton went off to New York to live with a sister and spend the summer working. Bob Hamlin helped his dad at work after school let out. They figured they'd be back at their desks come September.

Ronnie's youngest sister, Betty Jean Ward, was playing in the school yard when a white man posted a "No Trespassing" sign at Mary Branch Elementary School No. 1 on Main Street. She ran home to tell her father what the man had just done. "He told us we had to leave because schools weren't going to open," Betty Jean told her father.

"They're just talking," her dad responded. "They're going to open."

Even Oliver W. Hill Sr., the civil rights attorney, couldn't accept that the schools were closed. In a meeting with black parents more than two weeks after the board of supervisors' vote, Hill hinted that the courts might intervene. "They're not closed yet," he said.

While white parents spent the summer building makeshift desks to be installed in church basements, the black community took a wait-and-see approach. Black leaders didn't strategize for the coming school year, because it wasn't clear how long the schools would be shut. Griffin's eldest son, Skippy, who was twelve at the time, remembers that his father thought the schools would be closed for a year, maybe two—only long enough for white leaders to make a point.

To establish backup plans for their children would send a message that the black community was accepting the status quo—segregated schools—and that was the last thing they wanted to do. They hadn't watched their children protest the conditions of the black high school in 1951 and then sued to end school segregation to give up eight years later. They had come too far.

As the summer of 1959 wore on, it became increasingly clear that schools wouldn't open in the fall. Griffin brainstormed how to help Moton High School's students finish their educations. He was especially concerned about the seniors. He figured younger kids would be able to make up the lost time later, but if the older students didn't finish in a few years, the odds of them ever graduating were slim. "They were so close," Skippy Griffin said.

The students had been getting a solid, albeit segregated, education at the brand-new Moton High School, built after the students had filed their lawsuit against the county. The teachers were talented and they believed in their students, encouraging them not only to work toward a diploma but also to study for the sake of acquiring knowledge. The brick facility, located two miles from the old school, was such an up-grade that Betty Jean Ward's middle school teachers at Mary Branch No. 2—the old Moton High School—teased the students by saying that when they finished middle school they would go to "heaven."

In this period, a high school diploma was an important achieve-ment for both whites and blacks—but particularly for blacks. It sym-bolized an opportunity to accomplish more, to escape the lives their parents and grandparents led, working menial jobs or sharecropping. A diploma was also money in the bank. After graduating from high school, a black teenager could get a job at a hospital, enlist in the mil-itary, and even attend college. If the Moton students didn't graduate, their parents knew they'd all be working dead-end, minimum-wage jobs, struggling through life as maintenance workers, short-order cooks, farmers, housekeepers, or tobacco factory workers, as so many had before them.

ONCE GRIFFIN ACCEPTED THAT THE schools wouldn't open in the fall, he walked across Main Street to see the Reverend Alexander Isaiah "AI" Dunlap at Beulah African Methodist Episcopal Church. Dunlap suggested sending some of the high school students to the his-torically black Kittrell College, which the African Methodist Episco-pal Church (AME) ran in Kittrell, North Carolina, outside Henderson and some twenty miles from the Virginia line. Dunlap taught several days a week at the college, which was founded in 1886 by the North Carolina Conference of the AME and was struggling financially.

Dunlap lobbied the church bishop to allow Moton students to attend Kittrell so they could complete their educations. The school was already educating a handful of high school students, and Bishop Frank M. Reid agreed to expand its program to accommodate Prince Edward high school students, using the same facilities and teachers as the college. In the end, sixty-one Prince Edward students would enroll that year. Reid asked that the students pay half the tuition, but those who couldn't afford to contribute to their education were still allowed to attend. The Prince Edward County Christian Association, chaired by Griffin, would help pay their way. The school also granted work scholarships, and some students spent the year doing the menial jobs they were trying to avoid by getting an education—answering the phone at the college's reception desk, working in the cafeteria, and firing up the stove to heat the college president's home.

After Griffin made the Kittrell arrangements, he announced the news to parents and students. He knew some families were already making other plans for their children, and he told them that if it was possible to send their children north to live with family members, they should pursue that path. If that wasn't possible, "You really have no options but going to Kittrell," Griffin told them.

Black parents who had lived or traveled outside the county, those with some means, accepted that sending their children ninety miles away was the easiest, best solution and immediately signed on. Dozens of Farmville students would be together on an intimate campus, and they'd be studying under the tutelage of college professors. Other parents had reached out to relatives who lived outside the county—and out of state—to ask if they could send their children to live with them. Children climbed aboard buses bound for Philadelphia, Boston, and New York. There they would start new schools and make new friends but endure painful separation from their parents and siblings. Some would live with relatives they barely knew. Other children would stay on the weekdays with grandparents in counties that neighbored Prince Edward, and some would even be ferried across the county line daily. The separation of children from their parents echoed the indignities of slavery and the irreparable harm done when the closest of relationships were suddenly severed.

The great majority of parents, including Elsie and her husband, took a wait-and-see approach. Many didn't have the money, or the wherewithal, to send their children to live somewhere else. Others didn't have relatives they could call on to help. Their children simply stayed home. Early the next year, Griffin, aided by female volunteers, would establish training centers in the basements of black churches to keep children engaged in learning by providing math and reading instruction. The centers, attended by six hundred children, were supported with donations of books and money by black sororities and fraternities and other community organizations. They were meant to build morale, and they had no curriculum by intention.

But most black children received no formal schooling while the schools were closed. The older ones spent their days working in a tobacco field instead of learning algebra. The younger ones, unable to work, simply played at home, day in and day out.

ON SEPTEMBER 6, A MOTORCADE of twenty cars bound for Kittrell College lined up outside Griffin's church. The line stretched past the white State Theater on Main Street and around the corner at Southside Sundry on High Street. Some students were nervous because they had never been outside Prince Edward County, much less Virginia. They worried about how the college students would treat them. And they were scared to be away from their parents.

But the mood was festive as they prepared to leave for Kittrell.

Ronnie Ward was giddy as he climbed into his father's 1957 Plymouth. He and his sister Phyllistine would be among the first students to arrive at the college, and their parents were relieved to be sending them to school. As the vehicles headed out of town, with Dunlap and Griffin leading the way, the black parents drove their children toward a new life, honking their horns. A policeman yelled, "Shut up all that noise!" Students stuck their heads out of the windows, shouting at friends and waving good-bye to the community where most had lived their whole lives.

On the same day, Marie Walton, the rising Moton senior and the fifth of eleven children, left the rural Prince Edward community of Rice, an incorporated farming community six miles east of Farmville, where she lived with her mother and six younger siblings. Earlier that week, a teacher impressed with Marie had mentioned her to Dunlap, and he had dropped by to ask her mother if she could attend Kittrell. Marie, the oldest child still living at home, had just returned from New York, where she'd spent the summer waitressing while staying with an older sister. Friends had told her not to bother coming home because the schools weren't open.

"I didn't know what I was going to do," Marie said. "My mother hadn't made any decision."

For years, Marie had performed at the top of her class. A straight-A student, she loved school, but now she was terrified of what the future held. "I'm going to be a dropout," she worried. That was her likely path until Dunlap, a total stranger, arrived at the front door of their house. Her mother, Amanda, who had dropped out of school in the twelfth grade and now worked at the Dunnington Tobacco Company factory in downtown Farmville, agreed to let her go. "She didn't have any other options," Marie said. "She wanted us to go to school."

A younger sister who stayed home would become pregnant. Another sibling would go to live with relatives in New York. The others simply stayed home.

Three days after Dunlap's visit, Marie climbed into the car with another Rice family bound for North Carolina. "It just happened so fast," Marie said. "You prepare for college mentally and physically. You know you're going to leave home. We weren't really prepared for that."

In Kittrell, the black students found a leafy brick campus that was intimate and approachable. They registered at the school and settled into their dorm rooms. As the excitement wore off, the homesickness set in. That first night, a group of them built a bonfire in the parking lot of the administration building and sang songs, changing the words to a favorite tune. "I wanna go home," they crooned. "I want to go right back to Farmville."

As night fell, they sat around the bonfire, crying. "We wanted to be there to go to school," said Marie, "but we just wanted to go home."

THE DAY BEFORE SCHOOL WAS to start in 1959, Charlie Taylor caught a Greyhound bus back to Farmville from Atlantic City, where he'd spent the summer working. The previous spring, Charlie had told his parents he was tired of washing dishes for seventeen dollars a week at Longwood, where his father, Alonzo Hicks, was the head chef. Charlie told Hicks and his wife, Velma, a registered nurse at the one-hundred-bed Southside Community Hospital, that he wanted to work in New Jersey, where some of his friends were getting jobs. It was his first chance to get out of town.

In New Jersey, he stayed at a boarding house for six dollars a week and worked as a dishwasher at an Italian restaurant that paid three times more than any job in Prince Edward would. Plus, meals were provided.

The short, wiry eighteen-year-old called home only once the whole summer. In their brief phone conversation, Velma Hicks tried to tell Charlie about the school closures, but he wouldn't listen. He had things he wanted to talk about. He was free for the first time, tasting life outside the South. He told her how he regularly interacted with white people. His white boss even invited Charlie to his home for dinner, and Charlie was friendly with his boss's daughter. It was nothing like his sleepy hometown, where Charlie rarely spoke to white people.

Charlie came back to Farmville excited to begin his senior year at Moton High School. He was thrilled that he would be the editor of the school paper, the vice president of the senior class, and the cocaptain of the baseball and basketball teams. Velma Hicks had to break the news to him that the schools had closed.

His biological mother, Julia Taylor, who had a third-grade education, was a single mom, desperately poor and worn-down. She worked twelve hours a day at the Dunnington tobacco factory, shaking out tobacco leaves and hanging them to dry. His biological father wasn't in the picture. A few years earlier, Julia Taylor had taken in her two young nieces, and she had little energy or time left over for Charlie. When, at sixteen, Charlie befriended a classmate, Jerry, and began spending all his spare time at the boy's house, Jerry's parents offered to adopt Charlie. His mother allowed it so that his education and living expenses would be covered.

"I went home with their son one day and never came home," Charlie said.

Over their lifetimes, the Hicks family would take in several other children, a common practice for black families with means in the South. They gave Charlie the emotional and financial support he needed. They opened a bank account in his name and deposited a weekly allowance. Julia Taylor had missed Charlie's all-conference and all-state basketball and baseball games for work, but the Hickses sat in the stands nearly every game.

For once, everything was going Charlie's way. He wanted nothing more than the chance to shine in his final year of high school. "Seniors don't want to miss their senior year," Charlie said, "and they sure don't want to have it somewhere else."

When his mother told him that his friends had already left for a school in North Carolina, Charlie packed a paper grocery sack with pants and shirts. The next day, he climbed into the backseat of Dunlap's white Oldsmobile 88. Griffin, a family friend, and Dunlap, whom he had known for years, drove Charlie to Kittrell.

He sat quietly, listening to the pair of preachers talk as the car weaved down country roads. The men didn't think the school closures would last long, words that brought relief to Charlie. By the time they arrived in Kittrell and he set foot on the small campus, he thought of it as a temporary stop.

That night, Charlie and his friends sat on the steps of the administration building catching up on what had happened over the summer. Charlie told stories about his first encounter with openly gay people—waiters he had met working in New Jersey—and the white restaurant owner who had invited him to his home. They discussed their futures until the early morning, considering what the coming months would hold. All Charlie could think about was getting back to Moton.

For the first weeks of school, Charlie walked around in a daze. Sports were his life, and this year was supposed to be his chance to perform. College recruiters had already expressed an interest in him. But after he arrived in North Carolina, he learned that high school students weren't eligible to participate in Kittrell's athletic programs. He was heartbroken. "The thing that I loved the most had been taken away from me," he said. "I was miserable. My world had come to an end."

Angry and confused, Charlie slipped on his coat and shoes and walked a quarter mile from his dorm room down the dark, winding road to the gymnasium. This was his therapy. Whenever he felt sad or depressed, he walked back and forth on the road, praying as he pounded the pavement. He wondered if things would ever get better.

For many of the students, being away from their families was the most difficult part of their new life at Kittrell. For Charlie, who had only recently formed a strong bond with his adoptive parents, the separation was particularly challenging. The one thing that made this new life easier to accept was that so many members of his senior class were in the same boat. They were all living without their mama's cooking, eating the bland, mushy grits served in the cafeteria. They got used to the run-down school and the chilly dorm rooms. They made do.

They had been taught not to complain, and they'd been told not to concern themselves with what they didn't have. Instead, they focused on the reason they were in North Carolina—to continue their educations. "At least you were going to get a diploma," Charlie said.

The faculty looked out for them, scheduling Friday afternoon tutoring sessions to help the high school students complete their assignments. Some professors even offered to work with the Moton students on weekends.

Over time, the students became each other's families. On Saturdays, they went for walks around campus. They attended Sunday school and church together. Afterward, the boys visited the girls' dorm for a few hours, hoping to be offered a sandwich or a piece of cake from the baskets that parents sent weekly.

They stayed busy with schoolwork and their campus jobs. Charlie was a firefighter in a girls' dorm. He also hung around the gym during the college basketball team's practices, and the coach asked him to serve as a trainer for the team. He made dinner and hotel reservations for away games. Before long, he was helping to run practices, subbing as a guard to run the team up and down the court. "Some of the things that I wanted and needed were coming back to me," he said.

The Moton students kept up with news from Farmville. Once a week, Griffin would visit and update them on the progress—or lack thereof. By December, Charlie had accepted that he would not graduate from Moton. Other students poured their energy into making the year as much like high school as possible, planning a prom and putting together a yearbook. But this year away from their families would never replace the year they were supposed to have as Moton seniors.

ONE SUNDAY MORNING DURING A visit to Farmville from Boston in 2010, I ask my parents if I can leave Amaya and Selma with them for a few hours. I want to go hear Elsie sing. After breakfast, I drive downtown to the First Baptist Church, on South Main Street. It is my first visit to the historic black church. I slide into a curved pew, the wood cold on my bare legs. For years I have wanted to come, but until this trip to see my parents, I've never worked up the nerve to walk in.

Elsie's reaction to me when I first arrive confirms why I had reservations. As I enter the church, I introduce myself to Elsie's preacher and to some members of the congregation. When I see Elsie in the back of the church, I say hello and give her a hug. She seems uncomfortable, like she wants to escape. Does she dislike having me in her space, where few white people worship? Was I wrong to have come?

I lean forward to say hello to the elderly black woman seated in front of me. Nellie Coles, who served as the county health nurse for decades, introduces herself. She asks about my family, then tells me that my great-grandmother, Epsie Vale, was a friend. Coles tells me that she knew my father when he was a boy. I tell her I've known Elsie since I was a child and that I've come to hear her sing.

I sit back, soaking up the atmosphere of this sacred place where Griffin preached, where Hill met in the basement with Barbara Johns and her classmates and agreed to take their case. For years I have wanted to hear Elsie's voice in harmony with her church choir, to see her in her element, where she is most herself. But I can tell my presence is awkward for her. I understand, since most of our interactions over the years have been in my parents' or grandparents' home.

Only a couple of dozen people attend the service. Summer is a slow time, and as with many black churches around the country, the size of the congregation has dipped. But this one-room church was once the core of the county's black community and considered by some the birthplace of the modern civil rights movement in education. While it still sits on the corner of South Main and Fourth Streets, the shopping center behind it was leveled and rebuilt. The church, off to the side of a brick mixed-use housing and retail complex geared toward Longwood students, is an artifact of an earlier time.

Sitting alone, I am anxious. I pull out my recorder and my notebook. I fiddle with my phone. Then I sit in the airy sanctuary, still, concentrating on my breath. I try to embrace the few minutes of quiet. I notice the church's tall ceilings and gigantic brass chandeliers, the pale yellow walls and beveled glass windows. I notice the cool temperature, the air blowing over me, as soothing as a summer breeze on a hot day. And then, as the choir begins singing, I watch Elsie in front of the congregation, dressed in a white robe, swaying.

> *Glory, glory, hallelujah.*
> *Since I laid my burden down.*
> *Glory, glory, hallelujah.*
> *Since I laid my burden down.*

As the choir sings, I feel something welling up inside me. The music is so beautiful, and my life so hectic. I spend my days locked in a monotonous cycle of chores, caring for and cleaning up after small children. I don't have the energy to do anything else, not to call friends, not to write, not to exercise. In these long days that slide into each other and blur, my thoughts rarely turn inward. I can't remember who I used to be, who I am, except someone's mother.

But in this sanctuary, I am free. The tightness in my neck and shoulders, even my jaw, loosens. A feeling of great sadness washes over me, and unexpected tears stream down my face. Something is missing from my life. I wonder if I am reacting to being back inside a church after years away. Maybe I need a higher power. Or am I simply touched by being in such an important place in Farmville's history?

Then it dawns on me: this is one of the first times I have been among a group of black Farmville residents in *their* space. Growing up in Prince Edward, I rarely considered that other people existed beyond the community of whites I encountered at school and at church. For thirty-five years I have known only a few blacks in my hometown. I never participated in their cultural events. I didn't have black friends, black teachers, or black neighbors.

My cheeks wet with tears, I am mourning what could have been, not just for me, but for this community.

CHAPTER 8

Nigger Lovers

S ix miles outside Farmville, in Rice, eight-year-old Beverly Bass heard the screen door slam again and again. Black fathers and mothers from around the rural community drove up the gravel road to her family's farmhouse and knocked on the rickety back door at all hours of the day. They came to ask her father, B. Calvin Bass, who was white, "What should we do with our children?"

Poor white parents came to the front door with their own questions. They couldn't afford to send their children to the new private school that the white leaders were starting. How were their kids supposed to get an education?

Bass, an educated country boy who worked as a dairy farmer and a college professor, was a county school board member who had served as chairman. One of the few dissenters, he had pleaded with the board of supervisors not to close the schools. He had started speaking out in 1955, when the Defenders first proposed that the supervisors limit school funding. He had told the supervisors that a vote was premature—no black children had even applied to attend the schools that fall. Besides, the school board's attorney had advised board members that the courts would probably allow Prince Edward to operate segregated schools for another year. They disregarded Bass.

After the supervisors voted in 1959 to close the schools, Bass set up a meeting with then attorney general Albertis S. Harrison Jr. to propose that the white school receive funds equal to the county's regular contribution to public schools and that the state provide matching funds to keep the public schools open. His suggestion went nowhere.

AS A CHILD, BEVERLY DIDN'T know much about the contrarian stance her father took. They didn't talk about it over supper and he never explained his position to his children. Yet she had picked up on what was happening.

When she and her mother, Beatrice, went to Farmville to shop, certain stores wouldn't wait on them. Her mother also avoided shops on the corner of North Main Street and West Third Street, where the particularly unfriendly E. Louis Dahl, the treasurer of the Prince Edward School Foundation and a leader of the Defenders, operated his Army Goods Store. Sometimes, as they walked down the sidewalk, her mother would grab Beverly's hand and lead her across the street to avoid white residents who called her father "nigger lover."

Journalists had also become a regular presence in her house. They sat on the front porch, sipping tea and interviewing her dad. She knew why they were there, but unlike Skippy Griffin, whose preacher father had given him a front row seat to the civil rights movement happening in Prince Edward, Beverly wasn't allowed to listen to her father's conversations. When she walked onto the porch, he shooed her off. "Go away, little girl," he told her. "We're talking."

Her father had grown up working side by side with blacks on the "homeplace," as they referred to their family farm. Now B. Calvin Bass ran a dairy farm on the property, which he and his mother owned. Most white leaders in town didn't personally know as many blacks as he did. Bass, who also worked as a chemistry professor at Hampden-Sydney College, believed they deserved an education.

"Dad was always in favor of education, period," Beverly told me. "He did not want to see the schools closed, and that put him out of favor with the county." He knew the agrarian era was ending, and he thought schooling would enable blacks to find other meaningful work. "The only way these kids were going to come off the farm was to be educated," she told me.

But her father was no bleeding liberal, not by any stretch of the imagination. At his core he was conservative. "He was probably as prejudiced as the next person," she said. He referred to blacks as "darkies." He and her mom were shocked the first time a black person knocked on the family's front door instead of the back. Still, the stance he took against closing the schools was unique and brave.

"He did push the limits with his thinking," she said. "For his time, he did push it out."

Bass also opposed the premise of the white academy, given that it was founded by many of the Defenders who had argued against him. But with the public schools closed and Hampden-Sydney College offering to foot the academy's tuition bill for professors' children, he had no other options for his children.

"Where else would I go?" Beverly asked me.

PRINCE EDWARD'S RESIDENTS PRIDED THEMSELVES on keeping this disagreement about integrating the schools both civil and nonviolent. As Virginians, they were horrified by what was happening farther south: slurs being yelled at children, the Ku Klux Klan burning crosses, lynchings. The death of Emmett Till, a fourteen-year-old black boy from Chicago who had been attacked by two white men after he whistled at a white woman in Mississippi in August 1955, had been especially gruesome.

This wasn't the way Southern gentlemen behaved. Virginians considered themselves different from the people who lived in the Deep South. More refined, genteel even. "They imagine themselves in the highly racialized South, yet somehow above it," the historian and University of Richmond president Edward L. Ayers told me. "It really is a deeply ingrained identity."

"Politics in Virginia is reserved for those who can qualify as gentlemen," V. O. Key wrote in his 1949 book, *Southern Politics*. "Rabble-rousing and Negro baiting capacities, which in Georgia or Mississippi would be a great political asset, simply mark a person as one not to the manner born."

The Defenders wanted to keep segregation in place, but they didn't need to do it by killing, maiming, and burning. They relied instead on psychological tactics and economic repercussions, such as denying blacks credit at the grocery store without explanation. Otto Overton, the Farmville police chief, wanted to make sure the town wasn't further stained by violence, Skippy Griffin told me. He and other white leaders reached out to L. Francis Griffin, asking him to ensure that blacks did not commit acts of violence. They both agreed to work with their communities.

Those were "the terms of the struggles," Skippy Griffin told me. "It wasn't accidental. . . . It was a deliberate, conscious decision on their part."

White leaders were proud of the display of civility. Farmville's mayor, William F. Watkins Jr., noted the "wonderful relations" between blacks and whites. The *Farmville Herald* praised residents for their behavior. "It's a credit to the people of this county," said Robert Taylor, one of the academy's founders. "We haven't had so much as an argument between the races."

Indeed, it was a blessing that no one was badly beaten or lynched, as in other Southern communities. But the lack of violence also meant that the school closures never attracted the amount of media attention that they deserved, attention that might have put pressure on the county to reopen its schools sooner.

ON A BALMY FEBRUARY DAY in 2013, I walk down Main Street, past boarded-up storefronts and into a store I frequented for years.

While I am interviewing the owner, who has known me since I was a child, a young black man in his early twenties walks in wearing a down coat. He asks to use the phone, and the owner, keeping a close eye on him, agrees after being assured the call is local. After a brief conversation, the young man hangs up and walks out of the store without another word.

When he leaves, the business owner turns to me and explains that *this* is precisely the reason he has considered keeping a gun. I don't know what he means. The encounter seemed innocuous.

"Why?" I ask, and the owner explodes. "Because Farmville still has *niggers*!" he shouts.

A few minutes later, he acts as if it never happened, as if his behavior was perfectly normal. He tells me that he likes black people. He doesn't need to have them over for cocktails, but he likes them.

As I began researching this book, I had hoped that the racism my hometown was known for had faded away. But I have realized that it's still there, just not out in the open the way it was in the 1950s, when people uttered hateful slurs as they passed Bass's wife and children on the street. Now people reveal their racist beliefs in Farmville the same way they do in towns across America: when they are comfortable, when they think they are among like-minded people, particularly when they have a glass of alcohol in hand. At a Farmville bar, a high school classmate of one of my brothers asks how he likes being around so many "niggers" in northern Virginia. The "Indian pony" comment came during a Christmas party.

On occasion, someone spews racist slurs, seemingly without provocation. I keep replaying the scene with the young black man in the store, wondering what he had done to spark such vitriol from the owner. But I come up empty.

CHAPTER 9

"You Go Where Your Parents Tell You To"

On September 10, 1959, the new private school's buses rolled down rural county roads and up Farmville's streets, picking up white children and delivering them to makeshift schools. Nearly 1,500 white students from around the county, including my parents and uncles, would attend classes in a mix of churches, former homes, and vacant stores.

My mom, who was nine, walked up High Street, stopping in front of the handsome Farmville Women's Club House, staring up at its elegant second-floor balcony. Four wide Grecian columns graced the circular vestibule at the entryway of the former home, painted white with a red roof and shutters.

For four years, Mom had attended the brick Farmville Elementary School on the Longwood campus. That summer, her parents had informed her that she would be switching schools, but they didn't explain why. "You protected your children from what was going on in the world," she told me.

Her classmate Jim Ennis, now the county's commonwealth's attorney, had been kept in the dark, too. Ennis, the son of a Farmville television salesman, cared about his circle of friends, what he was going to do after school, and how much homework he had to complete each night. He was oblivious to everything else, particularly the politics surrounding the school closing. "You go to school, and you go where your parents tell you to," he explained.

In 1959, Mom didn't know that black students had walked out of Moton High School eight years earlier, when she was a baby, and she wouldn't learn about it for decades. Mimi and Papa had told her the court ruling was the reason she was changing schools, and she had heard Papa talking about how he disagreed with the courts forcing schools to desegregate. "My dad did not want us going to school with black children," she said. "He was very angry at the government for making that choice." Papa thought it should be up to him to decide if his children attended school with black children. He didn't want the Supreme Court making that call for him.

Mimi and Papa prepared Mom for the change by telling her that she would be able to walk to her new school and that she'd be with her classmates from Farmville Elementary. They made the transition seem ordinary. She didn't know that black children like Elsie's daughter, Gwen, didn't have a school to attend. She didn't know that the schools for black students were closed and that parents were sending their children to live with relatives in other counties, even other states. She had never had black classmates. She had never played with any black children other than Gwen. All she knew was that she was going to a pretty new school.

"We had no idea what a big deal it really was to the black community," Mom told me.

JUST OUTSIDE TOWN, BEHIND THE county fairgrounds off Route 460, my father, Chuck Green, along with two of his younger brothers, Steve and Mike, waited at the end of their gravel driveway for a bus to pick them up and take them to their new schools.

The bus dropped Dad at the Farmville Moose Lodge, a bare hall with wooden floors. He didn't like this school, which smelled of stale beer and cigarettes. His seventh-grade class was separated from other classrooms with a simple partition, and he could hear everything being said next door. There was no playground, so at recess he and his friends tossed a ball next to the building.

The previous year, my dad, Steve, and Mike, who ranged in age from eight to twelve, had attended Farmville Elementary School. They had just moved to the county with their strict grandmother, who lived in an old farmhouse her father had built on twenty-three acres. Epsie Vale, who had brought up eleven children of her own, was now raising her four young grandsons. Their father, a chief warrant officer for the navy, died of leukemia when my dad was nine, and Granny Vale stepped in to care for the boys when their mother's alcoholism progressed. Within a year of taking them in, Granny Vale would sit the boys down on her bed and deliver the news that their mother had died.

After briefly staying with relatives near Richmond, where she had been working, Granny Vale returned with the boys to Prince Edward, to the house on Fairgrounds Road. Vale, a religious woman who was twice widowed, spent hours each day praying and reading the Bible, and she required the boys do the same. They lived a meager existence, surviving off their father's military pension and money from her grown children. When I asked my dad how his grandmother managed to pay the academy's tuition, he wasn't sure. It's possible they were given scholarships.

Granny Vale collected and distributed clothes and food to families in even greater need. The back porch was piled high with donations that she would sort and deliver to both black and white families living in country shacks. The Bible told her to take care of those in need. It also told her that blacks and whites should be segregated, and she found scripture passages to support her reasoning. When she fed a needy black man who worked on her farm, he ate on the back porch. But a little black boy was invited to sit at her kitchen table.

"She loved black people," my dad told me. "She just thought she was better."

Granny Vale believed black people deserved respect and care. She forbade the boys from speaking negatively about them. She particularly disliked disparaging terms like "nigger," which many white kids in the rural community used freely. My dad and his brothers wouldn't have dreamed of uttering the slur. "She thought that was extremely demeaning," my uncle Steve told me. "As far as she was concerned, everybody had a soul."

When the white academy was formed, she didn't object to her grandchildren attending a segregated school. It was the only option. She accepted the status quo, my dad told me, but she never condemned black residents for wanting to integrate the schools. Instead, she told her grandsons that she often thought about their children.

"It's terrible," she said, "that the black kids don't have anywhere to go to school."

THE ELEGANT EXTERIOR OF THE women's club where my mom attended school announced to the community that white children had everything they needed. In truth, the clubhouse was packed uncomfortably full. A pair of front parlors had been converted into classrooms. Students could barely walk through the rooms, where thirty desks were crammed.

My mom quickly learned that if she needed to use the bathroom, she should go before class began. After school, students would remove the desks and the chalkboard to prepare the parlors for the club's afternoon tea. The fourth graders studied from hand-me-down books with torn backs and unraveled bindings. There weren't enough books for every student, so they had to share. And teachers couldn't assign homework, because they didn't want to risk losing the few books they had. Recess was different, too. The clubhouse had a tiny yard compared with the playgrounds the students were accustomed to. Whenever the students played kickball or baseball, they had to run down the hill to retrieve the ball from the thick bamboo that rimmed the property on the banks of Buffalo Creek. It took time to get used to the tiny classrooms, but for the most part, school was school and my mom and her classmates adapted to the new setting.

Mom's teacher that year, Elizabeth Crute Goode, was one of the best of her life. When Mom had trouble with an assignment, her teacher spent extra time working with her. When Goode noticed my mom squinting at the blackboard, she told Mimi. Mom came back to school with glasses, and a whole new world opened up to her. She could finally see the blackboard. One night, she walked outside and saw stars for the first time.

Mom's favorite thing about her new school was being allowed to walk home, even though her new black-and-white saddle shoes dug blisters into her heels on the half-mile journey. The best part of her day was stopping at the neighborhood grocery, Butcher's Store, on the corner of Griffin Boulevard and High Street. It was the same grocery store that Griffin's son Skippy had dropped by with his friends after school. The black children stood in a corner, where George Fred Butcher would bring them a selection of candy and sodas. After they'd paid for the treats, they were expected to leave. On days when the store was busy, Butcher dismissed Skippy and his friends with a simple, "Not now, come back later." Skippy understood the rules of segregation, and even as a young boy, he recognized that he should adhere to customs. It was just the way things were.

When Mom walked inside Butcher's store to buy a five-cent bottle of Coca-Cola, she sat down at a little table inside the store, feeling the cold sweetness trickle down her throat, the tiny bubbles making everything brighter.

. . . .

THE STORE OWNER'S DAUGHTER-IN-LAW, REBECCA Butcher, taught at the academy from the day it opened.

She had graduated from Longwood, married Buck Butcher, and taught home economics for three years at Worsham Elementary, the handsome two-story brick school with indoor plumbing and heat where Robert Redd and J. Boyd Bagby had also worked. The school was located six miles outside Farmville in the community of Worsham, which had served as Prince Edward's county seat until 1872. Butcher took pride in her classroom's neat, homey appearance. She decorated the bulletin boards, collected books, and hung posters to create an inviting space for students to learn. She relished teaching in such an organized setting.

When the schools closed, she lost all the teaching materials she'd spent years collecting. Academy administrators may have accessed public school supplies, but anything teachers had personally bought was locked inside the school. One morning, a county official opened the school doors for teachers to retrieve their belongings, and Butcher took a punch set that the home economics teachers had pooled their money to buy, but nothing else.

Like the vast majority of white teachers who worked for the public school system, Butcher transitioned to working for the private school foundation. A tiny, birdlike woman, she hopped around from makeshift school to makeshift school, working as a long-term substitute until she was hired as a full-time teacher. There was nothing fancy about any of the academy's borrowed facilities. Teachers in the new private school system felt that their struggles were overlooked.

"We suffered, too," Butcher told me. "And let me tell you how we suffered."

On opening day, she taught class aboard a yellow school bus parked outside Worsham Baptist Church. The school foundation was building an addition at the church for more classroom space, but it had not yet been completed. The conditions on the bus that opening day weren't so different from the ones the Moton students had protested in 1951, but white parents were willing for their children to endure these second-rate facilities for the sake of an all-white education.

The buildings varied by location, but they had much in common: There were no lunchrooms—students either ate in the classroom or left early enough to eat lunch at home. There were no playgrounds. In eighth grade, my father broke his wrist at recess running backward in a paved parking lot across the street from Farmville Baptist Church.

The academy couldn't offer art or music classes. Even basic classroom supplies were limited. Butcher scavenged her house for newspapers, sheets of cardboard inside her husband's new dress shirts, and brown paper grocery bags—anything she could find that the kids could use for drawing and painting. "It was a lot of making do," she said.

Because there were so few textbooks and no mimeograph machines, Butcher wrote worksheets by hand for each of her thirty students. She read test questions aloud and required students to write their answers on sheets of blank paper. Butcher grew accustomed to the lack of resources and the makeshift classrooms. Still, she dreaded dismantling and reassembling the room every week. On Friday afternoons, she took down the bulletin board decorations, then folded the metal chairs and put them away. When Monday morning rolled around, she set up the entire classroom again.

She was depressed by the surroundings, which included a Ping-Pong table and paper bags spilling donated clothing. She spent her second year teaching in the damp, unfinished basement of the Moose Lodge, and she had to tilt her head back and glance up at a row of tiny windows to glimpse any natural light. This classroom—if you could call it that—was nothing like that which she had envisioned as an idealistic college student considering a career in education. "It was such a mess," she said.

In the Moose Lodge's basement, the temperature never rose above 65 degrees, and Butcher stayed uncomfortably cold, even in a full-length wool pleated skirt paired with thick tights. She sat on her knees while she taught, keeping her legs warm underneath her.

That year, a paper-thin partition separated Butcher's class from Agnes Watkins's. Sometimes Watkins called out math answers while Butcher was testing her students. Having one bathroom was also a challenge. She lined up the girls to use the restroom, and then the boys got a chance. When the kids were thirsty, she sent a pair of boys upstairs to fill a bucket in the Moose Lodge's kitchen, and then she used a dipper to fill water cups her students made from sheets of paper. Eventually Butcher grew accustomed to teaching in these basic conditions, but she never liked it.

"We did our best teaching those years," Butcher told me, "because we couldn't do anything else but teach."

Butcher called what she and the academy students endured in those years "suffering." But I kept thinking about Shirley Davidson, a black six-year-old, who each day got dressed and pretended she was going to school, too, skipping down the hill from her home to the bus stop. I kept thinking about all the children who would never reenter a classroom.

Wasn't that the real suffering?

ONE OF THE TOUGHEST CHOICES parents make is deciding where to send their children to school. Now that it's time for Jason and me to think about it, I'm grateful we have options: How much should we shelter our girls, and how much should we expose them to? Can we strike a balance? Is that even possible?

We are considering whether to move Amaya, who is four, from her tiny church school to a public preschool center in a neighborhood near ours. I am touring the dated one-story brick building, constructed in the 1950s and badly in need of a makeover, yet bursting with life. Walking the hallways, I admire the children's paintings adorning the walls. I peek into classrooms with neatly arranged cubicles, where four- and five-year-olds are happily playing in learning centers, cooking meals in miniature kitchens, and sitting at desks writing their names.

Some parents aren't sure about sending their children to a preschool that is 80 percent black with children from tougher neighborhoods. But I like the idea of our girls in classrooms that are more reflective of our majority-black city with its growing Latino and Asian populations. I want to ensure that, from a young age, my children have a different experience than I did, learning with teachers and classmates of different races, who come from different socioeconomic backgrounds, who speak languages other than English. I want them to understand that not everyone's life looks exactly like theirs, to understand that our differences make life infinitely more interesting. Jason and I believe public school will expose our daughters to more diversity and more humanity than most private school educations.

We also believe vibrant public schools are essential to create thriving communities and that all children should have access to good, free education, as Jason did growing up in Texas. We know how important it is for parents to invest in neighborhood schools, and we want to be engaged in improving the schools our daughters attend.

But there's a catch. Richmond is a failing school district. Test scores and graduation rates are low. Students who manage to get a diploma often don't go to college. The city's high poverty rate is partly to blame, as is student truancy. And the schools in the region are increasingly segregated by income as well as race. In Richmond, most schools are overwhelmingly black, which, in this city, translates to poor. Seventy-seven percent of students qualify for free and reduced lunches, and there are many barriers to their academic success, from not having enough to eat to not having a parent at home encouraging them to do homework.

When we moved to Richmond, choosing a neighborhood with an excellent elementary school wasn't yet a priority. The girls were toddlers, and school was barely on our radar. Yet we liked that the neighborhood school was diverse. When our girls enter kindergarten, we will benefit from renting a house in a zone with a revered elementary school and engaged parents. Before walking their children to class each morning down wide wooden hallways, parents chat in front of the century-old brick elementary school while the children play in the grass and ride scooters. Parents devote hundreds of hours to volunteering for the PTA, a fund-raising machine that can bring in tens of thousands of dollars in a single night to support the school's programs.

If Jason and I had chosen to live in a neighborhood in Richmond with an elementary school that wasn't as highly regarded, I would have worked to make the school better, volunteering in my daughter's classrooms and joining the PTA, or we would have applied for our children to attend a different public school. But most middle-income Richmond parents who are comfortable sending their children to a public elementary school in their neighborhood—and plenty are not—tend to move to the suburbs for middle school or enroll their children in one of the region's many private schools. There is a sense that, in the upper grades, kids without learning or behavioral problems go unchallenged in Richmond Public Schools' classrooms. Many parents aren't willing to risk putting their children in that position, and, by middle school, they have tired of a curriculum that seems to revolve around standardized tests. Thus the number of children leaving Richmond's public schools every year is about half the number who enroll.

Many white children in this city never set foot in a public school. They follow in the footsteps of their parents and grandparents, attending private schools from the moment they hit kindergarten. This private school pipeline contributes to the racial disparity of the public schools, the same way my alma mater does in Farmville. Richmonders, like many in Prince Edward and around the country, have effectively given up on public school education. And the abandonment of Richmond's public schools by white and middle-income parents creates a self-fulfilling prophecy of schools that continue to perform poorly.

But when I consider how I might respond to Amaya or Selma being ignored or bullied in a public school setting, Redd's words echo in my ear: "You'd do the same thing."

He's probably right. Jason and I would find another option in a heartbeat. A private school, perhaps. We want what's best for our children, just as my grandfather did for his.

CHAPTER 10

Elsie's Other Life

Elsie had worked as a housekeeper for our family for as long as I could remember. Before that, she worked for my grandparents for as long as my mother and aunt could remember. As a child, I never imagined that Elsie had a life before us.

Elsie Mary Anderson was one of seven siblings, born in 1926. She grew up six miles outside Farmville in Hampden Sydney, in a mixed-race community just beyond the gates of the all-male Hampden-Sydney College, founded in 1775. Elsie's father, John T. Anderson, worked as a chef at the college, and Elsie was sometimes allowed to accompany him to work. At home, she played with white and black children.

At first, the family lived in a rental house, but her father saved to build a two-bedroom wood home with front and back porches, becoming the first black homeowner Elsie knew. He bought a television, too, and their neighbors and friends from church came over to watch boxing.

In high school, Elsie began dating a man seven years her senior. Melvin Lancaster, a cousin of her older sister's husband, was good in algebra and offered to help her with homework. She graduated from high school in 1945, and she wanted to go to college. Instead, she married Melvin and gave birth to Gwen the year after she graduated. While many of her siblings would move—north to Massachusetts, south to North Carolina—Elsie made Prince Edward County her home.

When Gwen was small, Elsie stayed home with her in a little house in Farmville. Then, around 1954, she filled in for her injured mother-in-law cleaning Mimi and Papa's house and looking after my mom and her siblings, and they later offered the job to her. Melvin didn't want Elsie to take it. He preferred her being at home, and he didn't want her working for a white family. But once she started earning money, Elsie never left. She liked the freedom the job gave her. She didn't want to have to ask Melvin every time she needed a few dollars.

She lived two blocks away from my grandparents on West Third Street, in a wood house on a hill. Several mornings a week, she walked to Mimi and Papa's brick house, where she would vacuum, iron, and help my grandmother care for the three children, nine-year-old Chuck, my five-year-old mother, and Beverley Anne, the newborn baby.

Mimi sometimes left Elsie alone with the children, slipping on white gloves and driving with a friend to Richmond for lunch and shopping at the downtown department store, Thalhimers. While Mom and her brother were at school, Elsie would dress my aunt, Beverley Anne, and brush her hair with a soft-bristled brush. Then they would walk downtown to the five and dime, J. J. Newberry Department Store. Elsie wasn't allowed to sit at the counter, but shopping was acceptable. Elsie and Beverley Anne would wander around the store until it was time to get the girl home. At naptime, Elsie pulled the child onto her lap or sat next to her on the bed, reading a story.

Occasionally Mimi and Papa would host bridge parties and ask Elsie to work at night. They set up three card tables in the living room, and Elsie would serve the guests and refill drinks. On New Year's Eve, she would stay with the children so Mimi and Papa could attend a party, and when they returned home at 2:00 a.m. with another couple, Elsie would prepare an early morning breakfast of eggs, bacon, and sausage.

But on days Mimi was home, she did the cooking herself. She would serve Elsie's lunch at noon, which Elsie ate alone, seated at the round table in the sunny breakfast nook. By the time my grandfather walked in the back door at precisely 1:10 p.m., Elsie was back at work, ironing in the basement. Papa would sit on the green pleather cushions at the same table where Elsie had eaten. Mimi had already swept away the crumbs and laid out his plate of food.

WHITES IN PRINCE EDWARD DIDN'T want their children going to school with black children, but, like whites all over the South, they were plenty comfortable having black women work in their homes. The domestic landscape of my grandparents' house looked similar to other professional families in town. White families typically hired black women to help with the laundry, the cleaning, the cooking—especially if they had children to care for. Some had their help come every day, while others shared housekeepers. Elsie split her time between my grandparents' house and the home of another family. Whites were comfortable with the intimate relationship they had with housekeepers as long as blacks knew their place. For Elsie, these unspoken rules meant not discussing the school closures and riding in the backseat when my grandparents drove her home.

In public life, the rules were stricter. In Farmville in the 1950s, just about every aspect of life was segregated. The churches were separate. Blacks and whites didn't eat in the same restaurants. Their children attended separate schools. They swam in adjacent lakes at a state park. They didn't sit together in the movie theater. One movie theater was just for whites; the other theater allowed blacks to sit upstairs. Water fountains and restrooms were separate. Often, the black facilities—if they were even offered—were grossly inferior. At many restaurants, blacks could order food for take-out but there was nowhere for them to eat inside. They weren't permitted in the library's reading room, either. Even the creek that ran through town was segregated. Black kids played in it one day, whites the next. For the most part, blacks and whites lived in distinct but close neighborhoods. They also had separate shopping districts, though blacks often shopped in white-owned stores and were given credit to buy the things they needed.

Across the South, most blacks didn't even speak to whites on the street—not unless they were spoken to. A black man was expected to keep his head low, avoiding eye contact if he passed a white woman. It's hard for me to imagine that this kind of divided society was the norm at the time, almost one hundred years after the Emancipation Proclamation. But the Supreme Court's 1857 decision in *Dred Scott v. Sandford*, which ruled that people of African ancestry were not and would never be eligible to be US citizens, had profound implications. Though the case was never overruled, the Fourteenth Amendment, ratified after the Civil War, gave equal citizenship to freed slaves and promised them "equal protection under the law." After Reconstruction, whites tried to take back the power they had lost by adopting laws state by state to legally enforce segregation that disadvantaged blacks.

Though the 1875 Civil Rights Act entitled all races to equal treatment, an 1883 Supreme Court decision clarified that the law did not apply to private persons or corporations. In 1892, Homer Plessy, a mixed-race man, challenged that ruling by boarding a train and sitting in the whites-only car. After years of appeals, the Supreme Court ruled in 1896 that "separate" facilities for blacks and whites were constitutional as long as they were "equal" and were not a violation of the Fourteenth Amendment. The *Plessy v. Ferguson* decision signaled the federal government's unwillingness to challenge segregation. It also upheld the constitutionality of the states' Jim Crow laws, which mandated segregation in public venues such as restaurants, hotels, beaches, theaters, and restrooms. Facilities for blacks were often inferior, if they even existed. Southern politicians worked to further restrict blacks from voting and to make them ineligible to serve on jury pools or run for office by instituting poll taxes, literacy requirements, and grandfather clauses that restricted the right to vote to people whose ancestors had voted before the Civil War.

WHEN THE SCHOOLS CLOSED IN 1959, Elsie had been working for my grandparents for five years. Yet my grandparents never talked with Elsie about the decision or its ramifications, even though her daughter, Gwen, was twelve and her school was closing, too. A few times, Gwen accompanied Elsie to my grandparents' house, where she played with my mother. But my grandparents didn't ask where Gwen was the rest of the time.

As the white community was enjoying its newly opened academy, Mimi made an offhand comment. Elsie and her friends should "get a group together and open up a school," Mimi told her. Elsie understood exactly what Mimi meant. My grandmother hoped the black community would follow in the white leaders' footsteps "so we wouldn't be bothering them to integrate."

Elsie never told her friends or family what my grandmother had said. She didn't dare mention it to Melvin, either. His cousin John Lancaster had been a PTA leader who had urged county leaders to improve the black high school, and his support of the student walkout had cost him his job as a county extension agent.

Elsie knew if she told Melvin, he would have made her quit working for Mimi and Papa. He didn't like his wife working for my grandparents in the first place. But Elsie wanted to keep the job. She went about her work as if nothing was wrong.

CHAPTER 11

The Hour Is Late

Most white parents felt good about what they were doing for their children, and they told themselves that they were doing right by black children, too. Without discussing the idea with black leaders, Prince Edward School Foundation officials announced in June 1959 that they would be willing to create a private school for black children. When there was no response from black leaders or parents, white leaders acted baffled. They seemed not to comprehend that the offer came across as disingenuous and was contradictory to the black struggle for integration.

White leaders moved ahead with their idea anyway. When, in December, the black community hadn't made plans to educate its children in a private school, the white academy's leaders chartered Southside Schools for black children. They secured a certificate of incorporation from the State Corporation Commission and made an announcement in the *Farmville Herald*. The black private school's board consisted of the same white leaders who headed the new white academy, including Robert E. Taylor and J. Barrye "Bo" Wall Jr., the son of the *Herald*'s publisher and a lawyer, who predicted that six hundred to eight hundred black children would apply.

Roy B. Hargrove, the president of the board, sought applicants by sending a note to the parents of every black student in the county. The letter said that the location of the schools would be determined after applications had been received. The board intended to set up good schools and get qualified teachers. Hargrove wrote to parents that the private black school would run the full academic year "so that the Negro children of this county will not lose time from school."

The idea of a black private school apparently didn't have the backing of a single black leader in the community. Many believed the white school leaders were bluffing because no funds had been raised for a new school and school buildings hadn't been identified.

Griffin despised the white leaders' idea. "The very fact that they did not call in any responsible Negro leaders to plan the school would indicate that there were no good intentions," Griffin said.

Others suggested that white leaders wanted to start a black private school only because it would help sustain the white academy. If black students also applied for state-funded tuition vouchers to attend a black private school, the vouchers—which white parents needed to help finance tuition at the white academy—might not be deemed unconstitutional, white leaders thought. They also believed the school board would be more willing to go along with their plan to buy public school buildings if some were sold to a black private school.

The NAACP attorney Oliver W. Hill Sr., who attended a Christmas party for black children in Prince Edward County on December 23, days after the letters about Southside Schools were mailed, considered the white leaders' efforts downright duplicitous. He told the five hundred people in attendance that he viewed the proposed creation of a black private school as an attempt to derail desegregation efforts, and he urged them to boycott it.

"They are enticing you away from your goal by offering schools," Hill told the assembled parents and children. "They are doing this only because either their own schools are failing or they are afraid of the spotlight of public opinion on them now."

He instructed the parents to hold out for integrated schools. "All you are losing now is one or two years of basic education, but if you succeed you'll get far more than you ever would in Jim Crow schools," Hill told the children and their parents.

Roy Wilkins, the NAACP's executive secretary, told the crowd that the people of Prince Edward County had "bowed to the idol of segregation and special privilege."

A few days later, on January 1, 1960, Martin Luther King Jr. raised the issue at the Second Annual Pilgrimage of Prayer for Public Schools. King, an emerging civil rights leader, had in 1954 succeeded Barbara Johns's uncle Vernon Johns as the minister of Dexter Avenue Baptist Church in Montgomery and was the president of the Southern Christian Leadership Conference.

In Richmond, about 1,500 blacks had gathered to ask the state assembly to repeal the massive resistance legislation that had stripped localities of the power to assign students to schools and instead had given this power to a board of state appointees. They also asked the general assembly to give Governor Almond emergency authority to reopen the Prince Edward schools. By then several dozen black children were in school with white children at school districts across Virginia.

King, then twenty-six, had been instrumental in the Montgomery bus boycott—a protest of racial discrimination on the city's public transit system after Rosa Parks's arrest, and a seminal event in the civil rights movement. He weighed in on the offer by Prince Edward's white leaders to build a private school for black children. "I hope these citizens won't sell their birthright of freedom for a mess of segregated pottage," King told the audience gathered at the capitol after walking seventeen blocks from the Mosque theater. "I hope they will continue to have the power of endurance. . . . There can be no growth without pain."

King reflected on the larger civil rights movement. "We stand today on the threshold of the most creative period in the nation's history in race relations," King said. "We stand on the border of the promised land of integration."

He believed the moderation that even President Eisenhower favored was no longer prudent. The president reportedly told a friend in private conversation, months after meeting with King and other black leaders in 1958, that integration should proceed more slowly.

"To those who say slow up, I say the hour is late," King told the Richmond crowd. "We can't stop because this nation has a date with destiny. We're moving up the highway of freedom to the city of equality."

White leaders announced later in the month that they would delay plans to open the private school for black children until September 1960, saying they were surprised and disappointed with the lack of interest. Hargrove, who believed a number of black parents wanted to enroll their children in the school, accused the NAACP of threatening reprisal to keep black parents from applying on their children's behalf.

Hill denied Hargrove's claim. "I think the Negro parents have not been signing up for the schools because they recognize it is simply an effort to preserve segregation, and more and more Negroes are awakening to the fact that segregated facilities are not to their benefit," he said.

The effort to establish Southside Schools was abandoned after only one child applied to attend. But its failure nagged at Harry F. Byrd, the US senator and mastermind of massive resistance. He viewed blacks' unwillingness to support the private school as evidence that the NAACP was responsible for keeping black children out of school in Prince Edward. "The NAACP is more interested in the integration of public schools than it is in the education of colored children," he said later. "The NAACP, alone, is responsible for the fact that 1,700 colored children in Prince Edward County are not now attending good schools with qualified teachers."

. . . .

THE WHITE ACADEMY HAD BEEN open only a few months when leaders of the Prince Edward School Foundation began working to move the schools out of church basements and into a permanent building. They asked the county school board to sell the closed Farmville High School to the foundation.

B. Blanton Hanbury, the president of the foundation, told the school board that the school buildings were not being used and could not be used in the foreseeable future. The high school building was a liability to the school board, which had to keep it insured and repaired, he argued. "You have the basis to sell it," Hanbury told board members. "The people of the county don't want integrated schools."

The *Farmville Herald* supported the idea, too. The paper argued that the foundation and its patrons were the taxpayers who paid for the very building they were asking the school board to sell to them, insinuating that the building belonged to white residents and not to the public. But the school board's leaders feared that if schools were sold, public education in Prince Edward County would never resume.

B. Calvin Bass's successor as school board chairman, Lester E. Andrews Sr., opposed selling the school buildings. He and his supporters on the board were now realizing that the board of supervisors and other county leaders considered the schools to be permanently closed unless the *Brown* decision was miraculously reversed. When pressed to sell Farmville High School in an April 1960 school board meeting, Andrews and four other board members, including Bass, walked out and later resigned their positions. "The school board has been guided by the fundamental belief that education must be provided for all the school-age children of the entire county," the resigning members said in a statement.

The *Farmville Herald* opined that the board had been "harassed by court proceedings," referring again to the experiment that the editor believed was in play in Prince Edward. The NAACP, meanwhile, was preparing to file a motion in federal district court in Richmond to force the reopening of the public schools and to prevent the sale of the school buildings. But the school board members' resignation had been effective. The leaders of the white school changed course, launching a fund-raising drive and looking for property on which they could build the academy from scratch.

IT DIDN'T TAKE LONG FOR them to find a suitable seller: the town of Farmville. Just six months after the private school opened, the foundation bought a thirteen-acre wooded parcel from the town for $2,400. The property at Catlin and Church Streets, on a hill above downtown, was located next to a planned thirty-acre development by the Farmville Memorial Recreation Association.

School leaders launched a $300,000 capital campaign—reaching out to the same 2,700 people who had contributed to a $265,000 operating fund the year before. The fund, B. Blanton Hanbury said, was "necessary to assure progress in education in Prince Edward County." The Richmond newspapers, which rarely discussed the impact of the closed schools on black children, ran weekly updates on the private school's fund-raising efforts.

Prince Edward's residents and businesses stepped up to give money, as well as labor and materials. By November, all the needed bricks had been donated and a third of the needed cinder blocks had been provided, too. Construction began early the second year of the academy's existence.

The high school campus was completed in September 1961, in time for the third year of private school classes. It included twenty-seven classrooms, a library, and a woodworking shop. The buildings were valued at $400,000 but had been built for $256,000.

Tuition, free the first year, was now creeping up. By the end of the first school year, the foundation announced that it would charge tuition for the 1960–1961 school year—$240 for elementary students and $265 for high school students. Parents were expected to be able to access state and county grants to cover the costs.

Some white families couldn't afford it, and their children dropped out. Others were forced to move with their families to neighboring counties. And some ran up debt that would take years to pay back. But these children were scarcely mentioned. In a television interview soon after the white school opened, Roy Pearson denied their existence, insisting that every child who had attended the white public schools was now attending the academy.

BASS, ONE OF FEW TO publicly oppose the school closings, was still looking for a way to get the schools reopened. In November 1959, he began meeting privately, in living rooms across the county, with other concerned businessmen and leaders, including Lester Andrews. Academy officials began referring derisively to the members of the fledgling group as the Bush League, insinuating that its members lacked sophistication. The group's supporters had different ideas about what should be done, but all agreed that they wanted the public schools to be reopened as soon as possible. They were businessmen who saw the school closures as an economic and social disaster for the county. For their desire to provide schools for all county children, they were harassed and called "integrationists," the ultimate insult.

Gordon Moss, the associate dean at Longwood, persuaded the group to meet with black leaders. White leaders involved in the discussion suggested a three-year moratorium on school desegregation and proposed that, in exchange, the principles of the *Brown* decision would be accepted. A biracial committee would be established to move the concept of integration forward. But the suggestions went nowhere.

An all-white group of forty met in June 1960 at a Cumberland County cabin owned by Andrews's business partner, Maurice Large. A Defender, he had stood before the crowd at Jarman Hall years earlier to urge the founding of a private school, but he also wanted the public schools open. At the meeting, the group discussed asking the supervisors to reopen the schools. But news of the meeting had leaked, and segregationists used various means to intimidate those in attendance. When Bass left, a car parked nearby shined its headlights on exiting cars. An academy official reportedly jotted down the names of each person who came and went. Some who attended the meeting reported being followed, even run off the road. Back at the Bass farmhouse in Rice, his wife sat staring out the window, terrified he wouldn't make it home.

The next day, the so-called minutes of the Cumberland meeting were photocopied and distributed around town, listing—and embarrassing—those who had attended. Business at Andrews and Large's newly constructed shopping center slowed. Lifelong friends stopped talking. Community leaders "would not discuss resumption of schools with anybody," Moss said. And the Bush League never met again.

The opinions of white leaders who believed the public schools should be reopened all but disappeared from public view.

Students walked out of the black Robert Russa Moton High School in Farmville on April 23, 1951, to protest the conditions of the school. Tar paper shack classrooms that had been added to relieve overcrowding looked like chicken coops, reeked of petroleum, and leaked when it rained. *(Richmond Times-Dispatch, 1951)*

This photograph of students seated around a potbelly stove in a Moton High School classroom was a defense exhibit in the case *Dorothy Davis et al. v. County School Board of Prince Edward County*, filed in May 1951. *(National Archives, 1951)*

Attorney Oliver W. Hill Sr. His Richmond law firm filed the suit against the Prince Edward school board that would later become one of five cases in the Supreme Court's landmark *Brown v. Board of Education* decision. *(Courtesy of Oliver Hill family, circa 1950)*

The new Moton High School for black students, which was hurriedly constructed and opened in 1953 after NAACP attorneys filed the *Davis* lawsuit, shut down six years later when the county board of supervisors voted not to fund public education rather than desegregate the schools. The building, now called Prince Edward County High School, is the county's sole public high school.   *(Richmond Times-Dispatch, 1959)*

The Reverend L. Francis Griffin visited the training center he helped establish for black children in the basement of his First Baptist Church in February 1960. The training centers were not designed as schools, but instead were intended to keep up morale and reinforce basic skills while the public schools were closed. *(Richmond Times-Dispatch, 1960)*

Farmville High School, the public school for white students in Prince Edward County, never reopened after the schools were closed in 1959. In 1993, the colonial revival building on First Avenue was demolished after Longwood College purchased it.   *(Richmond Times-Dispatch, 1979)*

The September 1961 dedication of the new Prince Edward Academy building, held two years after the white school was founded, was attended by 1,500 people.   *(Richmond Times-Dispatch, 1961)*

Young people protested the school closures in front of the shops on Main Street in downtown Farmville during the summer of 1963. *(Richmond Times-Dispatch, 1963)*

Youth from Prince Edward County traveled by bus to Washington, DC, to attend the March on Washington in August 1963 and carried a Prince Edward sign. *(Library of Congress, 1963)*

In September 1963, after the public schools had been closed for four years, Prince Edward County students entered the Free Schools, private schools for white and black children with integrated teaching staffs. The schools were located in public school buildings, including the former Moton High School, which is now home to the Moton Museum.   *(Library of Congress, 1963)*

Teacher Sheila Hartman of New York joined teachers from around the country in instructing students at the Free Schools, which existed for one academic year. The county was ordered by a federal court to reopen its public schools in 1964.   *(Richmond Times-Dispatch, 1963)*

Attorney General Robert F. Kennedy visited Prince Edward County in May 1964, going to the Free Schools to talk with parents and students. He got out of his car to address students at the all-female Longwood College who blocked his motorcade on the streets of Farmville. *(Richmond Times-Dispatch, 1964)*

Author Kristen Green and her husband, Jason Hamilton, with their daughter Amaya, one, and their newborn daughter, Selma. *(Crissy Pascual, 2009)*

Elsie Lancaster, the longtime housekeeper for author Kristen Green's grandparents and parents, visits with the author's children, Selma, four *(left)*, and Amaya, five *(right)*, outside her Prince Edward County home in 2013. *(Kristen Green, 2013)*

CHAPTER 12

A Bus Ticket and a World Away

Ever since fourteen-year-old Betty Jean Ward could remember, she, her parents, and her siblings gathered around the dinner table each night, talking and laughing and telling stories about their day. Friends filed in and out of the brick house on Main Street in Farmville to hang out with her older brother and sister and to play basketball on the backyard hoop. They were a happy, normal family.

And then they weren't.

The summer that the schools closed, Betty Jean's parents, Phillip and Doris, accepted the reality that they wouldn't reopen in the fall. They could see two of the locked and chained schools from their yard. Betty Jean's parents came up with a plan to educate their children that called for sending them in different directions.

They didn't see any alternative, not when they had such big dreams for their kids. They were relieved that, unlike many of their relatives, they had options. Ronnie had only one more year of school before graduation, and Phyllistine, two. Betty Jean wasn't far behind.

Phillip, who, like his father and grandfather, was a baker at Longwood, had completed eleventh grade, a big accomplishment at the time. But his exposure to higher education at Longwood and through family members who had attended college made him expect more of his children. His wife, Doris, had moved from Amelia County to

Prince Edward as a teenager to live with a cousin so that she could attend the black high school. After the children were born, Doris commuted to Richmond to attend nursing school so that she could become a licensed practical nurse and provide more income for the family. From the time the children were small, the couple tried to instill in them the value of schooling. "Get an education so you can take care of yourself," Phillip told them.

Their eldest son, Gerald, was already in college. Years earlier, the couple had sent him to high school in Washington, DC, where he had lived with a relative. Now he had a football scholarship to attend the historically black Saint Paul's College, an hour's drive away in Lawrenceville. The couple decided that Ronnie and Phyllistine would go to Kittrell, which was admitting juniors and seniors and would later take a few sophomores. Betty Jean, who was too young to attend, would live with her maternal grandparents in a neighboring county and enroll in its public schools. She wasn't happy about the news. "Why do we have to separate?" she asked her parents. A few days later, her brother and sister's bags were packed, and the teenagers left for North Carolina. "I just hated to see them go," Betty Jean said.

When school started for Betty Jean in September, her father dropped her off on Sunday nights at Willie and Betty Thompson's home on a tobacco farm twenty minutes outside Farmville. Their eleven kids were already grown, so Betty Jean had her grandparents' full attention. In the morning, her grandfather would put her on the tractor and drive her a mile down the road, where she'd catch a bus to Luther H. Foster High School in Nottoway County, an hour from her grandparents' house. The all-black high school built in 1950 had not yet been integrated. When she returned to her grandparents' home in the afternoon, they had snacks waiting for her. On Fridays, one of her parents would fetch her and take her back home to Main Street in Farmville. Some weeks, the Foster principal, who lived in Farmville, would drive her to school so that she could stay with her parents. "Don't tell anyone," he instructed her.

Betty Jean made new friends at Foster, but she often wondered if the education she was getting was as good as the one she would have received in the Prince Edward schools. Sometimes she thought about why all this was happening, why she had been separated from her brother and sister, why she had to go to school in a different community and live away from her parents during the week. She questioned her dad about the reasons the schools had been closed.

"The whites don't want black kids to be with their kids," her dad would tell her. "They feel you're below them."

"Because of the color of my skin?" she responded, trying to understand.

"Yes," he told her. "Because of the color of your skin."

He said he didn't think what the white leaders had done was right. "You're just as good as anybody else," he assured her. "That's why you need to get your education."

He could make sure she went to school, but he couldn't bring back the happy, innocent life she had had before her family was split by the school closures. With her brother and sister gone, there were no rowdy family meals, no friends coming and going, no arguing among the siblings. Her dad worked longer hours to help pay for the things his children needed away from home, picking up odd jobs painting or pumping gas after his shift at the college ended.

Betty Jean wished they were all back together again. But after the schools closed, the three children would never again sleep under the same roof, except during the holidays.

"It was terrible," her brother Ronnie told me. "We just broke our family up."

THAT SUMMER, DOROTHY LOCKETT WAS sitting on the back steps of her house in Prospect when her dad came home and broke the news that she would not be returning to school the next month. Leonard

Lockett, a railroad worker, assured his ten-year-old daughter that she would be educated. "Whatever's happened, I promise you're going to go to school," he told her.

Dorothy was devastated. She loved school and tried to keep learning at home. The family owned one storybook, which she and her brothers read repeatedly. Her dad bought the newspaper and asked the children to read articles aloud to him.

When Griffin opened the training centers around the county, Dorothy and her older brother Edward walked three miles each way to attend classes in the basement of a church. On rainy days, Lockett gave Dorothy his railroad-issued raincoat to keep her dry. She hated the walk, which was two miles longer than the one to her old school. When the white school bus passed by, children leaned out the window and spat.

Peaks Elementary, the three-room school she had attended before the schools closed, was nothing to brag about. Six grades were crammed into one room and an outhouse was the only bathroom. The schoolbooks were torn, and she would select whichever book had the most pages. It wasn't until the schools closed that she realized not all students read torn books, not all schools were overcrowded, not all children used an outhouse at school. Still, she couldn't help thinking that at least Peaks had been a real school.

Another older brother, a standout athlete who had been preparing to start his junior year at Moton, decided he was done with school. Dorothy's parents didn't want to split up their children, and, at eighteen, he didn't want to walk to the training center. But Dorothy and Edward kept walking. As one year turned into two, Dorothy often thought about her father's promise. She never stopped asking him about it.

"Dad, when are we going to go to a real school?"

Finally, he had had enough. Leonard Lockett decided he couldn't wait any longer for the schools to reopen. His three oldest children hadn't finished high school, and now his fourth had quit, too. He was determined not to let the same thing happen to his youngest two children. He and his wife, Alma, had completed only the sixth grade, but Lockett believed schooling was invaluable and wanted Edward and Dorothy to get a real education.

His white coworkers at the railroad helped him rent a house eighteen miles away in Appomattox County, where they were working on a railroad project. The decrepit two-story wood-framed house sat on the edge of a highway. He and Alma spent weeks working to make it appear habitable. He replaced broken window panes and cleared debris from the yard. His wife sewed burgundy curtains for the front windows.

It wasn't until the school year started that Dorothy realized her family wasn't moving. They would continue to live in the house they owned in Prince Edward, but they would pretend this rented Appomattox house was their home. Each school day Leonard Lockett dropped off Dorothy, Edward, and three grandsons behind the house. As he left his children and grandchildren to drive to work, he instructed them to stay outside, behind the house. The structure wasn't safe for them to be inside. He told the children that when they heard the bus roaring down the country road, they should walk through the back door, out the front door, and onto the bus.

Lockett told the children it was important to keep the secret. "You just get on the bus, keep your mouth shut, and go to school," he told them.

Edward didn't think it would be difficult. "We have pretended for two years that the church was our school, and now we just have to pretend that this is our house," he told his sister.

Dorothy and the other kids all played along. They knew this was serious business. "We didn't want to risk not being allowed to go to school," she said.

Carver-Price School, attended by black children in first through twelfth grades, was only miles from the elementary school she had attended in Prince Edward County, but it seemed a world away. It had a cafeteria, a gymnasium, and shiny, clean hallways.

Soon Leonard Lockett invited other Prince Edward families to bring their children to his rental home in the morning, too. Everett Berryman and his siblings had been dropped off on the side of the road so that they could catch a bus to the Appomattox schools. Now Everett sometimes joined the Locketts behind their rental house. At one point in the school year, twenty-one children from ten families boarded the bus there.

"We'd fill the bus up," Dorothy said.

The bus driver laughed and joked that they didn't look like siblings, noting that a number of the kids were in the same grades. The children didn't say a word. They knew their educations were at stake.

RICKY BROWN WAS SIX, AND he couldn't wait to start school. For years, he had watched his older brother and cousins go off every morning. Each day, as the bus approached to fetch the kids, they sang a song they'd made up. "School bus, school bus, give me a ride," they crooned.

Ricky's cousin Freck, named for a face full of freckles, had started school in 1958—the year before the schools closed. Ricky was next. "I was waiting for my turn," he told me.

He was excited for kindergarten. On what would have been the first day of school, he got dressed in his new school clothes. Then his mom broke the news to him that the schools wouldn't be opening, but he didn't understand. "Those damn crackers closed up the schools!" she said.

It was something they rarely discussed. His mother felt there was nothing she could do. Ricky's father had left the family when Ricky was two. His mother, one of ten children, was the daughter of illiterate sharecroppers. She learned to read and write, unlike most of her siblings, but she had dropped out of school at sixth grade. Now she did domestic work for white families around town and worked in a tobacco factory. She wasn't particularly concerned about her children being educated. Feeding them was a more pressing concern. Besides, she didn't have the resources to send her three children anywhere else.

Ricky's paternal grandparents, who lived in neighboring Cumberland County, took in Ricky's older brother, Walter, so that he could attend school. Ricky, who was five years younger and less independent, was not invited. His grandparents didn't think they could handle both boys. Instead, Ricky was stuck at home with his sister, Frances, who was four. He was angry about being left behind, and he was jealous of his brother. "I thought I should have been able to go, too," Ricky said. "I couldn't understand why it happened."

Instead of continuing his education, Ricky spent every day playing. He waded in the creek behind First Baptist Church, and, while his mom worked, he went to visit his aunts who lived nearby. He played ball in the soft green grass at the firehouse. At night, he went home to the duplex his mom rented for five dollars a month on South Street, where the walls were so thin he could smell the next-door neighbors' dinners and hear their conversations. Occasionally, he joined seventy-five students at one of the training centers in the basement of Griffin's church. Classes, which ran for three and a half hours, were taught by volunteers since most black teachers had left the county to find other jobs.

"The only thing I got out of that was how to spell my name and the alphabet," Ricky said. "That's all I learned."

NO ONE WENT LOOKING FOR Doug Vaughan when the schools closed. He lived in a poor neighborhood on the hill above Buffalo Shook Company, the Farmville sawmill. The saws ran all day long, until the whistle blew at 4:30 p.m. No one asked if the fifteen-year-old being raised by a single mother wanted to go away to school. During the week, she worked downtown as a cook at the Hotel Weyanoke, often bringing home pork chops or chicken for dinner. On the weekends, she liked to drink, so Doug and his three siblings had to look out for each other. Kids raising kids. "Nobody wanted to bother with us," Doug said.

When the schools closed, he was entering the eighth grade. He couldn't count on his mother or anyone else to plan for his future. It was in his teenage hands.

Doug asked an uncle in Philadelphia if he could live with him and attend school. Doug scraped together money for a bus fare and headed north, but the school charged tuition when officials realized that Doug was from Prince Edward. He was back in Farmville a few weeks later.

When Doug turned sixteen, he told his older brother, "We've got to get out of here." They left Farmville with a couple of his brother's friends for Mount Vernon, New York, where they rented a room in a spacious house for ten dollars a week. Doug worked for Good Humor Ice Cream Company, riding a bicycle from neighborhood to neighborhood for seven hours, selling ice cream out of a bucket. His brother and his friends didn't have jobs yet, so Doug would stop by the house they rented and feed them the ice cream he was supposed to be selling. Ice cream was breakfast and lunch, and Doug never made any money. For dinner, the boys bought heaping bowls of lima beans for a quarter from the corner market. It would be a month before they could afford a real meal.

Doug's brother found a job at a vacuum cleaner factory, which hired Doug, too. But soon, he would leave the North and head back home for a girl who had stolen his heart. He could barely read, but he would not return to high school.

Without an education, the road ahead would be a steep one.

WHEN THE SCHOOLS CLOSED, MICKIE Pride was nine years old and about to enter fifth grade. No one explained to her what had happened or why. "It meant nothing to me," she said. "All I knew was I was going to have an extended vacation from school."

Her family lived eighteen miles south of Farmville in a black community. Mickie attended the two-room Virso School, which housed grades kindergarten through twelve. There was no running water or indoor plumbing, and the school was heated with one big woodstove. The facilities were basic, but Mickie didn't know any better. She liked school, and her teacher told her she was smart, moving her ahead from second to fourth grade.

When the schools closed, Mickie did nothing for the first year. The next year, her mother arranged to send her to neighboring Lunenburg County. But after thirty days, Mickie was sent home when Lunenburg opted not to educate Prince Edward students. After that, she spent her days with her mother and three of her siblings. Mickie's mom, Mae, didn't drive, so attending one of the training centers wasn't an option. The children simply stayed home. The family didn't have a phone or a television, but a constant stream of friends visited. Her aunt and her aunt's sister were always around. "They'd come and sit all day," Mickie told me.

When she grew tired of listening to the adults, she'd go outside and play with her brothers and sister. They'd rake up big piles of leaves and hide in them, jumping out to frighten her dad, Arvesta, when he arrived home from work at the sawmill. And she spent hours playing jack rocks—the poor man's version of jacks, in which small rocks replaced jacks and a larger rock served as the ball.

Mae had a knack for styling hair, and friends popped by to gossip and get their hair pressed. Mae used oil, then a hot comb heated on the stove, to straighten their hair. While the adults talked and laughed, Mickie thumbed through magazines and mail order catalogues from Sears, Roebuck and Company, and Montgomery Ward. Her family didn't own any books, but sometimes one would be tucked inside the packages of hand-me-down clothes and shoes her aunts and uncles sent from the white families they worked for. "We read everything we could get our hands on," Mickie said.

· · · ·

THE FOUNDERS OF FARMVILLE'S NEW private academy had pitched it as a school for all the county's white children. But some of the county's poorest white kids, kids like John Hines, the son of a tenant farmer and logger, never set foot inside it.

White leaders had promised that the school would be free to all white children for the first year—its operating expenses would be covered by donations. But Shadrick Hines didn't see it as an option for his children. Maybe he knew he wouldn't be able to pay for bus fees or other costs that might crop up. Or perhaps he thought he would eventually be pressured to pay tuition.

No one from the academy tried to change his mind. No one told him to put his kids on the bus and that they'd figure out a way to cover the cost. No one said it was important for poor white children to get an education, too.

Besides, Hines, a second-generation logger, and his wife, Margaret, had attended school for five and seven years, respectively. Their limited education had served them well. Even though Shadrick Hines never learned to read and write, he could count money, and that's what mattered in his line of work. That, and working fast in the fields.

Now that the schools had closed, he had six extra sets of hands. John and two of his brothers could help the family earn more money. They might even be able to get ahead. The school closures were a blessing.

John would never return to school, nor would his siblings, who would struggle with illiteracy for the rest of their lives.

PUBLIC SCHOOLS DIDN'T SEEM ANY closer to opening. Gwen Lancaster had spent the last few months helping teach at Griffin's training centers, but Elsie and Melvin Lancaster knew it wasn't enough for her. They had a decision to make.

When Gwen was tiny, Elsie loved to sit with her daughter on her lap. They spent all their time together, and Elsie referred to the girl as her "sweet baby doll." By the time Gwen went to school, she could write her name and tie her shoes. Her teachers were surprised by how prepared she was. But not Elsie.

She had always known that her daughter was exceptional, and she wanted to make sure that the girl's intellect didn't go to waste. Gwen needed more stimulation. Elsie knew that if she kept her at home, in Prince Edward County, without access to the education she deserved, she risked history being repeated. She couldn't bear for her daughter to be trapped working as a housekeeper or doing other menial work. Elsie always regretted not leaving Farmville as her sisters had. She wished she had done more with her life, and she didn't want Gwen to end up like her.

"She was one of the smartest kids in her class, and she just wanted to go to school," Elsie told me.

She and Melvin talked about what to do. It was hard for Elsie to even think about sending her only child away. She loved children and had always wanted more, but they never came. Gwen was particularly close with her father, and he hated the thought of her living away from him. "Her daddy didn't want her to go, but I thought it was best for her," Elsie told me.

Elsie and Melvin discussed sending Gwen to Philadelphia, where Melvin had family. They also considered moving her to Cambridge to live with Elsie's sister. Elsie preferred to have Gwen closer, in Philadelphia. But Gwen told her parents she would rather go to Massachusetts because it was more familiar. She had spent summers with her aunt, uncle, and cousins there.

Melvin and Elsie agreed that Gwen would live with her aunt in Cambridge, a bus ticket and a world away.

CHAPTER 13

Then and Now

When Elsie took Gwen on the daylong bus ride to Massachusetts, she was still working for my grandparents three days a week. Mimi and Papa must have known about Elsie's trip to Cambridge, yet they never inquired how it went. They didn't ask how Gwen was adjusting or how Elsie was coping without her. They didn't tell her they were sorry, and they hadn't offered to help, not since Mimi had suggested that blacks start their own private school. They acted as though they didn't even know Gwen was gone.

"They never said a word to me about it," Elsie told me.

Elsie kept quiet, the way black people were expected to. Life was easier for them if they knew their place. Elsie kept her sadness to herself. She hummed and sang church hymns as she ironed my grandfather's pants and my grandmother's dresses.

One day after school, my mother, probably ten or eleven at the time, looked up at Elsie and innocently asked her why Gwen—whom she occasionally played with—was gone. Elsie saw it as an accusation, as if sending her daughter to Massachusetts was something that Elsie had wanted. Mom didn't know that it was a sacrifice Elsie had been forced to make for the benefit of her bright daughter.

"That was her only child," my mom thought to herself. "How could she just send her away like that?"

When Elsie went home that night, the child's words echoed in her head. She felt judged by my mom and her family for helping her daughter get an education, judged by a family whose children she had doted on for so many years.

For decades, Elsie held on to my mother's words—and felt the sting of them. She could never grasp that my mom had been a child at the time, protected from what was happening in the community around her. Elsie couldn't believe that my mom had been told little about the school closures.

All my mom knew was that Elsie had a daughter—and then she didn't.

AFTER SPENDING THE DAY AT Mimi and Papa's home taking care of their children instead of her own daughter, brushing my mom's and Beverley Anne's hair instead of Gwen's, Elsie walked back to her nearby house. Without Gwen, her home felt empty. Melvin had given away the girl's Hula-Hoop and sold her bike, toys that had made Elsie happy, too. Her precious child wasn't there to cook dinner for or discuss her day. The joy was sucked out of the house. Elsie told me that she longed to hold Gwen on her lap and read to her, just as she had done when Gwen was small. She longed to tuck her in at night and tell her that she loved her. She missed her daughter terribly. She wanted her little girl back.

But with the schools still closed, she had to remind herself that it was best for Gwen to be in Cambridge. She told herself that Gwen was adapting well to her new life in Massachusetts. She would see her over the holidays and send for her in the summer. Elsie grew accustomed to the long bus ride to Boston.

Taking care of my mom and Beverley Anne was comforting, too. She was glad to be around children. Staying home after Gwen left for Massachusetts would have made her even sadder.

"I just wanted to be around kids," she told me.

AMAYA PADS ACROSS THE WOOD floor in her patent leather ballet slippers to answer the front door, greeting guests arriving for her fifth birthday party. She is wearing a handmade dress, each tier a color of the rainbow, a satin red ribbon tied in a bow in the back.

I have invited children from all over the city to her rainbow-themed party—kids from the church preschool she attended and from the Richmond public preschool where she now goes. Her guest list is a rainbow, too.

Amaya laughs and smiles, talking with her friends as they make necklaces from Froot Loops in the kitchen and toss balloons in the living room. I serve them a brunch of waffles and fruit, then they slip old T-shirts over their party clothes and paint a giant mural in our backyard.

As the party winds down, I light candles on the six-layer rainbow cake I've baked and iced in buttercream frosting. I carry it to the kid-sized tables where the children are seated, and as I walk toward her at the head of the table, I take in the moment.

My little girl is growing up. She is happy and healthy, surrounded by her sister, a cousin, and her friends, among them black and multiracial children. Her classmates and their parents join Jason and me in singing "Happy Birthday." I am glowing with pride. This moment is exactly what I envisioned for her. Romantically naive as it may be, I love it. Jason and I want to open the world to our girls. We want them to have the diverse circle of friends that I didn't have growing up. Attending a public preschool where she is assigned to a classroom with black teachers and black students, she has made friends from a variety of racial and socioeconomic backgrounds. I am proud of Amaya, confident and beautiful on her birthday. And I am proud of what I think this party says about me: I am not defined by the history of my hometown.

When she closes her eyes to make a wish before she blows out the candles, I make one of my own: I hope that this day is just a glimpse of her future.

CHAPTER 14

Brown Stokes the Flames

A handful of communities around the nation began integrating peacefully after the *Brown* decision was handed down. The day after the court's ruling, President Eisenhower told Washington, DC, officials to make the city a "model" for the nation, and the superintendent for the district schools proposed a desegregation plan a week later. In September 1954, three-quarters of the schools in the nation's capital were desegregated, and the district planned to integrate them all by 1955.

But the District of Columbia turned out to be the exception, not the rule. Across the South, defiance of *Brown* was widespread. Even token attempts to desegregate led to protests, riots, and violence. Under a court order, Clinton High School in Tennessee became the first high school in the South to desegregate, in August 1956. John Kasper, who recruited members for the white supremacist White Citizens Councils, arrived in Clinton to mobilize opposition to the school's integration. On Labor Day weekend, cars were overturned and windows smashed in a riot. Tennessee's governor, Frank G. Clement, called in the National Guard to restore order. The violence quieted down, but it didn't end altogether. Three months later, in December, sympathetic white residents accompanied black students as they walked to school, and a preacher who served as an escort was badly beaten.

Also in 1956, a court ordered the desegregation of the New Orleans public schools by one grade per year, beginning with the first grade classes. After six-year-old Ruby Bridges passed a test and was selected to attend the white William Frantz Elementary School, her parents discussed the matter, disagreeing about whether it was a good idea, and finally decided to send her. On November 14, Ruby and her mother were picked up at home and escorted into the school by four US Marshals, two walking in front of her and two behind. As she approached the school, she passed crowds of people who shouted at her and shook their fists. She heard them scream, "Two, four, six, eight, we don't want to integrate!"

Ruby noticed a protestor carrying a black baby doll in a coffin, and she would have nightmares about it for years. A Norman Rockwell painting depicts Ruby's famous walk to the school.

Dressed in a starched white dress with white ribbons in her hair, she spent the day sitting in the principal's office as white parents withdrew their children from the school in protest. For the entire school year, she was the only student in her first grade class, taught by a white teacher from Boston, Barbara Henry. She was separated from the handful of other first graders whose parents kept them in school.

It was no better in Charlotte, North Carolina. On September 4, 1957, fifteen-year-old Dorothy "Dot" Geraldine Counts integrated the city's all-white Harding High School. Dot was greeted by white mobs that screamed racial slurs, threw trash, and spat as she walked toward the school's front door. Photographs of the confrontation ran in newspapers across the country. Concerned for her safety after receiving threatening phone calls, her family withdrew her a week later and sent her to Philadelphia to live with a relative.

And Little Rock had also desegregated the all-white Central High School in September with assistance of federal troops called in by Eisenhower. The federal troops stayed, allowing the "Little Rock Nine" to finish the school year. But the following school year, Governor Faubus closed all of Little Rock's high schools for a year.

Change was coming, but in the South, in particular, it was happening slowly. By 1958, Virginia was one of only seven states, including South Carolina, Georgia, Alabama, Florida, Mississippi, and Louisiana, that still maintained segregated public schools. In 1961, when Eisenhower's presidency ended, only 6 percent of black children across the country were attending integrated schools. Often only one school in a school district would desegregate, and the rest would do nothing at all. Instead, school districts waited for the issue to be brought before the courts. The burden of school desegregation fell on the shoulders of black parents.

Although *Brown* didn't have the desired effect of immediately desegregating schools across the nation, it did stoke the flames of the civil rights movement. Once segregation in schools was ruled illegal, blacks began to challenge other Jim Crow laws.

In 1955, Rosa Parks, a black seamstress, refused to move to the back of a bus in Montgomery, Alabama, so that a white man could have her seat. After she was arrested for violating segregation laws, blacks launched the country's first large-scale demonstration against segregation—and one of the most successful in history. The Montgomery bus boycott continued until the Supreme Court declared the bus segregation ordinance to be unconstitutional in November 1956, and, in December, ordered Montgomery to integrate its buses.

Next, sit-ins emerged as a popular and effective tool for students to force the desegregation of lunch counters and restaurants. In February 1960, four black students from the North Carolina Agricultural and Technical College in Greensboro, North Carolina, sat down and ordered coffee at the lunch counter of an F. W. Woolworth Company store. A waitress at the whites-only counter refused to serve the young men, but the students stayed until the store closed. They returned days later, bringing more students with them, until blacks occupied sixty-three of the sixty-six seats at the counter. The Greensboro sit-in spawned a movement, and by the end of the month, students from Florida to Tennessee had launched sit-ins, too. Hundreds of young people were arrested on trespassing charges. In April 1960, students from around the country gathered at the campus of Shaw University in Raleigh to discuss strategy. Martin Luther King Jr. urged the students to form their own direct action organization, and the Student Nonviolent Coordinating Committee (SNCC) was born. The sit-in movement even spread to New York. After six months of negative press and lost business, Woolworth's decided to desegregate its lunch counters.

J. Samuel Williams, a tall and lanky young man who grew up in Farmville, was studying for the ministry at Shaw during the sit-ins and helped to found SNCC. King's visit left a lasting impression on him. Jim Crow was the law of the land, King told the Shaw students, but the law of the land was unjust and unfair. "You don't have to obey unjust laws," Williams remembered King telling them.

Participating in the sit-ins reminded black Southerners that they had power. It reminded Williams of walking out of Moton High School in 1951 as a senior, "beating the streets for something you knew was right and proper." He had served in the US Army and worked a variety of jobs in the North and the South, and he was fed up with the way black people were treated, particularly in the South.

In Prince Edward, blacks were not only required to stand at lunch counters and swim in a separate lake from whites; at the drive-in, they parked their cars on one side of the parking lot while whites parked on the other. Blacks were allowed to purchase items at Baldwin's Department Store, but they were not permitted to try on clothes. Black mothers would trace their children's feet on cardboard and take the cardboard cutout with them to buy shoes for their children. They were allowed to buy ice cream at some shops, but only if they entered through the back door. Restrooms and water fountains were labeled "Whites Only," and blacks were buried in their own graveyards.

Blacks were repeatedly told that this was the way it was supposed to be. Some began to believe they were suited to work only as maids, chauffeurs, or barbers. "After a while," Williams told me, "you get that stuff inside of you."

The progress achieved through sit-ins across the South made Williams excited to carry Raleigh's activism to Prince Edward. The schools were still closed a decade after he had joined Barbara Johns's protest of the conditions at Moton school. But when he came home from Shaw on the weekends to preach with Griffin, he felt as though there was nothing he could do to help. He believed Prince Edward's problems were in the hands of the court. In 1961, a group of black parents had filed the case *Griffin v. County School Board of Prince Edward County* in federal court as an amended complaint to the *Davis* case, seeking for the schools to be reopened, and it was working its way through the judicial system.

In 1962, after Williams had graduated from Shaw and started preaching at Levi Baptist Church in the small Prince Edward community of Green Bay, he began serving as the president of the county's Voters Registration League. In his new position, he traveled around the county, encouraging black residents to register to vote so that they could elect blacks to local leadership positions and change the makeup of local government bodies. He realized that many blacks in the county were more determined to bring change than he had originally believed.

Finally, in the spring of 1963, it was time for action in Prince Edward, as students became inspired by boycotts of businesses and other demonstrations that King was leading. In May, Birmingham's police commissioner, Bull Connor, released dogs on protestors and sprayed a group of adults and young people with high-powered hoses, awakening the nation to the violence happening in the name of segregation. Eisenhower's successor, President John F. Kennedy, had sent three thousand federal troops near Birmingham and was preparing to federalize the National Guard. Birmingham's business leaders saw how the negative publicity was damaging their town and agreed to desegregate lunch counters, to allow blacks to try on clothes in department stores, to hire more blacks, and to remove "Whites Only" signs from drinking fountains and bathrooms. The action in Birmingham had spun off hundreds of "Little Birminghams" across the US, resulting in twenty thousand arrests.

The country was becoming increasingly disgusted by Prince Edward, which was making national headlines for its still-closed schools. Dr. Robert L. Green and a team of researchers from Michigan State University, funded by the US Office of Education, came to town, attempting to determine how black schoolchildren had been affected. They would soon learn that the illiteracy rate of black students ages five to twenty-two had jumped from 3 percent when the schools had closed to a staggering 23 percent. They found seven-year-old children who couldn't hold a pencil or make an X. Some didn't know how old they were; others couldn't communicate.

Immediately after the schools closed, nonprofits began arriving to offer assistance. The American Friends Service Committee (AFSC), a Quaker organization, established an office with the goal of helping black residents get the schools reopened. AFSC staff worked with Griffin to provide libraries in church basements and also organized a year-round youth recreation program, staffed by volunteers who drove in from Richmond. At the national level, the AFSC put out a call to its chapters, asking for volunteers to take in students so they could attend school. The organization placed forty-seven students in volunteers' homes in Pennsylvania, Ohio, Maryland, Iowa, Michigan, and Washington, DC, for the 1960–1961 school year. The next year, AFSC expanded the program, sending students to Berea College's Foundation School in Kentucky, and a Farmville leader borrowed a funeral home's station wagon to drive six students across the mountains.

During the three years the program was offered, sixty-seven students stayed in homes scattered around eight states. Eighteen of the students completed high school, and several went to college after graduation, including Phyllistine Ward, who left Kittrell to spend her senior year living with a white family in Iowa. James Ghee also went to Iowa, where he lived with several different families while attending high school and would stay for college, too.

Now, in 1963, more than three dozen New Yorkers, students from Queens College and city teachers, partly financed by the American Federation of Teachers, were arriving to offer summer enrichment programs. Some of the teachers were white, and they lived with black families and swam in the black lake. They avoided going to white restaurants, eating in the homes of black families instead.

Eighty miles away on the North Carolina border, things were heating up in Danville, Virginia, where Dunlap, the AME preacher who had helped to place students in Kittrell, now lived. In March 1963, King had visited Danville and met with the leaders of the Southern Christian Leadership Conference. With his encouragement, Dunlap and other black ministers—men who were fed up with the segregation of everything from water fountains to hospitals—led a series of demonstrations. Assistance streamed in from volunteers in New York, including SNCC leaders who would later head to Farmville. Danville's white leaders ignored the protests, and local newspapers did not cover them. Arrests mounted. Then, on June 10, city garbage collectors, who had been deputized by the police chief, aimed fire hoses on full blast at demonstrators attending an evening prayer vigil. King would later describe the attack, which came to be known as "Bloody Monday," as among the most brutal of the civil rights movement. All but three of the fifty demonstrators were injured.

J. Samuel Williams, now a preacher, suggested to Griffin it was time to demonstrate in Farmville. Griffin had threatened white leaders with boycotts in 1959 and 1960, and in 1962 he had persuaded teens not to demonstrate. Williams was tired of waiting. "You felt guilty if you weren't doing anything and living in an environment of rampant segregation," said Williams, then twenty-nine.

The Reverend Goodwin Douglas, the new twenty-five-year-old preacher at Beulah African Methodist Episcopal Church on Main Street who had attended school with many Farmville students at Kittrell, also thought demonstrations were needed. After he went to a lunch counter in Farmville and saw employees break the glass from which he had drunk, he begged Griffin to let him organize marches.

Griffin, elected statewide leader of the NAACP in 1962, recognized that the young people were inspired by Birmingham and similar demonstrations. Some of them attended integrated schools out of state—a few even lived with white families—and they saw the possibilities beyond this little town. "The hardened attitude and techniques in Birmingham certainly has served to arouse a great many lethargic and complacent Negroes to action in Virginia and elsewhere," he told the *Richmond Times-Dispatch*. In late June, he called a meeting of the Virginia State Conference of the NAACP and implemented a new plan that would support selective buying campaigns—boycotting businesses that supported or tolerated segregation.

With the new focus on direct action, Griffin worked to revive youth councils across the state and gave approval to Douglas and Williams to work with young people in Farmville. The goals were twofold: they wanted to integrate the segregated facilities downtown and open the school doors for locked-out black children. The campaign would eventually include sit-ins at restaurants, "kneel-ins" or "pray-ins" at white churches, demonstrations at local government buildings, and a boycott of Farmville stores that didn't employ blacks.

National media saw the demonstrations as evidence that blacks were finally willing to stand up to the county's white leaders. "In the sweltering heat of Virginia's Prince Edward County," *Time* magazine wrote, "Negroes woke from long torpor . . . to demonstrate against the most infamous segregationist tactic in the US—the closing of public schools there since 1959."

First, the young people needed to be trained in nonviolent demonstration tactics.

A pair of SNCC officers led the two-week training. Betty Jean Ward, who had lived with her grandparents for four years in neighboring Nottoway County, wanted to participate. She drove her dad's new '57 Plymouth to and from Vernon Johns's farm for the training sessions, piling in a bunch of her friends.

On the farm, the trainers taught Betty Jean and the other teenagers how to protect themselves if the police intervened during the demonstrations. If officers approach you, the trainers told them, drop down and don't move. If they are wielding water hoses, curl into a ball to protect your face. If they have dogs, grab something to shield yourself. After the training, the students practiced the new tactics, getting into each other's faces and shouting *"Nigger!"* The trainers doused them with ketchup and mustard. They were being prepared for the hatred they might encounter on the picket line.

One July night after the training, the students decided they wanted to start demonstrating right then. "Let's see if the College Shoppe on the corner is open," one of them suggested. Blacks were allowed to enter the College Shoppe and make purchases, but then they were expected to leave. On this night, a dozen young people walked through the front doors and sat down at the counter.

"What are y'all doing?" a white man behind the counter asked them. "Get out of here. I'm going to call the cops."

When the police arrived, they talked with Douglas, who had

accompanied the students, and then called Griffin, who rushed to the store. "We'll leave tonight, but we'll be back in the morning," Griffin informed the manager. The next day, Griffin told the students he would support them as long as they followed the law.

Everett Berryman, the fifteen-year-old who had been attending school in Appomattox County for two years, borrowed his father's '55 Chevrolet each day and trucked seven students from Prospect and other far western reaches of the county into Farmville to demonstrate. One day, Williams sent Everett and several others into J. J. Newberry's, a five and dime store chain, which had a long counter—maybe fifteen to twenty seats—and instructed them to sit down.

Everett was served a cup of coffee filled with salt. He and the others left after twenty minutes. When they came back the next day, the stools were gone.

"They took their stools up and never put them back," Betty Jean remembered.

The students demonstrated in front of other businesses that didn't employ blacks. By late July, they had become a permanent fixture downtown, carrying signs that read, "I Have Lost Four Years of 'Education.' WHY FIVE?" and "While the 4th Circuit Court Continues to Wait, Education for Negro Children Suffocates." The young people gathered every morning at First Baptist Church, where Williams assigned them each a location for the day. The demonstrators broke at lunchtime, often gathering on Williams's front lawn, where he and his wife served hot dogs and hamburgers. After the students ate, many of them returned downtown to demonstrate.

The young people walked up and down both sides of Main Street, carrying placards with slogans like "Let's Make Jim Crow Look Like a Rainbow" and "We'd Rather Line Up for School." A boycott of Farmville businesses was also under way.

In the mornings, teenager Sammie Womack would protest in front of Pairet's Discount House, where he was employed. Then, later in the day, Sammie put down his sign and went inside to work his shift. Sunny Pairet, the white owner, called him out. "How the devil you think I'm going to pay you to work when you walk back and forth in front of my store with a sign that says don't shop in Farmville?" Pairet asked Sammie.

"Mr. Pairet, I've got to do it," Sammie responded. Pairet, who that summer was running for a seat on the supervisors and calling for the schools to be reopened, allowed the teenager to continue working for him.

White students from the north, including some who had volunteered in Danville, joined Prince Edward's demonstrations. Some told Williams they were glad to serve food or paint posters, but they didn't want to be on the picket line because whites had been injured in demonstrations in other towns. Other students who admitted that if they got hit, they'd hit back were given other assignments. The strike's leaders didn't want the demonstration to turn violent because they knew it would bring negative attention, distracting from the mission. The goal of those demonstrating was to be placid.

"You could have smacked most of us down and we would have gotten up and said thank you," said Tina Land, the president of the NAACP Youth Council.

Only one grocery store and one drugstore were exempted from the boycott, so black residents drove to Lynchburg or Richmond to buy items they couldn't find at those stores. A truck driver confided to the students demonstrating in front of one of the targeted grocery stores that he was delivering a fraction of the normal supplies. The campaign seemed to have gotten the attention of white leaders.

"They knew by then that people were not playing," Douglas said. "Kids were tired. They wanted to see the schools reopened."

Then came a turning point. On July 27, a Saturday, black protestors paraded through town, requiring Main Street to be cordoned off and traffic detoured. A small group of protestors walked to the College Shoppe. When they refused to move, ten people were arrested.

The next day the teenagers staged pray-ins or kneel-ins at white churches around town in an attempt to integrate them. The black students organized a rally of four hundred people at Griffin's First Baptist Church and then dispersed to white churches around town. A group of black students went to Farmville Methodist Church, where they were turned away at the door. When young people entered the Wesleyan Methodist Church, the entire congregation got up and left except for five people and the brand-new minister, who was preaching for the first time. He begged the students to leave, and they complied. At Johns Memorial Episcopal Church, ushers planned to seat black students in the front of the church to embarrass them, but Gordon Moss, now the dean of Longwood, invited the seven students and an adult to sit in his pew. The next day, he would be dismissed from his position as the church's treasurer.

Wearing a new hat and purse, Tina Land joined a group walking toward the Farmville Baptist Church, the same church where my grandparents worshipped. As they made their way down the street, Land noticed police cars and officers who had been tipped off about the group's plans. The students who had been turned away from the Methodist churches joined the young people walking to Farmville Baptist, and by the time they arrived, the crowd had grown to several dozen. A leader of the group went to the front door and knocked, and the owner of a local business answered. Robert Burger, who owned a funeral home, also met the students at the door. "What are y'all doing down here?" the first businessman asked, standing army style, legs separated with his arms behind his back. "You got your own churches. You're not coming up in here."

"Well, we will pray here and sing freedom songs right here," Williams responded.

White churchgoers arriving late were directed to enter through a side door as Williams led the students in prayer and sang "We Shall Overcome" on the front steps.

Inside Farmville Baptist Church, where my grandparents sat on a pew near the rear of the church with their three children every Sunday, the service was already under way. The chanting and singing from the front of the church was so loud that a choir member seated directly behind the minister couldn't hear him. Police officers soon arrived.

"If you don't leave, we're going to arrest you," the officers told the young people.

The students sat down on the front steps, and some of them responded, "Arrest us." The Farmville police officers ordered the students into the cruisers, telling them that they were under arrest.

"The only way you're going to move us is you have to lift us," the students responded, and then went limp. Betty Jean was chubby, and it took four officers to pick her up by the arms and legs and lift her into the station wagon. She didn't say a word. An officer told Tina to get up and walk to his police car. "You want to take me, you're going to have to take me some other way," she told him. "I'm not going to walk."

"I was carried by my arms, I was carried by my feet, and I was actually dragged," she said.

Williams was the only demonstrator who walked to the police car. He was taken to a holding cell at the Farmville Jail. "We didn't care if we went to jail or not, because King had taught us that it is good to go to jail for a just cause," Williams said, recalling the civil rights leader's words at Shaw University.

Burger, the chairman of the church's board of deacons, signed the warrant for charges of interfering with worship services. Ivanhoe Donaldson, a field worker for SNCC of New York who had also been in Danville, was among those arrested. Most of the demonstrators were rolled on stretchers to the police station around the corner.

The students had warned their parents that they might be taken into police custody before they left home that morning. Don't come and get us, they had instructed their parents. The students wanted to be locked up in order to attract media attention. But when the police started calling parents of the children who were under eighteen, threatening to send them to different counties, parents like Betty Jean's headed down to the police station to pick them up.

Deputy Jack Overton, the brother of Farmville Police Chief Otto Overton and the future county sheriff, went to Williams's cell and told him that Griffin was there to see him. Williams didn't believe Overton—he thought he was about to be beaten. Downstairs, deputy sheriffs from neighboring Lunenburg County were waiting to transport him to their jail—out of sight of reporters, who had gotten word that students and organizers were in custody. Williams was loaded into a sheriff's car and driven down Main Street in Farmville. He waved to a woman he knew from the back of the cruiser and she immediately alerted Griffin.

Over the weekend the police had arrested thirty-three demonstrators, twenty-five of whom were juveniles released to their parents. In preparation, white officials had requested space in eight surrounding counties' jails, enough "to house every citizen of Prince Edward County, Negro and white, including horses, cattle and dogs," one black county leader noted. More than a dozen young men had also been deputized to help law enforcement officers.

It took nearly a week for Williams to be bailed out of jail. He was sentenced to twelve months in prison for interrupting and disturbing an assembly met for the worship of God. But the sentence was appealed and Williams did not return to jail.

CHAPTER 15

Two Steps Forward, One Step Back

P rince Edward County's black residents believed they had a
friend in President Kennedy.

When the schools closed, Virginia legislators and congressmen turned their backs on the black residents of Prince Edward
County. And President Eisenhower had seemed to pay little attention
to the shuttering of schools and its effect on black students. Although
the president acknowledged in correspondence with a Charlottesville
parent deep regret that the schools were closed and said the impact on
children could be "disastrous," he never offered to intervene in Prince
Edward.

Black county residents had all but given up on their local representatives, but they hoped the next president would step in. During the
1960 presidential campaign, Griffin wrote letters to both candidates,
Senator John F. Kennedy and Vice President Richard Nixon, asking
them how they planned to address the situation in Prince Edward.
"This little Virginia community has defied the courts and violated
every principle of democracy. Strong federal intervention is needed to
save us from ourselves and guarantee our children a fair chance in an
ever-changing world," Griffin wrote.

"If you are elected as president of this great nation of ours, will you
advocate measures to prevent this from happening to other children of

the nation?" Griffin wanted to know. "Will you use the powers of this great office to correct this evil that is negatively affecting the lives of approximately 1,400 white and 1,700 Negro children, and by tomorrow could affect the lives of untold numbers of the South?"

More than 70 percent of blacks around the country voted for Kennedy, helping him to win the election.

Soon after Kennedy took office in January 1961, he expressed public support for *Brown* and denounced the school closings. His administration wanted to help the children of Prince Edward, but without clear authority for the federal government to enforce the *Brown* decision, the Department of Justice needed to be invited by a federal judge to join a school desegregation case as a friend of the court, not a party to the action.

Months after taking office, Attorney General Robert F. Kennedy found a way around the friend of the court requirement. In April 1961, the Department of Justice filed a motion in federal district court to intervene in the Prince Edward suit as a party plaintiff, in an attempt to expand the NAACP's complaint. In its first school desegregation case, the department asked the federal court to add the Commonwealth of Virginia, the comptroller of Virginia, and the Prince Edward School Foundation as defendants. It also asked the court to order Virginia to withhold state money for all schools—and for tuition grants—until the Prince Edward schools were reopened.

Segregationists quickly denounced the Department of Justice's request to join the lawsuits. The Prince Edward Defenders held a rally attended by 250 people and adopted a resolution calling the department's move "totalitarianism." Congressman Watkins M. Abbitt of Appomattox, a member of Byrd's close circle of advisers who had once referred to the *Brown* decision as the "naked and arrogant declaration of nine men," said the department had usurped its powers. Senator Byrd suggested that the Kennedy administration was penalizing the whole state in order to punish one locality.

The Kennedys did not relent under the criticism. Bobby Kennedy questioned the morality of closing the schools and accused Prince Edward of circumventing federal courts. He promised to act if that claim were found to be true. "We will not stand by or be aloof," he said in a May 1961 speech at the University of Georgia. "We will move."

But the Kennedy administration would have to find another path. Federal Judge Oren R. Lewis denied the Department of Justice's motion to intervene, finding that doing so without clear legislation would defy Congress. Black leaders' hopes for quick action by the new president had been dashed. Lewis's decision implied that the executive branch of the federal government was powerless to reopen the schools.

It already seemed that the state had no power—or no will—to act. During his gubernatorial campaign, Albertis S. Harrison Jr. had advocated reopening the schools even though he was responsible for defending massive resistance as attorney general. But since his 1962 swearing-in as governor, Harrison had taken no action in Prince Edward. His failure to act led many to believe that the state could not intervene to assist the county's black students while the case was in the federal courts.

The Prince Edward County Board of Supervisors could have re-opened the schools at any point. But each year when the issue came before the board, its members voted not to levy taxes, effectively keeping the schools closed. After the Bush League stopped meeting, public calls to reopen the schools came primarily from the black community.

The Kennedy administration focused its attention on voting rights after being turned away from the Prince Edward case and soon had to address violence and protests that were erupting farther South.

In May 1961, the Congress of Racial Equality led a group of thirteen black and white volunteers from Washington, DC, into the South on a pair of Greyhound and Trailways buses. Some whites sat in the back and some blacks in the front, testing whether buses and station facilities had complied with Supreme Court rulings that called for integrated interstate travel, including lunch counters, waiting rooms, and restrooms at bus stations.

The lawsuit had originated in Virginia. The NAACP had taken up the case of Irene Morgan, who had been arrested in July 1944 by the sheriff of Middlesex County for refusing to give up her seat on a Greyhound bus. In June 1946, the Supreme Court ruled that racial segregation on interstate buses was a violation of the interstate commerce clause. In December 1960, *Boynton v. Virginia* had expanded the ruling, prohibiting segregation in waiting rooms and restaurants at bus stations, but both decisions were largely ignored in the South.

The Freedom Riders—the individuals testing the laws—stopped in Prince Edward County on their route. They found that the "Colored" signs at the Farmville bus station had been painted over, and all thirteen riders were served. They left Prince Edward unscathed, but as the buses traveled farther south and new passengers boarded, the Freedom Riders experienced growing hostility. They were arrested in North Carolina and beaten in South Carolina. In Anniston, Alabama, a crowd of fifty surrounded the bus with encouragement from a Ku Klux Klan member. Holding chains, clubs, and metal pipes, the crowd slashed the bus's tires and broke windows before the police arrived. After the bus was escorted out of town by the police, it hobbled to a stop six miles beyond the town limits as its tires went flat. A mob surrounded the Greyhound bus, rocking the bus in an attempt to flip it. Someone threw a bomb inside, while another held the doors shut to keep passengers inside and screamed, "Burn them alive!" and "Fry the goddamn niggers!" As passengers escaped the burning vehicle, they were beaten with baseball bats. In response, rioting broke out in Birmingham and Montgomery. When the Trailways bus arrived in Birmingham, its passengers were attacked by another Klan mob.

Over the course of the protest, four hundred people participated in the Freedom Rides, many of whom were imprisoned. After continued rioting and mounting arrests, the Interstate Commerce Commission in September 1961 ordered the desegregation of interstate travel at the request of Attorney General Robert Kennedy.

The following year, James H. Meredith Jr., a black air force veteran, attempted to enroll in the University of Mississippi after a court ordered he be admitted. President Kennedy intervened when Governor Ross Barnett blocked Meredith's path. Federal marshals and Department of Justice lawyers accompanied Meredith to campus—he was dropped off by a border patrol plane—so that he could register for classes, ending segregation at the university. The president sent twenty-three thousand Mississippi National Guard troops to the campus. Riots broke out, with youth throwing bottles and rocks and setting fires. Two men died and 375 were injured in the violence. Meredith was guarded around the clock and escorted from building to building.

It seemed to blacks in Farmville that, with headline-grabbing racial violence farther south, Kennedy had forgotten about their children. But, as time wore on, it became clear that the president was growing increasingly frustrated with the county's closed schools. "Prince Edward's educational wasteland troubled the consciences of many Americans, particularly President Kennedy," *Newsweek* wrote.

Just before Christmas 1962, the Department of Justice joined the NAACP as a friend of the court in a filing with the Court of Appeals for the Fourth Circuit to "order the schools opened promptly without racial segregation" in Prince Edward. Bobby Kennedy argued that the federal courts had the power to require the county to levy taxes to operate desegregated public schools.

But many in Prince Edward were tired of Kennedy's legal focus and wanted him to take action instead. Late in 1962 and into 1963, Griffin coordinated with other agencies to petition the administration to do more. Finally the national NAACP asked Kennedy to put together a remedial program for Prince Edward's children.

At the beginning of the New Year, matters were escalating in the South. When George C. Wallace delivered his inaugural address as

Alabama's governor in January 1963, the streets of Montgomery were packed with his supporters, some of whom wore white flowers symbolizing their commitment to white supremacy. Blacks were not welcome at the public event. Wallace pledged, in a vehement speech written by a Ku Klux Klansman, to protect the state's "Anglo-Saxon people" from "communist amalgamation" with blacks.

"In the name of the greatest people that have ever trod this earth, I draw a line in the dust and toss the gauntlet before the feet of tyranny. And I say, segregation now, segregation tomorrow and segregation forever."

Six months later, in June 1963, Wallace would "stand in the schoolhouse door" to block two black students, Vivian Malone and James Hood, from enrolling at the University of Alabama in Tuscaloosa. When the president called for one hundred troops from the Alabama National Guard to assist, Wallace stepped aside. But the violence Wallace seemed to condone, if not advocate, had followed his inaugural address with cross burnings, night ridings, and police beatings. Black youth would launch sit-ins and a boycott of stores to protest Birmingham's segregation policies, and the violence would only mount as the year wore on.

In Prince Edward, Bobby Kennedy and the president stepped up the pressure. In January 1963, Bobby Kennedy referred to Prince Edward as "a disgrace to our country." President Kennedy personally deplored the school closures in a special civil rights message to Congress in February. He pledged publicly to "fulfill the constitutional objective of an equal, nonsegregated educational opportunity for all children." In private, he urged his brother to make progress in the county before September. And if he hadn't already made it clear that he considered Prince Edward an embarrassment, Bobby Kennedy cited the county by name at the centennial of the Emancipation Proclamation in Louisville in March. "We may observe, with as much sadness as irony, that outside of Africa, south of the Sahara where education is still a difficult challenge, the only places on earth known not to provide free public education are Communist China, North Vietnam, Sarawak, Singapore, British Honduras—and Prince Edward County, Virginia," he said.

The NAACP kept the pressure on the White House to intervene, with more than seven hundred people signing a letter to the president requesting a more sophisticated remedial instruction program. The Virginia Teachers Association also planned to request a more concerted federal action on behalf of Prince Edward's schoolchildren, calling the long-closed schools a "blot on the American image."

After Wallace tried to prevent black students from enrolling in the University of Alabama, the president went on national television and proposed what became the Civil Rights Act of 1964. He deemed civil rights a "moral issue," saying it was "as old as the Scriptures" and "clear as the American Constitution," adding that America "will not be fully free until all its citizens are free."

> The heart of the question is whether all Americans are to be afforded equal rights and equal opportunities, whether we are going to treat our fellow Americans as we want to be treated. If an American, because his skin is dark, cannot eat lunch in a restaurant open to the public, if he cannot send his children to the best public school available, if he cannot vote for the public officials who will represent him, if, in short, he cannot enjoy the full and free life which all of us want, then who among us would be content to have the color of his skin changed and stand in his place? Who among us would then be content with the counsels of patience and delay?

"One hundred years of delay have passed since President Lincoln freed the slaves, yet their heirs, their grandsons, are not fully free," he added.

That night, Medgar Evers, a thirty-seven-year-old Mississippi field secretary for the NAACP known for his role investigating Emmett Till's death, was gunned down by a white supremacist in his Jackson driveway as he arrived home, where his wife and three children had been watching the president's speech.

IN FEBRUARY 1963, THE PRESIDENT had discussed the situation in Prince Edward County with his advisers and directed them to find a way the federal government could help. The challenge: the federal government couldn't operate schools or finance them. A few months later, Robert Kennedy assigned a Department of Justice aide to the county.

William J. vanden Heuvel, a tall thirty-three-year-old who was the president of the International Rescue Committee, spent much of the summer traveling between DC and Farmville, talking with state and local officials and sharing his progress with the Kennedy administration. The student-led demonstrations had peaked in late July when students were arrested on the steps of the white church. Vanden Heuvel, named an assistant attorney general, gradually established communication between black and white leaders in Prince Edward. Avoiding the legal dispute over whether the county was required to operate public schools, he was able to hammer out a solution that was amenable to the community and his boss: a temporary, free private school for black children and any white students who wanted to attend.

Governor Harrison, Griffin, and segregationists alike signed off on the plan, which called for an integrated staff and student body. The agreement to open the private school would enable state officials to continue fighting against public school integration in Prince Edward and black leaders to keep pressing for it. The Department of Justice assured Griffin that the court case would be fast-tracked and lawyers would argue before the Supreme Court for the schools to be reopened.

"The temporary solution has been endorsed by the Justice

Department, the NAACP—practically everybody involved in the seemingly endless dispute," wrote *U.S. News & World Report.*

The governor, who had taken no action in Prince Edward, was under pressure to find a solution after a summer of protests in Farmville. He announced in August that schools would open in the county the next month. A biracial board of directors of three whites and three blacks, and headed by former University of Virginia president Colgate W. Darden Jr., would establish an independently run school in four public school buildings. The new Prince Edward Free School Association, known as the Free Schools, would cost a million dollars to operate for one year and would be funded with donations from the Ford Foundation and the Field Foundation, as well as the National Education Association and parent-teacher organizations throughout the country. The private school would recruit its faculty from across the US.

In the same month, the Fourth Circuit Court of Appeals ruled against the NAACP and the Department of Justice's attempt to force the reopening of the county's public schools, claiming that "there is nothing in the 14th Amendment which requires a state, or any of its political subdivisions . . . to provide schooling for any of its citizens."

The decision was a blow to the administration. But after four years, black children would finally have a school to attend in Prince Edward County. The Free Schools would soon be up and running.

Two weeks after the governor's announcement, several dozen Prince Edward residents, most of them students, boarded buses before the sun came up. They were carrying fried chicken in shoeboxes, bound for the nation's capital to participate in the March on Washington for Jobs and Freedom.

For some, the road trip felt like a religious experience. It was many students' first time outside Virginia, and they sang fight songs on the long bus ride. They had spent the summer demonstrating, and at the March on Washington the students could celebrate the commonality they felt with other Southern blacks protesting segregation. When they arrived, they walked to the Lincoln Memorial carrying a huge "Prince Edward" banner, securing a spot near the steps where they witnessed Martin Luther King Jr.'s iconic "I Have a Dream" speech. Betty Jean Ward dipped her feet in the reflecting pool.

King referred to the summer the Farmville youth had spent protesting, boycotting businesses, and conducting sit-ins and a church kneel-in as the "sweltering summer of the Negro's legitimate discontent."

"Now is the time to rise from the dark and desolate valley of segregation to the sunlit path of racial justice," King instructed the crowd.

The end of his speech spoke directly to the ongoing struggles of Prince Edward's black families, who had sacrificed so much in their quest for desegregated schools. "I have a dream that my four little children will one day live in a nation where they will not be judged by the color of their skin but by the content of their character," he told the crowd.

It was their dream, too.

AFTER THE AGREEMENT TO OPEN the Free Schools came together, a superintendent, Neil V. Sullivan, was hired with three weeks to spare. Sullivan took a one-year leave from the same position at East Williston School District in Long Island, New York. His to-do list was long: prepare school buildings that hadn't been used in four years, oversee repairs to twenty buses, hire administrators and one hundred teachers, stock the cafeterias, and order textbooks and equipment. He had been warned that three of the school facilities—the former Moton High School, now known as Mary Branch No. 2; Mary Branch No. 1; and Worsham Elementary School—needed repairs to roofs, floors, and walls. Only the new Robert R. Moton High School was in decent shape.

When Sullivan finally toured the schools, he found them in "deplorable condition," with "dirt, dust, and rubbish" everywhere.

"I could only conclude that the powers that be in Prince Edward County had written [the schools] off entirely," Sullivan later wrote in his memoir *Bound for Freedom*. "Apparently they had never had any intention of reopening public schools once the private white academy was established. . . . Floorboards were rotting; plaster had fallen; water had penetrated walls. Wastepaper baskets had not been emptied when the schools were closed, and the stench from the contaminated remains was sickening," he wrote. Although maintenance workers had already begun cleaning, Sullivan wondered whether the buildings could be readied in a matter of weeks.

He was appalled by the lack of equipment in the schools, particularly in the brand-new Moton High School. There were few books on the library's shelves, no textbooks in the classrooms, and one lone microscope to teach 650 students biology.

The buses were in dire shape, too. "Those buses are still standing right where they were parked four years ago," the public school superintendent, T. J. McIlwaine, told him. "Drivers just turned off the ignition, got out, locked 'em up, and there they are."

At Mary Branch No. 2, which served as the headquarters for the Free Schools, parents had lined up to register their children, who were getting checkups and vaccinations from a doctor while they waited. Teacher candidates trickled in, too. Sullivan had hired several teachers from other states after interviewing them by phone. Other administrators had reached out to former colleagues and Peace Corps volunteers to staff the school. After several weeks of recruiting, Sullivan had lined up only fifteen teachers, including his wife. When he reported to vanden Heuvel the difficulty he was having, the assistant attorney general offered to reach out to the National Education Association to help locate qualified candidates. "I'll move heaven and earth to find them for you," he told Sullivan.

The superintendent didn't want just anybody. He warned candidates that they would have their work cut out for them. Many of the children returning to school would not be able to read, and some wouldn't be able to recognize the alphabet, count to ten, or tell time. But he told potential teachers that he was excited about the innovative way they would be teaching that year. The Free School would offer a crash program in reading and mathematics. The goal was to make up lost ground as quickly as possible. Instead of putting students in classes with other children their age, Sullivan planned to group them by need and ability—an innovation he had implemented in New York, with good results. The students would move up as they progressed, and teachers would spend all day teaching in their area of expertise, such as reading or math.

The plight of Prince Edward County's schoolchildren had caught the attention of the nation, and teachers from around the country wanted to help. Half of the teachers hired for the Free Schools were from out of state, and they took pay cuts to leave cities such as Boston, Philadelphia, and New York. Others came in from West Virginia, North Carolina, South Carolina, Maryland, Florida, Wisconsin, and California. One quarter of the teachers were white, making the Free Schools one of the first integrated teaching staffs in Virginia.

Days before the school was scheduled to open, Sullivan still needed twenty more teachers. He asked Virginia State College to send student teachers, and some left Petersburg for Prince Edward before learning if they would be paid a salary and reimbursed for their expenses. It was difficult for future teachers to say no to this challenge, to work with children who had lost so much through no fault of their own.

TENSIONS WERE HIGH ON SEPTEMBER 16, 1963, the day the Free Schools were to open. The previous morning, a bomb had exploded at the Sixteenth Street Baptist Church in Birmingham, Alabama, killing four black girls. Earlier that week, three all-white schools in the city had desegregated by federal court order. The church had served as a meeting place for civil rights organizers like King and as the starting point for many of the protest marches in Birmingham.

The bomb detonated on the east side of the building, killing fourteen-year-olds Addie Mae Collins, Cynthia Wesley, and Carole Robertson, and eleven-year-old Denise McNair. Fourteen others were injured, including Addie Mae's sister, twelve-year-old Sarah Collins, who was sprayed with glass and lost an eye in the explosion. After the bombing, riots broke out in Birmingham, and two black boys, Virgil Ware, thirteen, and Johnny Robinson, sixteen, were also killed. Governor Wallace sent five hundred National Guardsmen and three hundred state troopers to the city. The next day, hundreds more police officers and sheriffs' deputies would join them.

This violence terrified Prince Edward parents, who worried that their children would be in harm's way as they returned to school. No physical violence against black youth had been reported in the county, but parents and school officials were edgy just the same. A handful of white children would be attending the Free Schools, and Sullivan's reception in town had been icy. He had received threatening letters at his hotel, and calls came in nightly demanding that he leave town. "Go on home, you nigger lover!" one caller advised him. Another night, when a call came in at 2:00 a.m., an exasperated Sullivan shouted back. "Go to hell!" he yelled into the phone. "I'm staying."

J. Barrye Wall, the editor and publisher of the *Farmville Herald*, had little to say about the Free Schools. "We have never been happy about the lack of schools for Negroes," he told *U.S. News & World Report*. "We do not oppose education for Negroes. We just oppose integrated education."

Gordon Moss, the Longwood dean who had publicly derided the school closings, was the first white parent to enroll his son. He hoped it would encourage other whites to send their children to the Free

Schools. Moss had never explained to his son, Dickie, a seventeen-year-old rising senior at Virginia Episcopal School in Lynchburg, why he had opposed the school closings, but Dickie understood how much his father had sacrificed. When his father asked him to consider leaving boarding school to attend the Free Schools, Dickie immediately agreed. His father warned the six-foot-tall young man that classroom time would be devoted to helping the black children catch up. He told his son that he might not do a lot of book learning that year, but he would learn about people from the experience. In the group of twenty-two seniors, Dickie Moss told me, "I stood out like a sore thumb."

William W. Tews, a white tobacco farmer, and his wife registered their eight-year-old daughter, Letitia. After officials at the white academy learned that the couple planned to send their daughter to the Free Schools, they offered to help pay for her education. Her parents declined because they believed that school should be free for all children, and their response was met with threats. The girl's mother was told in a store, "Your head will be cut off if you let Letitia go to school with the niggers."

McCarthy Eanes, a twenty-year-old black student who also worked as a bus driver for the Free Schools, told his supervisor about two white children, Brenda and George Abernathy, who lived up the road from him and might attend. Sullivan went to visit the children's father, a tenant farmer who had recently moved from Portsmouth, Virginia. He wanted to send his children to public school. Sullivan assured him that he would keep his children safe, and their father agreed to send them to the Free Schools. "My parents were not prejudiced people," George Abernathy said. "They were salt of the earth people."

Betty Lewis and her brother, Thomas Lewis, who had spent four years in the tobacco fields helping their dad, were also enrolled. When the academy had called on their father, Walter Lewis, "Daddy told them straight up he didn't believe in segregation," Betty told me.

On the first day of school, Eanes drove Brenda and George to class. They sat directly behind him on the bus. He had been instructed not to open the doors for anyone. As he pulled up to the schools and joined the line of buses, photographers and reporters jostled to get on. Eanes focused on his instructions from school officials—do not open the doors for anyone. A pair of teachers was waiting to escort George and Brenda to their classrooms when his bus pulled to the front of the line.

At 9:00 a.m., children gathered around the flagpole at Mary Branch No. 2, the former Moton High School. The children were quiet as the American flag went up. Inside the building, the school bell sounded for a full thirty seconds, a symbolic tribute to the four years it had remained silent.

Sixteen hundred children, all but a few of them black, had returned to the classroom. Half were attending school for the first time in their lives. Sullivan delivered the opening prayer. "We ask you to bless the students," he said, "and to encourage them to take advantage of an opportunity denied them for four years—one which, we pray, will never again be denied an American child."

WHEN MCCARTHY EANES WENT BACK to the classroom, school was a distant memory.

For four years, he and his siblings had stayed home without an ounce of education. One of twenty-one children, he had spent the time helping out in his family's tobacco fields, like the other kids who were old enough to work. His dad had a first-grade education and couldn't read or write, but he was good at math, and he had done all right for himself. He worked as a logger and a tobacco farmer, and he had purchased three hundred acres of land behind Moton High School in the community of Worsham. He didn't think his children needed more schooling. McCarthy's mom, Gertrude, had finished sixth grade, and she wanted her kids to be educated. But with so many children—as many as fifteen in school at one time—it seemed fairest, and most affordable, to keep them all home when the schools closed.

During the long hiatus, there had been no training centers or informal schooling for McCarthy. But not finishing school nagged at him. He wanted to go back for his senior year and get his high school diploma. His father relied on him at the farm, but he didn't try to stop his son. His mom supported him, too. McCarthy had applied to drive the bus so he could make some money while he was a student.

Betty Jean Ward also joined the senior class of the Free Schools. Her parents thought it was for the best, even though she had been attending school in Nottoway for four years with her new friends. She was torn about whether to return to Prince Edward, but after spending the summer protesting in Farmville, she wanted to stay home. She found that the schools were nicer than when she had left, and there was new equipment and new books, donations sent from around the country. Dickie Moss was her first white classmate.

The teachers were highly qualified, and administrators bought an army surplus bus and took the students on field trips to Appomattox and Charlottesville. They went to New York, where they met the mayor, toured the United Nations, and ate lunch in Jackie Robinson's home.

Everett Berryman had been attending school in Appomattox for years. He had returned to school there and was driving a bus when, two weeks into the new school year, his dad announced the family would be moving back to Prince Edward, and he would go to the Free Schools. "You've got to be kidding me," Everett thought. He had settled in and made a life in Appomattox. Now he was starting over again.

Griffin's son, Skippy, came back, too, joining the sophomore class after spending the summer demonstrating in Farmville with other students. Since the schools had closed, he had moved back and forth between Prince Edward and Newton, Massachusetts—just outside

Boston—where he stayed with a black host family arranged by the American Friends Service Committee. He went to Newton High School, one of the best in the country.

Skippy decided to attend the Free Schools after he heard that Dickie Moss had enrolled. Griffin thought that Skippy's return would send a good message to other families in Prince Edward. Plus, the students had talked about continuing the demonstrations during the school year, even though Griffin didn't want them to. Skippy wanted to be close by for the outcome of the pending Supreme Court case in which he was a plaintiff, *Griffin v. County School Board of Prince Edward County*. The district judge Oren Lewis had ruled in the case that tuition grants be discontinued but did not address whether closing the schools violated the Constitution.

JUST WEEKS INTO THE SCHOOL year, President Kennedy was shot and killed, breaking the hearts of those in Prince Edward who credited him with opening the Free Schools and who had counted on him to get the public schools reopened.

Sullivan moved into a house five miles south of Farmville, where he continued to be harassed. People drove down the long semicircular driveway to his home early in the morning, blowing their horns and dumping garbage on his lawn. He and his wife began sleeping in separate bedrooms, reasoning that their two college-aged sons deserved at least one surviving parent. When a shotgun blasted through a bedroom window late one night, the superintendent dove under his bed and stayed there until the smell of gunpowder cleared.

After a weekend away, he returned home to find the yard covered in trash, the tires of his Buick convertible slashed, and the car's roof and rear window destroyed. The local police did nothing, he later wrote, and one officer even suggested that black youngsters were rebelling because Sullivan made them work too hard in school. "This is just their way of letting you know they don't like it," one of the officers told him.

Ultimately, federal marshals were assigned to protect him and his staff, and a threat against a white teacher from the North brought the Federal Bureau of Investigation to town. "It was a living hell," Sullivan said later.

Students at the Free Schools signed a scroll that was delivered to Jacqueline Kennedy. "Our beloved President John F. Kennedy once considered us in our distress," it read. "We, the students of Prince Edward County Free Schools in Farmville, Virginia, think of Caroline, John, and Mrs. Kennedy in their sorrow. It is also ours."

They collected donations for the John F. Kennedy Memorial Library. In the spring of 1964, Bobby Kennedy and his wife, Ethel, flew to the county for a four-hour visit—Colgate Darden met their plane. As Darden guided Kennedy and his wife through the Free Schools, the attorney general was "quiet and uncertain" as he met with parents and talked with students, the *Richmond Times-Dispatch* reported, noting that Kennedy accepted a package tied with a red, white, and blue bow that contained thousands of pennies. Kennedy warmed up when a throng of Longwood students blocked his motorcade through downtown, getting out of the car and shaking hands before heading to Hampden-Sydney College, where he had been invited to speak.

Two weeks after the attorney general's visit, on May 25, 1964, the US Supreme Court finally took action that would reopen Prince Edward's public schools. During the four years the schools were closed, 1,100 black children had received no formal education, the Michigan State researcher Robert L. Green found. Only twenty-five black children had enrolled in full-time school between 1959 and 1963, he found, writing that the school closings may have had "irreversible effects" on the children.

The prior December, the Virginia Supreme Court of Appeals had upheld Prince Edward County's decision to close the schools, declaring that the county had no duty to operate public schools and finding that there was no provision in the Virginia Constitution or state law that prohibited the payment of state and local tuition grants.

But the Supreme Court, ruling in *Griffin v. County School Board of Prince Edward County,* found the school closings to be unconstitutional. The court ruled that the county's decision to close all public schools while providing tuition grants and vouchers to white children to attend private schools denied black school children equal protection of the laws guaranteed by the Fourteenth Amendment. "The time for mere 'deliberate speed' has run out, and that phrase can no longer justify denying these Prince Edward County school children their constitutional rights to an education equal to that afforded by the public schools in the other parts of Virginia," the court found.

The nation's highest court ordered Prince Edward to reopen and desegregate its schools. It also found that a district court could require the county supervisors to levy taxes to raise funds for a county school system, and it outlawed Virginia's tuition grants to private education.

Ten years and eight days after the *Brown* decision, the county's black leaders finally got the answer they sought. Black children and their families had paid a heartbreaking, life-changing price.

IN JUNE, WEEKS AFTER THE ruling, the county board of supervisors set aside $375,000 for schools, $180,000 of it for tuition grants for the academy. A month later, the board held a late-night meeting.

Elsie was working at my grandparents' house when a call came in about the special meeting. Papa was still at work and Elsie was in the basement ironing when Mimi answered the phone. "I can't believe it's happening," my grandmother said into the phone, giddy.

Later that night, hundreds of academy patrons gathered at the town armory to accept grants that were being handed out in secret. A federal judge was expected to issue an injunction the next day to block distribution of the funds, and, to get around the ruling, the supervisors planned to immediately issue 1,250 tuition grants. Parents buzzed with excitement as they waited for the checks to be cut at 2:00 a.m. "You would have thought an atomic bomb went off," Robert Taylor recalled.

That morning, the town's three banks opened early for parents to cash the checks "before a new court order could stop them," Taylor said. Women wearing dresses and men in suits with hats or short-sleeved dress shirts lined up outside Peoples National Bank on Main Street, waiting to deposit the public funds into their own accounts. Two years later, a federal appeals court ordered the supervisors to return the money. The county asked parents to repay the grants, but some parents refused—or simply couldn't afford to do so. Still $68,000 short in 1967, the supervisors unhappily sued the parents who still owed money.

Not much had changed in Prince Edward. The Free Schools, always intended to be temporary, closed down, donating some of their supplies and leftover money to the public schools. When the public schools reopened that fall, only eight of the 1,500 students were white. But nationally, change was afoot. In July 1964, President Lyndon B. Johnson signed the Civil Rights Act into law, enacting the most sweeping nondiscrimination legislation since Reconstruction. It ended the use of Jim Crow laws, prohibiting discrimination in hotels, in employment practices and union membership, and in programs that received federal aid. Johnson called on the American people to "eliminate the last vestiges of injustice in America." He implored the nation, "Let us close the springs of racial poison."

I'M SITTING IN THE COOL, dark living room of a house I'm renting in Farmville for the summer, flipping through a thin phone book, looking for the number of one of my high school teachers. I have moved to town to get a feel for what Farmville is like today, to ensure that my views are not filtered through my parents' experiences.

I spotted Peggy Cave two days earlier, sitting across the aisle at Farmville Baptist Church at the fiftieth anniversary of the kneel-in. We greeted each other, and I asked if she had been in church the day of the protest, and she told me she had been singing in the choir. She agreed to talk with me about what happened.

But when I get her on the phone, she seems irritated. "I'm just so tired of this subject I could scream," she tells me. "I am tired of re-hashing this thing. I just want to move on."

I tell her that I have heard the same comment from a number of white residents of the county. She responds that I would hear it from a lot of black people, too, if I asked "the right people." Her tone grows increasingly condescending to me.

"Some people just want to keep on and on and on," she says. By "some people," I know she means me. I can almost feel her staring over her glasses at me like she did when I was her student. "It's been said a million times," she adds.

Now I'm annoyed, too, and ready to hang up, but I keep her on the line, hoping for a thread of information about my grandparents. She briefly opens up, expressing remorse that the schools closed. "I regret this whole situation," she tells me. "I regret that we imported slaves. There's a lot of things we did wrong in the past."

My frustration is mounting with people who tell me Farmville's story doesn't need to be shared. She has said it was wrong, yet she doesn't want to talk about it.

"Weren't you a history teacher?" I ask, incredulous. "How can it be wrong to discuss history?"

A classmate of mine recalled Mrs. Cave telling her students that buses integrated not because of Rosa Parks but because white women wanted their maids back and were tired of being inconvenienced by the Montgomery bus boycott. My friend remembered, years earlier, a different academy teacher conceding that the North had won the Civil War, adding that she was "Southern born and Southern bred and when she died she'd be Southern dead." Another academy graduate recalled that after she asked to write a report on *Uncle Tom's Cabin*, the groundbreaking antislavery novel, she was told to pick another book because "we don't read black authors." I think about how my classmates and I deserved a more balanced version of history, a chance to reflect on our town's—and the South's—past. How even now Mrs. Cave is shutting down the conversation and preventing deeper reflection.

Her message is loud and clear: She's done talking about this, and she thinks I should stop, too.

Chapter 16

Building a Life Without a Foundation

The black children whose educations were halted became known as the Lost Generation. Fifty years later, many still can't talk about what happened during that time. Not with their siblings, let alone with strangers. They carry around shame and sadness and anger, buried deep inside for decades. They don't swap stories with their sisters about where they were sent when the schools closed or talk to their brothers about working in the fields. They don't say how they were supposed to graduate high school but instead became dropouts, through no fault of their own.

Reopening those old wounds hurts. Even the "Lost Generation" label hurts. They don't feel lost. They have survived. Some have even thrived.

For younger children, like ten-year-old Ricky Brown, who had not yet begun his education and had no academic foundation, school would always be difficult. At the Free Schools, Ricky's teacher fussed at him instead of patiently explaining how he should do his work. The next year, when the public schools reopened, it was more of the same.

Ricky was poor, and his teachers wrote him off, applying the same low expectations that black children too often face in school today.

"They knew where I was from and knew I'd been left behind," he told me. "They couldn't hold back a whole class to help me."

His mother was busy working and she didn't have a car, so she rarely visited the school. It seemed that no one believed he would amount to anything. "For a while, I was beginning to believe that myself," he told me. He struggled without encouragement, trying to learn to read. The little boy who had been so excited to start school now despised it. "I didn't want to go because I didn't know what was going on in my classes," he remembers.

He had no confidence in the classroom, but he was a star on the athletic fields. Ricky shined in football, basketball, and baseball. Playing sports, he felt like he mattered. His mother never came to his games—she was usually working to support the family—but the coach took an interest in him, talking to college recruiters on his behalf. Ricky was offered scholarships to play basketball for three colleges, but when he looked around at the other high school seniors, he realized they had significantly more schooling than his seven years. If he was struggling now, he knew he wouldn't be able to handle the college workload.

He graduated from Prince Edward County High School in 1972, a stellar athlete but a demoralized, underachieving student. He still had a year of high school athletic eligibility left, but he couldn't stomach another year of classes, even if it meant he could play sports. "I'd had enough," he said.

He felt lost. Then he met his future wife, Shirby Scott, who had been raised by more progressive black parents. She grew up in a neighboring county and rarely traveled to Farmville as a child. "Black people just shouldn't be in an area that didn't want black people to be educated," her parents told her.

She was one of eight children, all of whom went to college. Scott saw something in Ricky that she hadn't seen in the college guys she knew. Ricky wanted to marry her, but he also wanted to be able to provide for Scott and her young son. That's when he had a tough realization—high-paying jobs are reserved for people with college degrees. "If I can't get a better job, I'm not going to marry you," he told Scott.

He finally landed a job as a guard at the Virginia Department of Corrections, which paid well, and the couple wed. When Ricky started his new career, he made up his mind to become a different man. He was not going to "be dumb" anymore. Every day he tucked a red miniature dictionary into his shirt pocket. Up in the watchtower, overlooking the corrections yard, he would pull out the dictionary and learn a few new words.

"Anytime I had a free moment, I would flip it open and just read," he said.

Still, each time he needed to take a routine test at the corrections department, he became nervous and upset. It was like being back in school all over again. "It's just reading," his wife would reassure him. "You can pass this."

He left the corrections position for a job as one of Farmville's first black police officers. A few years later, he took a higher-paying job with the power company.

At the end of his career, he would become a school resource officer, working day after day in the very school system that had denied him an education and a sense of worth. He founded an after-school program to mentor middle school boys like him.

He still thinks every day about what he might have accomplished if he had started school when he should have.

"Where would I have been," he wonders, "if my foundation had been built?"

WHEN THE SCHOOLS REOPENED, DOUG Vaughan was already married with a child. His wife JoAnn had become pregnant at sixteen, and neighboring Cumberland County, where she went to school, wouldn't allow pregnant girls to attend classes. It was important to Doug that she finish high school and get the education he had been denied. She was too smart not to graduate, and he was already thinking of the next generation of Vaughans. JoAnn's grandmother, a retired teacher, petitioned the Cumberland County School Board, gaining permission for JoAnn to attend school while pregnant. "I didn't want my kids to grow up uneducated," Doug told me.

After JoAnn gave birth to their baby daughter, she started skipping school. Doug adjusted his work schedule from a 5:00 a.m. to a 10:00 a.m. start so that he could walk her to the bus stop each day to make sure she climbed aboard. "I wanted her to finish at all costs," he told me.

When JoAnn graduated in 1964, the family moved to New Jersey so that Doug could find a better-paying job. He landed a position sewing children's clothes at a garment factory. At night, Doug attended school, working toward his GED. But, before he could earn the degree, he had to learn to read. When they got married, JoAnn hadn't realized how much difficulty he had reading, so good was he at hiding his weaknesses.

JoAnn worked to help him become a better reader. At night, they sat in bed, taking turns reading Harlequin romance novels aloud to each other. "I was so embarrassed. It was pathetic," Doug told me. "I'm a grown man, married, and I can't read."

It wasn't just his lack of education that was weighing him down. He was burning with a hatred for white people, who he believed had made it difficult for him to earn a living to support his family. "I blamed them," he told me.

Eventually Doug and his family returned to Virginia, where Doug worked for years as a brick mason and learned construction, building a house for his family. When construction jobs dried up, he applied to work with the Virginia Department of Corrections, which paid good salaries and provided benefits. After he completed the training academy, his instructor took him aside. "You barely made it through," the instructor told Doug, suggesting that he was not a good candidate for promotion and advising him not to bother trying.

The instructor's words were heartbreaking. "I hated him telling me that's as far as I could go in life," Doug told me. "I had always dreamed of doing something good and being recognized for it." He made up his mind to prove the instructor wrong.

"This guy," he told himself, "I am going to make a liar out of him." And so Doug did.

In the prison system, he was promoted through the ranks. In 2005, he was named warden of a high-security prison in a neighboring county, becoming the first officer in the state's prison system to be promoted to warden with only a GED, he said. As the top administrator of Nottoway Correctional Center, he was responsible for the safety of 1,400 prisoners and managed a $26 million annual budget. He also oversaw a work center that housed inmates who were eligible for work release.

As much as he had accomplished, he still wanted more. Over the years, he took college classes at a local community college and at Longwood, but his job was too demanding to keep at it, and he still didn't have a college degree. When the state rolled out a program that paid tuition for residents denied an education by massive resistance, he enrolled in Saint Paul's College, transferring the credits he had accumulated. Now he meant business. "This time I will not give it up," he told himself. "I'll give up corrections first."

In 2008, he graduated with a bachelor's degree in business administration, one of the proudest moments of his life. A few months later, he retired. But for all Doug accomplished, none of it erased what he had endured as a child. He still considers what might have been. "I always wondered, 'Where would I be if I had gone to school, completed it, and gotten a college education?'" he said. "Where would I be in life?"

. . . .

GWEN LANCASTER WOULD NOT MOVE back home, no matter how much Elsie begged and pleaded. A teenager by then, Gwen had settled into her new life in Cambridge, and she didn't want to come home even for the summers. Her aunt and uncle had three young children when Gwen moved in.

"She just became part of our lives," Elsie's sister told me. "We didn't even look back."

Gwen would stay in Massachusetts for decades. Elsie never got to be her mother again. Not the way she wanted.

PART THREE

Integration

The past is never dead. It's not even past.

—WILLIAM FAULKNER, REQUIEM FOR A NUN

CHAPTER 17

"We Are All God's Children"

As much as Mimi's and Papa's rejection of desegregation frustrated me, I accepted on some level that they were products of their time. But when it came to my parents, I had a harder time understanding their decision to return to Farmville and to send my brothers and me to the segregation academy they had attended.

My parents left Farmville when they graduated high school and headed off to Virginia colleges, Dad in 1965 and Mom in 1968.

My dad grew up poor, eager to escape his overprotective grandmother and her strict religious beliefs. For seven years, he and his three younger brothers had lived with Epsie Vale in her rural farmhouse. When the thick admission packet arrived in the mail from the University of Virginia, Dad was thrilled. He couldn't wait to put sixty miles between him and his rigid home life. He left Prince Edward County believing that blacks weren't as intelligent as whites, a country belief as deep as the work ethic he also had learned. Granny Vale could be critical, but she had taught him not to disparage anyone. "We're all God's children," she told her grandsons.

In the bucolic rolling hills of Charlottesville, he was exposed to different ways of looking at the world. He encountered few black students at the University of Virginia, and he believed the ones he met were exceptional. After graduating in 1969, he moved to Richmond to attend dental school at the Medical College of Virginia, now Virginia Commonwealth University, which had graduated only two black students. The urban campus felt foreign and frightening after growing up in Farmville and spending four years in Charlottesville.

He ran into my mother one morning on the dental school campus, where she was visiting her brother, also a student there. My mom had followed in the footsteps of her brother and father, attending the University of Richmond. Dad mentioned to her that he had never visited the campus. "You should come out and see me," she told him, so he did.

They married in 1971 and moved into a university apartment for married students in Richmond, then a city writhing with racial animosity. In April, a federal district judge had ordered a citywide busing program after the Supreme Court had approved the measure to integrate schools. Twenty-one thousand children would be bused in the new school year to bring each of the district's schools into a balance of 70 percent black and 30 percent white.

Dad spent the summer working for the city's Department of Recreation in Creighton Court, a public housing community. It was the first time my dad had ever been around blacks. At first he thought he would never be able to differentiate one child from another. But in a few weeks, he knew most of the children by name and had developed a good rapport. He coached a baseball team, piling the children into his Volkswagen Beetle to drive them to games. When an opposing team's coach picked a fight with one of his players and then tried to press charges, my dad stood up for the boy, winning the children's admiration.

"I really liked those kids," he recalled. They liked him, too, and some of his prejudices began to fade away. He was realizing that blacks weren't "slow thinking," as he had been taught.

Mom took a job teaching swimming, physical education, and drama at Janie Porter Barrett School for Girls, a school founded to rehabilitate black females who had been incarcerated. School officials called her their "token WASP," as she was one of only two white employees. She quit in April 1973 when, five months pregnant with me, a student pushed her down.

Dad graduated from dental school and joined the US Army as a dentist. He was assigned to Fort Campbell, Kentucky, and I was born weeks after they arrived. There he worked with a gifted dentist who happened to be black. It finally occurred to Dad that race and intelligence were not connected.

His views had been based on his limited exposure to blacks and on beliefs passed down to him by his grandmother and the country people he grew up around. But in Kentucky, working side by side with a capable black dentist, he admitted to himself that he had been wrong.

As Dad's two-year stint with the military wrapped up, he and Mom considered where they should settle down. When he had left home for college, he couldn't get out of Farmville fast enough. But returning to his hometown to start a business and raise a family made sense. Granny Vale was getting older and feebler—she was in her seventies—and none of her children lived in town. Dad wanted to be able to help her after all she had sacrificed to take care of him and his brothers. Mom liked the idea of being near her parents, and Mimi and Papa still lived in the brick house where Mom had grown up. It also made sense for Dad to start a dentistry practice in a town where he already knew a number of people.

When they thought about what they wanted in a town, Farmville had the qualities they were looking for. They liked how quiet the town was. They liked that people were friendly, that they waved when you passed on the street, that they could leave the backdoor unlocked. They knew the whole community would be keeping an eye on their children as we grew up. My parents chose to return to Farmville because it was what they knew. To them, it didn't represent segregation—it represented family.

In 1975, soon after the birth of my brother Chaz, they bought a rambling Sears, Roebuck and Company–designed craftsman home a block from the abandoned Farmville High School. Our family quickly grew into the house. Three years later, the twins were born.

I went from toddler to child, sitting out long summer rainstorms on the front porch swing, watching the magnolias and dogwoods bloom. I waved at passing neighbors, all of them white. I played hopscotch on the sidewalk out front. I chased fireflies in my nightgown and captured bumblebees in glass jars. My brothers and I ran through the neighbor's yards, sledded down the hill behind the school, and rode bikes to an ice cream shop.

The house was our haven. In the summer, we spent all day in the pool my parents had installed. Mom whipped up cream cheese and cucumber sandwiches on white bread and trimmed off the crusts, and she served bowls of popcorn with glasses of bright red Kool-Aid. When Dad got home from work, he threw ball after ball to us as we jumped off the diving board, trying to catch one midair. We played dodge Frisbee and basketball in the backyard, then jumped in the pool again.

Helen Henson, our elderly neighbor, hosted her granddaughter from California every summer, and I peppered the girl with questions when she came over to swim. I grew up healthy and happy. And desperate for information about life outside my town.

As MY FIFTH BIRTHDAY APPROACHED in 1978, my parents considered where to send me to school. I didn't get a spot at J. P. Wynne Campus School, a publicly funded laboratory school that had been established on the Longwood campus for the children of faculty and staff. That left my parents with two options: the public schools or Prince Edward Academy. Their alma mater was still open and still all-white, nearly twenty years after its founding. Prince Edward County Public Schools were still mostly black, though the number of white students was creeping up and would reach 23 percent by 1980. Many liberal newcomers to town, professors at Longwood and Hampden-Sydney colleges, enthusiastically supported public education and encouraged their friends to do so as well.

Mom and Dad talked with other parents of young children, mainly people they'd grown up with, most of whom sent their kids to the academy. They toured the public schools, and they weren't sold. When I asked Dad about it years later, he told me, "It just didn't look like a dynamic, well-functioning environment."

They debated their options. It wasn't just me they were making a decision about, but also my three younger brothers. They believed Prince Edward Academy was academically superior, in part because a majority of students—about 80 percent by then—attended college after graduation. They had heard reports of bullying and violence in the public schools, and they worried about my safety. The rumors about rapes in the bathrooms scared my mother, even though the reports were unsubstantiated. Besides, my parents liked the discipline the private school offered, and they figured the odds of us playing sports were higher there. Tuition was an expensive proposition for a family with four children. Mom and Dad disliked the school's segregation history, but it was their alma mater. My grandfather still sat on the board of directors.

They struggled for weeks with the decision until my father came home from work one evening and asked my mother where she would send me if money was no object. Without hesitation, she told him she wanted me to attend Prince Edward Academy. She believed it would be best for us.

"I tried very hard to convince myself that the public schools would be fine, but I just couldn't send you there," Mom told me.

With their decision made, my mother and father followed in the footsteps of her parents and his grandmother, enrolling us in a school that represented segregation to the nation. "Maybe we can make some changes at the academy," they told themselves.

Prince Edward Academy became central to our lives, a second home. When I was in middle school, my mom, with a fresh master's degree, was appointed the school's guidance counselor, a position she would hold for twenty-five years.

The academy was a cocoon, protecting and sheltering us. For thirteen years, I moved through the grades with the same group of white friends—save the occasional addition of a student new to town whom my classmates and I viewed in wide-eyed amazement. Some of the teachers had taught my mom or dad when they were students, including the gym teacher who called me by my mother's maiden name. My parents knew not only the teachers and administrators but also my classmates' parents, many of whom had been their classmates.

On paper, I was well rounded, a student athlete and a leader. And yet, I was rarely exposed to people who were different from me. For most of my time at the academy, all the students were white, and so were the teachers and administrators.

CHANGE WAS AFOOT. IN 1978, my first year at the academy, the Internal Revenue Service pulled the school's tax-exempt status for its failure to desegregate. When I was a child, my mom told me there were no rules forbidding black children from attending Prince Edward Academy—a line Robert Redd repeated to me more than twenty years later. No black children had applied to attend, and Mom understood why: without any black students, it was difficult for the academy to attract them.

My grandfather still wasn't ready for the school to integrate. When he started thinking about retiring from the private school board, he asked my father if he was interested in replacing him. Years earlier, my dad and another coach had invited a black boy to join the baseball team they were coaching on the Prince Edward Academy fields—the first instance of a black child participating in any formal activities on the campus, my dad believed. He told my grandfather he thought it was time for the school to integrate, too, and that he would quietly push for it. "I don't think I can recommend you," Papa responded.

He asked my dad why he supported integration. Nearly half of my dad's dental patients were black, and he thought admitting black students to the academy was the right thing to do. But he told Papa he also believed that the school would not survive without making the change. My grandfather didn't react. Dad got a seat on the board, and he believed Papa had nominated him. They never discussed it again, and Papa stayed on the board a few more years.

The school's leaders were beginning to realize that without tax-deductible contributions, the academy could not survive. Redd accepted that the school would have to change its admission policy, and he worked for years to persuade key board members that it was time to do so. He had secured every vote except one—an unnamed board member who was steadfast in his opposition. Redd asked the board member to accompany him to the elementary school. Redd walked into a classroom and asked the board member to tell the students that he was the reason they would no longer be able to attend their school. The board member cussed at Redd, but finally agreed to the policy change.

In 1984, rather than watch the school they had worked diligently to build close its doors, the board members adopted a new admissions policy. The next year, the IRS restored the tax-exempt status the school had lost seven years earlier. Prince Edward Academy began working to actively recruit black students, publishing its new admission policy in advertisements in the *Farmville Herald*. "Prince Edward Academy admits students of any race, color and national ethnic origin," its brochures read. The school also appointed a black board member and established a scholarship fund for minority students.

Some county residents were critical of the decision, and they suggested that the academy was desegregating only to keep its tax-exempt status, which likely was the reason some board members agreed to the change. Redd is careful in his description of what happened. The school did not integrate, he tells me, correcting my word choice. Rather, it changed its admission policy.

During my eighth-grade year, five black students attended the academy. Given the school's twenty-seven-year history of segregation and the resistance many people had to integration, the reaction was surprisingly muted. White parents did not pull their children out, and black parents reported that their children were making friends. "There are no problems," Jerry West, the father of two black children attending the school, said.

When a *Richmond Times-Dispatch* reporter interviewed my father, who was serving as the president of the PTA and as a member of the school's board of directors, Dad said he was pleased that the school had accepted black students, calling the change "inevitable." Many younger parents of academy students had supported desegregation, he said. He told me later that he had not been comfortable sending me to the public schools, but he wasn't in favor of segregation, either. "I didn't want my kids to go to a racially separate school," Dad told the newspaper. "They are missing a true reflection of the cultural composition of this community."

Although Dad acknowledged that the admission of five black students did not constitute "a significant change," given that nearly half of the county's population was black, he predicted that more black students would matriculate. "I think, eventually, the school will reflect a better cross section of our local society," he told the paper.

But soon a new wrinkle would arise. A $676,000 trust left to the school in 1968 by a tobacco plant manager from Lynchburg had been subject to a provision in his will that all the students be white. After the academy admitted black students, the trust became the subject of a lawsuit, which the school lost when the US Supreme Court refused to hear the case.

"It doesn't make any sense," my mom told the *Richmond Times-Dispatch* when the ruling was handed down in 1990. "We have worked so hard to turn around history. We have overcome the past, but the government is penalizing us for that."

As the case was winding through the courts, a black teenager joined my class. In her role as guidance counselor, Mom worked to help diversify the school, encouraging black students to enroll and providing support when they arrived. Over the course of her career, she helped organize a diversity forum to introduce students to other cultures and religions and supervised a black intern who founded a support group for students of color. As an administrator, she quickly dealt with racial slurs, calling offending students into her office and explaining why the words were hurtful and would not be tolerated.

She urged me to be friendly to my new classmate and help him feel welcome. I made a point of saying hello but I felt awkward and rarely talked with him. In junior English class, where we spent days discussing *The Scarlet Letter*, I found myself staring at his sad, round face, framed with black glasses. I wondered what it was like to be one of few black students on campus. He seemed unhappy, and I could understand why.

In 1991, he walked across the stage at Longwood's Jarman Hall with our class. It was the same stage where, in the 1950s, the county's white residents had discussed their plans to open a private academy. Thirty-two years after the school was founded to keep blacks and whites from attending school together, my classmate became the second black graduate of Prince Edward Academy.

Soon after I left for college, Prince Edward Academy's officials faced a pressing reality: the school was in danger of closing. The money that for years had flowed in from segregationists around the

South had dried up, and the school had been denied the significant inheritance after admitting students of color. Plus, the academy had never charged enough tuition, and the administrators didn't try especially hard to collect it, even though it accounted for most of the school's operating budget. Prince Edward Academy was more than a million dollars in debt.

That's when Robert Taylor, the chairman of the school's board, thought of his old friend J. B. Fuqua, a successful seventy-three-year-old businessman who had grown up poor, raised by his grandparents on a Prince Edward tobacco farm. Now he was a multimillionaire living in Georgia. Fuqua hadn't attended college but had educated himself in law and business by reading books he borrowed by mail from Duke University. He had served four terms in the Georgia legislature before founding Fuqua Industries Inc., a conglomerate of businesses that included movie theaters, radio stations, and oil distributors, some of which were on the New York Stock Exchange. Fuqua was also a philanthropist, donating more than $140 million in his lifetime, including $40 million to Duke University, which named its school of business for him.

Taylor thought Fuqua might be willing to contribute to Prince Edward Academy, too, and he called him to ask for help in 1991. Fuqua, who said he "never gave a penny" to the school while it was all-white, offered to pay off the one-million-dollar debt if the school would raise one million dollars in matching funds.

Redd wrote a ten-page letter outlining the full extent of the school's financial problems and what it needed. In 1993, Fuqua announced he would give the school ten million dollars and that it would be renamed for him. He said he hoped his gesture would "close the door" on the county's history of racial division. He stipulated that the school be open to children of all races and religions and that it focus on becoming a model school that utilized best practices. For years, he had been embarrassed to be associated with a community that had closed its schools and denied black children an education. "I wanted to wipe out the stigma of that horrible school closing," Fuqua said, adding that he thought it had held back the whole community.

Perhaps he believed that changing the school's name, as well as its black and orange colors and Wolverine mascot, remnants of the white Farmville High School, would enable the town to forget the school's racist history and the reason it was founded. Perhaps he thought that the changes he ordered would be enough for the town—the nation even—to think of it as an altogether different school.

With the money Fuqua provided, the academy installed air conditioning, added a cafeteria and a gym at the elementary school, raised the teachers' salaries, and purchased hundreds of computers. Fuqua installed a new headmaster, and he and his wife took seats on the board and visited Farmville annually. The school, he said, would be "changed in its entirety."

A few days after his announcement, seniors at the former Prince Edward Academy began the new academic year by driving to the renamed school in a motorcade, passing through an arch of balloons in the school's new colors, red and gold. Students pinned red and yellow flowers to their shirts, and many teachers wore Fuqua School T-shirts. The school reported that it had enrolled twenty-eight students of color, twenty of whom were black.

The academy, Fuqua said, "disappeared." It was the dawn of a new era.

But was it?

IT'S LATE JULY 2013, AND it's hot. Southern hot. Muggy, sticky, uncomfortable. I'm over summer, and I'm over this town.

I'm still living in Farmville, doing research. It's not so much the small-town vibe that's driving me crazy or even how little there is to do. I welcome the slower pace of life. It's more the white men glaring at me while I interview a black man in a restaurant. It's the way some whites, even people I've known since I was a child, seem wary and suspicious when I approach them, especially if I try to talk about the town's history. Even my parents want to avoid discussing what happened here so many years ago. They barely ask about my research. My mom, in particular, gives the same tired defenses, and I'm left wondering if we'll ever move beyond them.

Walking the streets, I notice a tension hangs in the heavy summer air. People seem angry. Sometimes I feel as if this whole town is still protecting a secret.

I thought coming back to Farmville as an adult, with children of my own, would allow me to see more clearly the town as it is today, maybe even let me make peace with its past. For the sake of research, I moved here for the summer with the girls, renting a brick two-story house up the street from my parents.

So many years have passed since I left for college, but in my day-to-day life with my children in Farmville, not much has changed. Here I am, living in my parents' neighborhood, floating in their pool. After I pick up my daughters from day care, we sometimes head to the public library or grab a milkshake. But usually the girls ask to go swimming in their grandparents' pool. We stop at our rental house, where they slip on bathing suits, and then close the front door behind us, cross High Street, and skip down a tree-lined gravel alley to my parents' home.

This summer is eerily similar to summers past. All these years after community leaders closed the public schools here, I still exist in Farmville in a mostly white world. My parents' neighborhood—the one in which I am living—is almost entirely white. The bakery is frequented by white customers. Even town-sponsored music events attract a white crowd.

Over lunch with a white Longwood professor, Heather Edwards, I ask her if this is how her life looks, too, and she seems surprised by the question. She has a diverse set of friends, as do both her children.

She can't even imagine a segregated life in Farmville, and she assures me that if I lived here full-time and sent my kids to public schools, as she does, it would be different. Her son plays with black children on youth sports teams, and her daughter takes dance classes with black children. Edwards's life in Farmville sounds similar to mine back in Richmond, but it's hard for me to imagine that scenario for myself here. My hometown still seems so stuck in the past, unable to redefine itself.

Of course, there has been much progress since I left more than two decades ago. The community has diversified, like Virginia as a whole. At Walmart, I notice mixed-race children, Muslim women shopping in burkas, and Hispanics. The newspaper that once called for the schools to be closed in the name of segregation has helped promote healing. And there are more ways than ever for residents to interact. Whites and blacks run on treadmills next to each other at the new YMCA. They check their e-mail side-by-side on computers at the new community library. They swim together at Farmville's community pool, which the town purchased from a private country club. All these places give blacks and whites a chance to strike up conversations, get to know each other, and find commonality, even if their kids don't go to the same schools. Blacks serve on the board of supervisors and the school board, and hold other elected offices. Still, the progress seems limited, the racial divide deep. Many people don't reach outside their established lives.

Even important turning points seem to veer off track. In 2005, when Congressman John Lewis and Senator George Allen visited the county as part of a three-day "Reconciliation Pilgrimage," demonstrators waved Confederate flags, expressed displeasure that segregation had ended, and referred to Allen as a "turncoat."

Three years later, the all-male Hampden-Sydney College hired its first black president, Chris Howard, a Rhodes Scholar and graduate of Harvard Business School. The decision by the college's board made national news, evidence of how far the community had come. Howard, the great-great-grandson of a slave, grew the number of students of color. But four years into his presidency, on the night of President Barack Obama's reelection, forty students shouted racial slurs, threw bottles, and set off fireworks outside the Minority Student Union. The "harmful, senseless episode" made national news. One student would be expelled and three more placed on probation and ordered to perform community service. The event became not only a stain on Howard's presidency and the college, but yet another on the county.

The social constructs in place in Farmville, for someone who attended Prince Edward Academy and was raised in a white neighborhood with only white friends, mean my life here looks much the same as it did growing up. Yet it is different in one significant way: I now know dozens of black residents. I spend Mondays in the town's civil rights museum, the Robert Russa Moton Museum, learning about the community's history, and afterward I sometimes go out for lunch with a mixed group. During the week, I interview black residents about their experiences during the school closures. I regularly visit with Elsie and feel comfortable attending her church. I bump into J. Samuel Williams at the library, and we embrace. I take my daughters to the museum and introduce them to its leaders, and I invite my parents and other family members to join me at Moton events. Personally, it's a huge change.

But I want more.

CHAPTER 18

The Schools Today

Prince Edward County Public Schools look entirely different than they did forty years ago. Whites now make up 36 percent of the student body, not 6 percent. Black students account for 57 percent, not 94 percent. And a growing percentage of students—about 7 percent—are some other ethnicity or mixed race.

Still, black students are disproportionately represented, comprising the majority of the student body but only one-third of the county's population. Lacy Ward Jr., the director of the Moton Museum, believes that this racial makeup is why county leaders do not allocate the public school system the money it needs to prosper. "They still see the system as the black system, so they fund it as such," Ward said.

The board's chair, Howard F. Simpson, elected by a coin toss after a split vote, acknowledged as much to me, and he gets upset talking about how this county has historically treated its black residents. Yet in the last five years, the only increases in local school funding went to teachers' salaries, health insurance subsidies, contributions to the state's retirement fund, and a reading specialist's salary. During that time, average daily attendance plunged and the school district's overall budget dropped by $3.5 million, or 12 percent.

The supervisors don't seem to hear concerned parents, who have asked them to raise taxes to support education. Simpson and other members have refused, even though the county's tax rate has historically been among the lowest in the region. The supervisors also ignored a five-year proposed capital improvement plan laid out by the school board to fix leaky roofs, replace a failing heating system, and renovate a rutted football field. As the problems become critical, the school board is forced to go back to the supervisors for emergency funds. Yet more than a million dollars of the county's money was spent constructing a road to an undeveloped site of a hotel that may never be built.

In 2014, when the school board requested nearly one million additional dollars in local funds to pay for kindergarten aides, a preschool teacher, and a replacement bus, a new member of the board of supervisors questioned why the county's per pupil spending was higher than surrounding counties. Supervisor C. R. "Bob" Timmons Jr. was seemingly unable to understand how the county's poverty rate and history of denying blacks an education has affected its population. "But that was 50 years ago," he protested.

A school board member told Timmons if he compared Prince Edward's per pupil spending with other localities, he also needed to consider student needs in those counties. After the discussion, *Farmville Herald* editor Ken Woodley called for a study of the school closures' generational effects. Twenty-four years earlier, the paper had named him the first non–family member editor. The former editor, Bid Wall, a grandson of J. Barrye Wall, had left the position for a new career, and the direction of the paper was left to Woodley, a young reporter who had joined the staff out of Hampden-Sydney College without knowing the county's—or the paper's—history. Woodley would become an advocate for the many residents impacted by the school closings, though no members of the Wall family have apologized on behalf of the newspaper.

"For too long this subject has been the giant elephant in the room that nobody talked about when school funding and academic programs are discussed," Woodley wrote. He told readers that he has long believed the school closures have affected generations of Prince Edward residents. "It's common sense," he wrote. "Children raised in homes where parents cannot read, for example, are going to be impacted by their parents' illiteracy." In fact, 16 percent of county residents were estimated to be illiterate in 2003, the latest numbers available. The county's illiteracy rate is 4 percentage points higher than the state's.

Woodley envisions a document elected officials could turn to each time they make decisions about how to spend the county's money. But it was too late for the 2014–2015 school year. The board voted to raise taxes by 5 percentage points, but not a penny of the new funds would go to the schools.

RUTH S. MURPHY SPENT THE first part of her career as an educator trying to desegregate public schools in North Carolina. But when she arrived in Farmville in 1994, handpicked by J. B. Fuqua to lead the private school, she did not grasp how difficult the job would be.

Fuqua School, still a predominantly white, independent school, sits on a sixty-acre campus at the top of a hill above downtown Farmville. Six one-story brick buildings, each with six classrooms, make up the upper school. The classroom doors open onto sidewalks and manicured lawns lined with wood benches and dogwood trees. The cafeteria and administration building is located across the street from the school, and behind it a huge pool buzzes with activity all summer long.

When Fuqua took over, Robert Redd was pushed out after serving as headmaster for decades. Another leader was put in place briefly, but Murphy essentially took the reins from the man who had designed and built the school, in some cases with his own hands. Brash and determined, Murphy viewed herself as an agent of change. The way she saw it, there was a lot about Fuqua School that needed changing. Instead of having teachers stand in front of classes lecturing, she wanted them to use hands-on learning. She wanted to fashion a board that operated independently and wouldn't fold to parents' every whim. She needed to develop a curriculum and write new school policies. And she wanted to create a learning environment that embraced diversity.

After she had been in Farmville a few years and learned more about the history of the school's founding, she realized that overcoming its racist past would take more time than she had thought.

The school she has invested two decades rebuilding might never outrun its legacy.

Over the years, many of the segregation academies scattered across the South have shut down. In Virginia, one merged with another private school, while others simply closed their doors. But some of those that started around the same time as Fuqua School remain, despite dwindling student bodies. When Redd was questioned in the early years about Prince Edward Academy's viability, he told reporters the school would be around for decades, and he was right.

In recent years, enrollment has plunged to fewer than four hundred students, down from seven hundred when the academy integrated in 1986. The recent economic downturn hit rural counties particularly hard, and the public school population has dropped, too. Two-thirds of the Fuqua student body travels from outside Prince Edward, and the school sends buses to pick up children who live as far as sixty miles away. Tuition for middle and high school students has climbed to $7,800 per year—a fraction of the $20,000 starting price for elite Richmond-area private schools. But Fuqua's tuition is still steep in Prince Edward, where the median household income is $36,700 and parents work as professionals, small business owners, and farmers.

Parents I talked with, including former classmates at the academy, told me that they believe the education their children are getting at

Fuqua will better prepare them for college than a public school education would. They like that the school offers honors and advanced placement classes, that class sizes are small, that Fuqua utilizes multi-aged classrooms so students can learn at their own pace, that there is a focus on technology. Others said that their children are happy in the intimate setting. They appreciate the honor code and the requirement that students perform community service to graduate. Most of all, they are drawn to the feeling that the school is "a family."

Murphy told me that she has worked diligently from the moment she arrived to make Fuqua an open environment. With the board's approval, she discounted tuition for students of color. "Diversity strengthens a school community and should be embraced," the school website reads. The school's mission and beliefs were developed by a committee made of teachers, parents, and alumni. "My goal has been to welcome people of every nationality and race," Murphy said. "We have done that."

Despite her best efforts, it has been difficult to attract black students. In the 2013–2014 school year, about 5 percent of the student body was black. She believes many blacks in the community can't afford the tuition, even at the reduced rate. The bigger impediment, she told me, is that the black community "refuses to acknowledge what we've done." Black residents still refer to Fuqua as a racist school, as do white liberals, she said.

Murphy insists it's not true. As she tells the parents of black children who apply: "We want more black kids. We value diversity. We want you to tell people that Fuqua welcomes minority kids and values them."

Murphy asked the board in 2008 to approve a pair of full four-year scholarships for black students, with the goal of making Fuqua's successful black students more visible. She wanted the recipients to act as ambassadors for the school in Prince Edward's black community. Since it was approved, the scholarship program, funded with private donations, has been modified to assist not only black students but also any economically disadvantaged student. In 2013–2014, ten students—some black, some white—received a combination of partial and full scholarships. Most were athletes.

In 2013, the school had its first valedictorian of color, an Asian student. In 2014, a second Asian student was the valedictorian.

Murphy doesn't know what more she can do to persuade the community—and black residents in particular—that Fuqua School is not the same place it once was. By adopting a textbook that addresses the school closures, she has ensured that Fuqua's students are taught the county's past in fourth and fifth grade history classes. In 2014, high school students marched in a reenactment of Barbara Johns's walkout, an event Murphy attended. Fuqua classes visit the Moton Museum, and Murphy has served on its board of directors since 1999. When a fellow board member asked her how she dealt with her school's history, she reminded him that it was just that—*history*. "That's what makes where the school is now a miracle," Murphy says.

For a school to make a decision to completely change its heritage—to go from being a school established specifically for white children to a school accepting of and open to diversity—is a dramatic change, she says. "It is not the same place," she tells me. "It is not the same school."

But even with a new name, the school will continue to be a vivid symbol of racism for some.

Perhaps Murphy's drive to diversify the school has had unintended consequences. By recruiting black students, she has lured away some of Prince Edward County High School's best athletes, infuriating some black residents.

In 2008, Murphy met with Charles Williams, a freshman and the starting quarterback on the public school's football team. Charles wanted more opportunities than he saw at Prince Edward County High School, and one of his best friends had transferred to Fuqua. Murphy offered Charles a full scholarship on the condition that he would promote Fuqua, telling other blacks what he liked about the school.

His mother urged him to transfer. Within a week, he had decided that Fuqua was best for his future, in part, because he liked that the school felt like a family. "I didn't . . . worry about the history," said Charles, a college sophomore. "I was looking at Fuqua today."

But some of Charles's fans on the football field, even a close family friend, told him they'd never watch another of his games if he transferred. When he made the switch, some of the county school's boosters were livid. They believed Fuqua was cherry-picking the public school's best athletes, "the future of the football team," Charles recalled. They viewed Fuqua School as being more interested in a strong athletic program than true integration.

Charles made history as Fuqua's first black team captain and was regarded as one of the best—if not *the* best—athletes in the school's history. After Charles came to Fuqua, it was easier for the school to attract black athletes from around the region. By the 2012–2013 school year, the basketball team had seven black players. A year earlier, the school had brought in its first black administrator, Marcus Gregory, a former assistant coach at Prince Edward County High School. Gregory now coaches Fuqua's varsity basketball team and serves as its athletic director. He is the only black faculty member—the only faculty member of color, period—though the school does have black staff.

Ricky Brown, the former basketball star at Prince Edward County High School, is angered by Fuqua's recruitment of black students. He doesn't believe that the school is a different place. If Fuqua really wanted to diversify its student body, he told me, it would not recruit black athletes. Instead, the school would focus on black academic stars, or even nonathletes who are struggling academically and need help to succeed.

Brown refuses to set foot on the campus, even when the public school's basketball team, coached by his brother-in-law, James Scott, played Fuqua for the first time during its regular basketball season in 2012–2013. In back-to-back games, Prince Edward County won on its home court. A week later, when the public school lost at Fuqua, Brown wasn't there.

Doug Vaughan, the retired prison warden, can't get past Fuqua's history either. "I never liked Prince Edward Academy," he told me. Just hearing its name bothers him. "The academy was built solely to keep the races from mixing," he told me, "and I felt that was just wrong."

Its founders didn't care whether he got an education or not, Vaughan says. When he received an invitation to a retirement party for one of his fellow corrections officers at Fuqua, Vaughan considered not attending. His wife, JoAnn, called him out. "Are you going to let a building stop you?" she asked him.

He relented and went to the party, but it didn't change his feelings. The school has a different name, and black students now attend classes and play sports, but, to Vaughan, it is still the same school that was founded to keep black kids out.

Those children who lost years of their education will never be able to trust that Fuqua is a different place. And who can blame them?

TWENTY-TWO YEARS AFTER I GRADUATED from Prince Edward Academy, I return to my high school senior English classroom. The fluorescent lights are identical. The painted cinder block walls are the same. It is still an unattractive brick school with a leaky roof and modest facilities, not the sanctuary some have imagined it to be.

Senior English is still taught in the small classroom where I remember taking classes with Daphne Mason, my funny, Shakespeare-loving next-door neighbor. The new teacher, Diane Stubbins, is also funny and engaging, but in a different way. She allows the students to talk quietly, which creates a dull hum while she lectures. Students can leave to go to the bathroom, and they can roll Matchbox cars back and forth on a table to help them stay focused during the ninety-minute class. She talks about sex in their study of Shakespeare. She is quirky and cool, and I am surprised when she tells me that she sends her own daughters to the county's public schools. That would have been unimaginable when I was a student here. Stubbins represents a certain openness that didn't exist when I was growing up: you were either an academy person or a public school person.

Students are required to wear uniforms, but despite this change, the school seems more permissive and creative than when I attended. The library, once a staid, musty place, now is a vibrant space where students eat lunch and socialize with their friends.

The school feels decidedly more diverse. As enrollment fell in recent years, Murphy reached out to teachers and staff for ideas to bring in more students—and more income. She followed the lead of other private schools in Virginia and launched a foreign exchange program to lure international students eager to study in the United States and willing to pay higher tuition—students who would come for three or four years with the intention of attending an American college. A faculty member trained to teach English as a second language, and in 2013–2014, six students from China and one from Japan enrolled in the new program.

It is the ultimate paradox. The school founded to avoid desegregation, a school that for decades snubbed the black children born and raised in this county, is now welcoming brown students from halfway around the world.

. . . .

The successful integration of the Prince Edward schools is owed, in large part, to James M. Anderson Jr., who, like my grandparents, grew up in Buckingham County. As the principal of Buckingham's high school, he had been demoted to an administrative job when, in 1969, he refused to replace the school's black valedictorian with a white one, as his superintendent had suggested.

He accepted the job as superintendent of Prince Edward County Public Schools in 1972 at the urging of an academy official who told Anderson he wanted to see the taxpayers' money spent well. The county's spending on schools had remained low since they reopened, but the state had established a minimum threshold for localities to spend on schools, requiring the county to increase its allocation to schools by nearly 50 percent.

But a challenge facing the public schools was a new, publicly funded laboratory school on the Longwood campus that was drawing children away from the public system. Two hundred students, most of them children of Longwood and Hampden-Sydney professors, were attending the Campus School. Established in 1970, the school went only through the seventh grade, so it wasn't a perfect solution for parents who didn't want to send their children to the public schools. Anderson encouraged the presidents of Longwood and Hampden-Sydney to send their own children to the public schools, and a group of professors also agreed to enroll their children, dampening other white families' fears that they would be ostracized if they moved their children to the public schools. The campus school closed in 1982.

Over the twenty-five years Anderson served as superintendent, his policies encouraged integration, and the number of white children enrolled in the public schools gradually increased. Performance improved, as did the graduation rate, and the high school began sending students to esteemed universities and boasting National Merit Scholars.

A *Newsday* reporter, visiting the community prior to the fortieth anniversary of the *Brown* decision in 1994, found that, of the five localities in the suit, Prince Edward was the "success story." It had truly integrated its schools. Summerton High School in Clarendon County, South Carolina, had one white student. The state of Delaware was trying to bring an end to the busing that had enabled it to successfully desegregate its schools. Linda Brown, the girl whose surname was the namesake of the Supreme Court decision, spent years in federal court, fighting to get schools desegregated for her own children and grandchildren in Kansas. The Washington, DC, schools were overwhelmingly black and poor. Next to them, Prince Edward County was a star.

By 2009, the picture had changed. Student performance fell after Anderson retired in 1997. As superintendents circulated through, teachers left for jobs in neighboring counties, and money from the state dropped off. The graduation rate hovered at 67 percent, and academic performance on state assessments in core subjects did not meet state or federal standards.

Prince Edward County High School scored in the bottom 5 percent of schools in the state when the Obama administration announced in 2009 that the US Department of Education would distribute eight billion dollars to improve student achievement in the country's lowest-performing schools. The Virginia Department of Education wanted to enroll Prince Edward County High School in the federally funded turnaround program to boost student performance. The school district would get $500,000 per year for three years to raise test scores, close achievement gaps, and boost the graduation rate. The funds could be used to hire an education consulting company to help make the improvements and put instructional aides in every classroom to improve teaching.

Before the district could get started, a new principal needed to be hired.

. . . .

DRESSED IN A SHARP TAN suit, Craig Reed greets me inside the high school's lobby. The morning bell has just rung and the hallway is still buzzing with students. Parents sit on benches, waiting to talk with school administrators, and tardy students sign in at the front desk. Reed leads me into the administrative suite, and we sit down at a table in a conference room where he has laid out neat stacks of papers detailing students' progress.

The forty-one-year-old Reed signed on as principal in 2010. He grew up in Farmville and graduated from Prince Edward County High School, and working to improve his alma mater appealed to him. When Reed interviewed for the job, school district administrators told him that the school had enrolled in the turnaround program. Reed questioned whether he wanted to be in the tightly regulated environment but told himself he would develop a new skill set.

Reed seems the ideal principal for this failing school. He's black, like most of the students. He understands Prince Edward and its history, but his parents weren't directly affected by the school closures. Reed is also a county success story, having earned a bachelor's degree at Hampton University and a master's degree in education leadership from the College of William & Mary, where he is currently pursuing a doctorate. He previously worked as a teacher and as an assistant principal at schools around the state.

He also has a presence. He is short and sturdy, with a shaved head and a clean-shaven face. He comes across as confident and bold, unconstrained by old ideas of how blacks should act in Farmville. He rented a house on First Avenue with his wife and stepdaughter, becoming the first black family to live on my parents' block. At school, he speaks frankly. He reaches out to students to explain why they must perform better and why it's important for them to graduate. "We're not an agrarian society anymore," he tells students and their parents. "You can't just be a farmer. You need a high school degree to do something with your life."

He isn't the disciplinarian some people think the high school needs. Instead, his priority is transforming Prince Edward County High School into one of the highest-performing schools in the state. He wants the teachers and students to believe they can do it, too. He is trying to focus the attention on academics and ignore other distractions.

The high school presents plenty of challenges for Reed. More than half the students live in poverty; 58 percent are receiving free and reduced lunches. Many of the students are being raised by a single parent or by grandparents, and they need more support to thrive in school. Soon after his arrival, Reed quickly identified two more problems—teachers who felt helpless, and students who weren't hungry to learn.

The two-story brick building is the same school that was built to appease black students in the 1950s after the strike at Moton High School. Upgrades have been made through the years and new sections have been added, but it feels worn-down. To make the school seem more welcoming, Reed and his father spent a weekend repainting the entryway and clearing out glass trophy cases filled with mementos of decades past. Word spread among black county residents that Reed was dismissing the school's history, but he simply wanted to focus his students on learning, not on the county's troubled past. "That's a burden our community carries," Reed tells me. "That's not a burden for our kids."

Reed homes in on his primary objective: bringing an academic focus to the school attended by nearly seven hundred children. He wants it to reach its academic benchmarks and to develop a reputation as a great school. And he has a partner to help him do it—Cambridge Education, a consultancy that helps school districts around the nation improve students' performance.

To ensure students get the rigorous and engaging instruction they deserve, he and other administrators spend the bulk of their days in the classroom, observing teachers and providing feedback about instruction. He stands in the hallways, greeting students as they change classes, then pops into classrooms, typing up notes as he watches teachers and students interact. By the end of the day, he e-mails teachers his critiques. Instructors work one-on-one in the classroom with some teachers. Teacher turnover, already high in this rural community, has increased because some teachers can't meet the new standards or don't want to try. But other teachers have embraced the hands-on instruction from Cambridge and are taking more pride in their work.

Reed is also attacking the low graduation rate, a priority for the state. He created a graduation wall in the conference room, pinning photos and short biographies of each of the seniors on a bulletin board, grouping them into categories based on their readiness to graduate. The list includes students on track to graduate with an advanced degree, a regular degree, or a special education diploma. There is also a "danger" category for students not on track to graduate, a label that fit nearly one-quarter of the senior class when Reed arrived. "Those are the learners you want to focus on because those are the ones that need the most help," he tells me.

He has established a team of teachers, administrators, and guidance counselors who meet on Monday mornings to identify ways to help these children graduate. Most need to pass a required standardized test or an elective class. Over the year, Reed, other administrators, and teachers seek parents' help encouraging at-risk students to meet the graduation requirements. Reed suggests that a student who needs help to pass a state-required test come in before or after school to work with a teacher, and he asks students to sign a contract agreeing to work harder. He has even brought students' preachers on board.

Reed takes a mathematical approach to improving the school's test pass rate, attempting to predict which students may not pass. He tests students every six weeks and then crunches the data. He requires at-risk students to work more closely with teachers or enrolls them in an algebra camp where they are drilled in the basics.

Using these tools, his team has boosted the school's standardized test scores. In a three-year period, his team has cut the number of students who do not graduate by more than half. After the final year of the turnaround program, 87 percent of seniors will earn a diploma.

But, on graduation day, Reed will be packing up to leave the job at his alma mater. His success in Prince Edward has caught the attention of a Norfolk middle school, and he is ready to try to replicate what he's done at another turnaround school. Without Reed, parents and teachers wonder if the high school can maintain the momentum.

THE NOTION THAT PRINCE EDWARD County High School could become one of the best schools in the state seemed implausible, given its history and given the current state of the schools. Yet Virginia's education department considers the changes that occurred during Reed's three-year tenure to be remarkable. Of the twenty-five high schools in the state's turnaround program, Prince Edward County High School made the most gains. Kathleen Smith, the director of the Office of School Improvement at the Virginia Department of Education, told me the county embraced the state's mandate to increase the graduation rate. "Prince Edward has historically not cared one way or the other if a black student graduated from high school," she told me, "and now they are caring.

"High schools are not easy to change," she added. "That school has come a long way."

But despite the long hours put in by teachers, and despite the academic success the school has seen as a result of that work, Reed still sees a persistent belief in the community that the public schools can't achieve academically.

"There is the expectation—more of an expectation here than in other places—for the school to fail," Reed confides. It's even worse than that, he says. "It's almost like we have a population . . . of parents that, for whatever reason, *want* to see this school fail because of what happened then," he tells me.

They aren't persuaded by data showing the improvements the school has made, and they aren't moved by praise from the state Department of Education, Reed says.

I wonder if parents aren't able to see changes because of their limited involvement in the school. Few turn out for parent-teacher conferences. Maybe the lack of parental engagement, typical at the high school level, is exacerbated by the school closings.

"They've been taught their entire life that going to a council meeting and being an advocate . . . is not a good idea, you'll get in trouble," Kathleen Smith reminded me. "They have a natural fear of those kinds of things."

Maybe parents don't value education because either they or their parents were denied the chance to attend school. Or maybe there's simply lingering resentment.

CHAPTER 19

"We All Wish It Hadn't Happened"

I slide back into a cold wooden booth at First Baptist Church. It is the fiftieth anniversary of the black students' 1963 march from this church down Main Street to the white Farmville Baptist Church. The black students tried to join the white church's worship service and were blocked at the door. The students knelt and prayed and sang on the steps, where they were arrested for disrupting a church service.

This time, in 2013, will be different. This time, black county residents have been invited inside the same churches that once turned them away. This time, the police force that decades earlier arrested twenty-three people will recognize them for their bravery. This time, a sea of white people sits inside the historic black church. Diane Stubbins, the Fuqua English teacher, is here with her daughter. I see Farmville city councilwoman Sally B. Thompson and her husband, the Reverend William E. Thompson, a historian. Patsy Watson, a member of Farmville Baptist Church whose children attended Fuqua School, is here. Donna Peery Andrews, the widow of Bush League leader Lester Andrews, is here. Dozens more whites affiliated with the churches and the universities have already been seated.

As I look around the church, I realize that I've interviewed many of the black people in the sanctuary. Doug and JoAnn Vaughan. Ricky Brown and Shirby Scott Brown. Everett Berryman. Farmville vice mayor A. D. "Chuckie" Reid. Lacy Ward Jr. and Justin Reid from the Moton Museum. Lacy's father, Lacy Ward Sr., a former county supervisor. James Ghee. The church's pastor, the Reverend James Ashton. Elsie is seated in the front with some of her friends from the choir.

The Reverend J. Samuel Williams, one of the strike's leaders, addresses the congregation, noting how much things have changed since he was arrested. A year earlier, the leadership of the church that denied him entrance asked him to read the scripture there, and later, to preach.

A. Q. "Andy" Ellington, a lieutenant with the Farmville Police Department and a graduate of Prince Edward Academy, tells the congregation that he got goose bumps looking at photographs taken in 1963 of Farmville police officers preparing to arrest protestors, whom he referred to as "unsung local civil rights heroes."

"Because of these students, we are a reconciled and united community that I'm proud to be a part of," Ellington tells the crowd. I wait for him to go further, to say that his department shouldn't have arrested the students, to make some sort of apology, but he doesn't. Still, it feels like an important step to have a representative of the police department speak at all, to acknowledge what the officers did that day and to recognize the contributions of the students they arrested.

Williams asks the crowd to sing the civil rights anthem "We Shall Overcome." As I stand to join in, I visualize him leading students in the protest song five decades earlier, on the steps of my grandparents' church. I wipe tears on the sleeve of my jacket, coarse against my cheek. My faith in this community is renewed watching white churches welcome the very people they once excluded. If some members of the black community are willing to walk through doors that had been closed to them, that's progress. If the town's biggest employer, Centra Southside Hospital, donates water for the event, and the town of Farmville provides a bus to transport elderly people from church to church, maybe there is hope yet.

I walk with the congregation down the sidewalk to Farmville Baptist Church, following Williams and the former student protestor Tina Land on the same path they took five decades earlier. The group also visits the Farmville Methodist Church and Johns Memorial Episcopal Church, where the church vestry, without fanfare, extends a public apology for participation "in the complex webs of racism that gripped this community fifty years ago and since."

"Insofar as our brothers and sisters, especially our African American brothers and sisters, were harmed educationally, socially, and spiritually," a church member reads, "we wish to say that we are sorry and ask pardon although we recognize that no pardon is deserved."

The next day, a handful of people, most of them black, turn out for the Monday brown bag lunch at the Moton Museum. After watching a movie about Bobby Kennedy, they are talking about the previous day's anniversary of the kneel-in and considering why more black residents didn't participate. Some point out that whites attended in higher numbers, bringing their children along. "It was twice as many of them as there were of us," one woman says.

"Our children should have been there," says Mary Reed, a retired reading specialist at the public schools and the mother of the high school's outgoing principal, Craig Reed.

They agree that blacks need to teach their children Prince Edward's story. "We have to blame ourselves," Mary Reed tells the group, which includes me and one other white person. "We don't know our history."

The museum director's father, Lacy Ward Sr., tells the people assembled that he believes the Prince Edward story is one of the most exciting pieces of American history, in part because the struggle of a group of young people against discrimination resulted in a Supreme Court ruling. He says that he doesn't understand why more residents aren't engaged in learning the history. "The people here, it doesn't move them, it seems," Ward Sr. said, sounding sad and resigned.

Mickie Pride, who lost four years of education, suggests that apathy among black residents is a direct result of the education denied them. She wonders how to reach the large segment of the community that hasn't set foot in the museum and doesn't attend the school reunions she helps to organize. She thinks it's important for black residents in particular to face the past, as she has, but she's not sure how to connect with people who don't want to be reached, to tell them about what the museum is doing, to encourage them to attend the Moton reunions.

"A lot of blacks in Prince Edward County want to put it behind them," Mickie tells me. "They see it as hashing up old feelings." It's a sentiment I have heard repeatedly from whites, too.

"We're not bringing it up out of anger," Mickie says. "This is part of our history."

For some, the memories are still vivid and difficult to face, even now.

BETTY JEAN WARD CAN'T BRING herself to walk back into Farmville Baptist Church, where she was arrested in 1963.

She attended Virginia State University after graduating from the Free Schools, spent thirty-two years working as a teacher, and is now retired. But try as she may, the memories of being shut out of school and being arrested on the steps of the white church don't fade.

Sometime in the late 1970s or early 1980s, she accompanied her husband to his company's Christmas dinner at Cedar Brook Restaurant, where blacks were required to order food from a window on the side of the building when she was a child. When Ward sat down at a dinner table with her husband and his coworkers, she realized that his boss, seated at an adjacent table, was one of the police officers who had arrested her on the steps of the church and dragged her out to a police car.

"I wanted so bad to let him know," she told me. But her husband begged her not to say anything, reminding Ward that his boss was hosting the couple "here at an integrated table." And so she did what black people were expected to do back when the schools closed. She kept her mouth shut.

She didn't want to be put in that position again. A few years later, when the pastor of Farmville Baptist Church invited her congregation to join in a worship service, she declined to attend. "I could just picture that man standing at that door saying, 'Y'all go back up the street where you came from, y'all got your own church,'" she said.

She happened to be out of town on the fiftieth anniversary event, but told me she wouldn't have attended anyway. When I asked her how she feels now about what happened more than five decades ago, she became quiet.

"I'll never forget what happened," she told me. "I'm trying to forgive."

ONE MORNING, LATE IN THE summer of 2013, when my girls are at preschool, Mom invites me to stop by for lunch. I walk the familiar alley from my Farmville rental home to my parents' house. I sit down at the counter in the pale yellow kitchen, watching her slice tomatoes fresh from her garden.

She asks how a conversation with one of my former teachers at the academy went, and I unload. I'm tired of hearing the same rote lines from so many white people in town. I have encountered few who offer a fresh perspective, who admit to having grappled with the seriousness of what happened here. Instead, so many seem defensive. Mom seems defensive, too.

She has always stuck by her story. She has defended Fuqua School's place in town, defended her father for doing what was best for his children. It disappoints me that her position hasn't shifted, and I know she can sense my frustration.

Today, slicing tomatoes in front of me, she speaks the words I have been waiting to hear, the words that will help me to move on.

"You know, Kristen," she says, putting down the tomato and looking at me, "we all wish it hadn't happened. I wish it hadn't happened."

She cuts through the space between us with her words, acknowledging the destructiveness of the school closures, acknowledging regret. I realize that, since I started work on this project, I have been waiting for this admission. Mom says she has always been sorry the schools closed, but I needed to hear it from her. I needed her to spell it out.

With those words, she frees me.

DAYS LATER, I AM SITTING outside the French bakery downtown, drinking a cup of coffee. An enormous logging truck rumbles down Main Street.

I see Robert Taylor's son, Bob, crossing the street, and I call out to him. He walks over and sits across from me at the café table. I explain that I interviewed his father years earlier, and I am curious how Bob, the owner of a kayak and canoe business, views the school closings.

"It's ruined the last fifty years," he tells me. "It's just stigmatized Prince Edward County. Every time we try to get beyond it, something stirs it up again. Why can't we put it behind us?"

I know what he's thinking: he wishes I would let sleeping dogs lie. The negative publicity from the school closures has hindered Prince Edward's progress, he tells me. He wishes it could have happened in one of the neighboring counties instead.

Talking about it, he says, is like "digging up a Johnny house"—an outhouse. "Every time you dig it up, you just make a stink," he tells me. "Just leave it be."

It is a common refrain. We've discussed this enough. While many of the people I've talked with are sorry the schools closed, I sense there is still a disconnect between regret about what happened and empathy for the people it happened to. I think of a story a friend shared about teaching her young son how to apologize. After he knocked over a classmate on the playground, he mumbled "Sorry" under his breath. My friend pulled her son aside and told him the apology alone wasn't enough. He also needed to inquire about the other boy, listen to his response, and help him get up.

It's as if Farmville didn't get this lesson. The apologies to students shut out of school have never been adequate. Sometimes the community reminds me of a child who expects everything to return to normal once he says he is sorry. In this way, the town never grew up.

CHAPTER 20

A Healing Place for the Community

In 2013, a beautifully renovated Moton Museum was unveiled. The floors of the original Moton High School had been stripped and polished. The wood trim, painted kelly green. Heavy purple curtains hung in front of the auditorium's stage. Every detail matched the appearance of the former high school in 1951 when Barbara Johns strode across the stage and told her fellow students of her plans to strike. Moton had been transformed into a real museum—the state's only civil rights museum.

It almost didn't happen.

The public school system planned to stop using the building as an elementary school in June 1995. The board of supervisors announced its intention to designate the building as surplus so it could be sold and possibly demolished. Farmville High School had met that fate in 1993 after it was purchased by Longwood, and now the college had offered to buy Moton High School and the adjacent playing fields for one million dollars. The supervisors wanted to use the money to pay for an addition at the middle school and requested that the Virginia Department of Historic Resources defer consideration of the building for historical landmark status, a designation that would prevent it from being demolished.

"Some people hope that if the school gets torn down, it will make us forget what happened to us in the past," Grace Scott Ward, a 1948 graduate of Moton, told the *Washington Post*.

Hugh Elliott "H. E." Carwile Jr., then the chairman of the board of supervisors, who had served on the board since 1964, believed that "the county may be better served if the building is removed." "People tell me it's a constant reminder," he told the *Post*, "like rubbing salt in a wound."

Before the county announced it would no longer use Moton as a school, black residents were already working to preserve it. The Martha E. Forrester Council of Women, a branch of the National Council of Negro Women, had been trying to get historical status for the building since 1990. After learning that it might be sold, James Ghee, who attended school in Iowa during the closings and later became the town's first black lawyer, suggested to the congregation of First Baptist Church that residents take up a collection and buy the building.

Support for the idea came from a place it was least expected. The editor of the *Farmville Herald* stepped in, calling for the school to be saved. "If we're going to tear down the former R.R. Moton High School . . . let's go ahead and tear down Independence Hall, too, and dump the Liberty Bell in the river," Ken Woodley wrote in a February 1995 editorial.

A few years earlier, after his appointment as editor, Woodley wrote an editorial that supported converting Moton to a museum. When he learned that the supervisors had objected to a historic listing of the building, he took his support to a new level, angrily hammering out a response. William B. "Bill" Wall, the publisher emeritus and younger son of J. Barrye Wall, told his new editor to tone down the editorial, but Woodley refused and went home early to avoid doing so. The piece ran as he had written it.

Woodley suggested that the town should embrace Moton. "The

building is a monument we should be proud of," he wrote. "We're not talking about a pile of bricks. We're talking about the soul of America."

Community support was building. Some of the older members of the Forrester Council who had been teachers rallied to secure tax-exempt status for their organization and raise funds. The Virginia General Assembly donated money, along with corporations like Wachovia and Dominion.

The supervisors agreed in 1996 to sell the school building for $306,000, including interest, to the Forrester Council, which paid the initial $100,000. The Robert Russa Moton Museum was incorporated as a separate nonprofit and took on the Forrester Council's $206,000 debt. Historians recognized the building's significance, adding it to the National Registry of Historic Places, and later designating it a National Historic Landmark.

The Robert Russa Moton Museum opened on April 23, 2001, the fiftieth anniversary of the school strike. For years, it was a sad space, mostly empty, rarely open, with displays mounted on faded cardboard panels. The roof and the heating system needed to be replaced, but at least the building had been saved.

WHEN LACY WARD JR. WAS named director in 2008, he believed the museum should tell a bigger story than black students being shut out of school. A black native of the county who had served in the military and lived in other states, he envisioned a museum that told the whole community's story of the school closures, a story that would bring blacks and whites together. The museum would describe one Virginia county's transition from segregation to integration.

Not everyone in the county embraced the vision, particularly black students whose educations had ended prematurely. "People were extremely hurt by this," Ward acknowledged. Some black students felt the story was theirs—and theirs alone. They didn't want the museum to recognize whites. "Why are we talking about students who attended Prince Edward Academy?" they asked Ward. Others told him flat-out, "You shouldn't be telling those stories." Even some members of his own board felt that way. During the renovation, Farmville's vice mayor, Chuckie Reid, questioned the decision to incorporate stories about the white academy's founding.

But Ward wanted to build a museum that acknowledged that race was a social construct. "Segregation was about an ill-informed view of how to look at people," he said. "I don't want to use that same view moving forward."

As Ward has worked to expand the scope of the museum, the county has done little to support it. When he prepared to embark on a massive $6 million renovation and construction of six galleries in 2008, he asked the county to contribute $750,000. In other important civil rights communities, such as Atlanta, Birmingham, Memphis, Montgomery, and Selma, the local government has invested in museums. "This local government has not acted like other local governments that are at the center of national civil rights stories," Ward told me. "They just haven't gotten it."

In a meeting with Wade Bartlett, the county administrator, and Howard Simpson, now the chair of the board of supervisors, Bartlett told Ward he wasn't sure the museum was a good investment. The county declined to donate to the renovation. Bartlett explained that he didn't think it was something county taxpayers should have to fund.

Although the county passed up the opportunity to make amends through the museum, the state has, belatedly, taken steps to repair the damage it did. The Virginia General Assembly in 2003 approved a resolution acknowledging "profound regret" over the closing of the schools. Woodley, ashamed of the *Herald*'s role in the school closures, believed the apologies had not gone far enough. In dozens of columns that ran in newspapers around the state, he called for the creation of a scholarship program for those denied an education. He lobbied the governor and called on state legislators to support him, finding sponsors for the legislation in the state House and the Senate. In 2004, the general assembly instituted a scholarship program to benefit students locked out of schools around the commonwealth, appropriating two million dollars, half of it donated. In the first eight years of the program, eighty-one awards of state aid were distributed to affected students to pursue job training, work toward a GED, and enroll in college classes. Woodley is encouraging the general assembly to also make the money available to the children and grandchildren of those locked out of school.

The state also built a civil rights memorial on the pristine grounds of the state capitol, steps from the governor's mansion. The $2.8 million sculpture, located across from a statue of Harry Byrd, the leader of massive resistance, was completed in 2008 and features Barbara Johns and other students engaged in the walkout, alongside NAACP attorneys and community members. It is a beautiful tribute to the civil rights struggle in Virginia, and Prince Edward County in particular. "How do you like the new Virginia?" then-governor Timothy M. Kaine asked minutes before the statue was unveiled. "Because this is the new Virginia."

And in 2014, Longwood University, a state-funded institution, apologized for failing to show leadership during the school closures and for causing "real and lasting offense and pain to our community" by taking black homes and a church through eminent domain. Under the leadership of President W. Taylor Reveley IV, the university announced it had established a scholarship as a way to show regret and has begun work on a partnership with the Moton Museum.

But what has the county ever done to repent?

In June 2003, the public schools hosted a Moton graduation to honor students who had been shut out of school. Many declined to attend, but the three hundred former students who wanted to participate were dressed in caps and gowns to accept their honorary degrees on the Prince Edward County High School stage. A graduation speaker, Dorothy Lockett, who had been appointed a school board member a year earlier, believed the recognition was long overdue. Her parents decided not to return to Prince Edward County when the schools reopened, and she graduated second in her Appomattox class and was awarded a full college scholarship. She came back to the county after graduating to help care for her sick father. She became the first professional black employee hired by the state employment office in town, where she would help illiterate former classmates who had never returned to school fill out applications for work.

"This should not have happened to you," she told the locked-out students.

Five years later, on the day the state civil rights statue was unveiled, the county illuminated a Light of Reconciliation. The idea had been proposed by Woodley, who was disgusted that "the county had never expressed its sorrow for the school closings, it had never done anything to honor Barbara Johns or those students for the birth of the civil rights movement." The supervisors embraced his suggestion, lighting the bell tower at the same county building where the decision not to fund the schools had been made.

The board of supervisors publicly denounced its predecessors' decision not to fund the county's schools, honoring Johns and her fellow students who had participated in the walkout. The board also had a plaque installed in front of the courthouse acknowledging that closing the schools was "wrong" and stating that they "regret those past actions."

"I think they felt that that was it," Joy Cabarrus Speakes, one of the litigants in the *Davis* suit and a museum council officer, told me. She didn't think it was enough. "You can't just put a plaque out and then nobody talk to each other. You have to come together as a community."

The question is, can anything ever be enough?

IF ANYWHERE CAN SERVE AS a healing place for this community, it is the Moton Museum.

For years, staff have worked to pull together black and white residents and to make the museum a place of unity where the whole community can gather to learn its shared history. Moton hosts events on anniversaries of important court decisions, the kneel-in, and the walkout. It hosts weekly brown bag lunches, a free monthly community prayer breakfast, and an annual community benefit dinner. It is also becoming a place where people can tell their stories, where they can work to forgive, where they can be forgiven.

For a long time, Everett Berryman, now a preacher in Lynchburg, didn't like to talk about what happened to him when the schools closed. His parents moved with their children to Appomattox, where they lived in the homes of two families before returning to Prince Edward and enrolling their children in the Free Schools. Everett never saw himself as a victim. Instead, he viewed the school closings as a wake-up call. If he wanted an education, he had to go out and get it himself. He has been successful in spite of being shut out of school, but he was ashamed to go to the museum and talk about how well things turned out for him around people who had fared worse and were still hurting.

But in July 2013, during the anniversary of the sit-ins, Everett returned to the museum to share his story, and I wanted to hear it. Tall and sturdy, Everett sat in front of a series of round tables in the auditorium where white and black residents of the county were gathered. My mom had joined me, and we were seated at a table with Mickie Pride. My aunt, Beverley Anne, and her youngest daughter sat at a table behind us.

Everett explained why, for a long time, he didn't like to talk about the school closings. He felt he had benefited because he had gotten opportunities he might not otherwise have had, opportunities other children in the community didn't get. He had survivor's guilt.

The audience members, including my mom, peppered him with questions. Pride, who lost four years of school during the closures, showed empathy. Petite with curly hair, Mickie told him that she was dealing with strong emotions of her own. The hate had been brewing for years, starting when she was shut out of school and building up when she was in her twenties.

By the time she had children, it had taken root in her heart. She worried she would pass this anger on to her kids. When one of her children came home from school and complained about an interaction with a teacher, she would get defensive and ask: Was she white or black? Any conflict always came down to race.

For her, the museum has been a place of healing. It began at a Moton reunion, when a former student's sermon made her think more deeply about the weight of the anger she was carrying around. Then it progressed to the museum, where she and Rebecca Butcher, the long-time teacher and administrator at Prince Edward Academy, were interviewed for a radio program. Mickie came into the museum feeling defensive, her shoulders tight, dreading the conversation. But during the interview, she heard something she hadn't heard before. Things were not perfect for white children and their teachers at the private academy. It was a difficult time for them, too. For the first time in her life, Mickie listened to a white person and gave her a chance. But Mickie also made a point to be heard. When Butcher talked about the difficulties of working at the white academy, Mickie responded that she would have loved to have attended school.

When the interview was over, the two women hugged. Now Mickie comes back to the museum every week to learn more about the past. She speaks in front of large audiences about her experiences. She has opened her heart, a little at a time, and she has begun to heal. And that healing has benefitted her children, too.

"I wasted some forty-seven years being angry," she told Everett and the audience. "I can't take it back. All I can do is move forward, and I'm not too old to do that."

THE MUSEUM IS A PLACE of connection for me, too. Jason and I visited on one of our first trips to Farmville from San Diego, and a new world opened up. Then, as I began work on the book, I conducted interviews in the auditorium, and as the museum began offering regular programming, I attended its events. I watched as Moton was transformed from a dingy relic to a shining monument.

The museum is where I meet former students affected by the school closures, who participated in the walkout, who were arrested at the kneel-in. Moton provides a safe space where I can ask about their experiences in an environment where they feel comfortable, even excited, to share their stories. It is also a place where I can talk about the role my family played in the town's history, about attending the white school, about knowing only one black person growing up. I can tell people that I have been researching my grandfather's role in the Defenders and in the white academy, and that I am grappling with the realization that he was an early supporter of massive resistance. I can be honest about my family's history, and, most of the time, I feel acceptance, not judgment.

The more I tell my story, the more black people I encounter who knew Papa or knew his name. They offer to absolve me of the guilt and shame I feel about his decision to embrace massive resistance and join the Defenders. At a celebration of the museum's reopening, Lacy Ward Jr.'s wife tells me Papa's role was typical. When I mention it to Henry Marsh, the Virginia Senator who worked for years as a civil rights attorney with Oliver Hill Sr., he reassures me that in the 1950s "most of the respectable white people were Defenders." Goodwin Douglas, who led the student protests, says my grandfather agreed to see patients of the town's black dentist at Southside Community Hospital because blacks were not permitted to practice at the time. He suggests that my grandfather might not have held on to the beliefs that led him to join the anti-integration organization. "A lot of the people who were Defenders changed as things went along," Douglas tells me.

Elsie's daughter, Gwen, declined to talk with me. Perhaps she holds my family accountable for what happened to her. I don't blame her. But many of Elsie's other relatives are open and friendly. At a Moton High School reunion at the county's Twin Lakes State Park, once run as two separate state parks segregated by race, I introduce myself to someone I recognize from Elsie's church. He tells me he is Elsie's nephew and introduces me to his brothers. One nephew who lives in Richmond wants to introduce me to his grandkids. He asks me to pose for a picture with him so he can show Elsie. At the dinner banquet that night, her nephews are kind, politely answering my questions and telling me about their lives.

Sometimes I wish I could follow the lead of my mother, who doesn't seem particularly troubled by my discovery that her father was a Defender. The way she views it, Papa's membership fit with his belief system at the time. He grew up on a farm, and, other than military service overseas and a handful of vacations, all he knew was Southside Virginia—isolated, rural, agricultural, conservative. Papa and Mimi embraced the beliefs common among whites in southern Virginia at the time, Mom has told me. Blacks were inferior, and race mixing was bad. It was a belief passed down from our own founding fathers, Virginians like Thomas Jefferson.

But then I think about this American president, who expressed a fear of miscegenation throughout his life, while fathering mixed-race children with Sally Hemings, one of his slaves. The hypocrisy reminds me of Farmville's leaders, who bragged about the lack of violence in

Prince Edward while exacting a severe punishment on all black children and their families, and then continued to blame blacks for seeking equal facilities, and later, desegregated schools.

In Farmville of the 1950s, whites who were courageous enough to call for keeping the schools open—or for reopening them once they were closed—faced enormous personal and professional repercussions, such as being humiliated, harassed, even run out of town. Neighbors jeered and grocery store clerks turned their backs on Farmville High School principal James Bash after the meeting in Jarman Hall, and he quit two months later. James R. Kennedy, the preacher at the Farmville Presbyterian Church, resigned under pressure in 1956 after his son was harassed. Gordon Moss, the Longwood dean, was removed from his leadership position in the Episcopal church after letting black students sit on his pew. Lester Andrews put his construction business in jeopardy and friends stopped speaking to him. If Papa hadn't supported the academy, he could have lost his dental practice.

I consider what to think of people's offers to absolve my grandfather. In my research, I haven't turned up information about the root of my grandfather's objection to desegregation. He is not quoted in newspaper articles or books, and he left behind no journals. Beyond his Defender membership and his role at the private school, I don't know exactly what he believed or why he believed it, and it's unlikely I ever will. Sunny Pairet, sitting at his store downtown, tells me that my grandfather "kept his thoughts to himself." I wonder: Did Papa feel pressured to go along with other white leaders who were fighting desegregation? Or was his silence, as is so often the case, a powerful form of consent?

We tend to view racism as extraordinary, as the exception. But at the time the schools closed, it was part of the fabric of American life, particularly in the South. It would be easy to absolve Papa, to say he was doing the same as other white leaders, but if no one will take the blame for the schools' closing, even on behalf of their family members, it becomes, as the historian David W. Blight writes, "a blameless act." "Responsibility for history can be generalized and spread around so diffusely that no person or people are ever deemed the source of radical evil," he suggests.

Yet people are responsible for what happened in my hometown. People like my grandfather.

I'M TIRED OF BEING DISAPPOINTED with Mimi and Papa. I'm done questioning my parents' decision to return to Farmville and send me to the academy. I want to come to terms with my upbringing—and to accept that I can never leave Prince Edward County behind. It's part of my identity. My family tree extends back generations in Southside Virginia. Just as Fuqua School can't erase its history, neither can I.

I am the segregation academy. I am the grandchild of prejudiced but loving grandparents. I am the sister of a Fuqua School teacher and the sister-in-law of a Prince Edward County High School teacher. I am the mother of multiracial children, the wife of a multiracial man. This quaint, damaged community is my hometown. I cannot be separated from any of it—not from Farmville, not from the white academy, not from Mimi and Papa.

Although I sometimes wonder how I would have turned out if I had attended a different school or grown up in a different community, I never wish for a different family. My parents and brothers are my world. I adored my grandparents, and their love made me the person I am today.

Still, I can't help wishing that Papa had been braver, that he had been willing to challenge the system. Surely he knew people who had risked their businesses to take a stand against the school closings. If only he had considered the impact of his actions on his devoted housekeeper and her daughter, and on black children around the county who would be forever damaged by his stance.

I want to find comfort in the words of blacks who generously let me off the hook. But, deep down, I wonder if it's important to not just recognize, but grapple with, the shame and guilt I feel. Perhaps it should be my legacy to regularly confront these strong emotions about what happened in Prince Edward and the role my family played.

And yet I realize that holding on to these feelings isn't progress. Progress is revisiting what happened here in a public way, connecting with both black and white residents and telling their stories. My contribution is to share the whole story, the complete story, of this town.

CHAPTER 21

The New Normal

The McDonald's on Main Street, across from Longwood University, buzzes with activity every morning. Cars stretch around the drive-through window and fill the diagonal parking spaces on both sides of the building. Inside, the flat-screen televisions are tuned to Fox News.

A group of older white men, along with a pair of women, sit on the right side of the restaurant around a long, rectangular table, drinking coffee and chatting. Black men and a handful of ladies sit on the other side of the restaurant doing the same thing. The franchise owner makes his way around the room, talking with the regulars and pouring free refills. The two sides of the fast-food restaurant occasionally interact—a white former town police officer walks through and says hello to black acquaintances—but, for the most part, they sit separately, segregated once more.

One summer morning I grab a seat on the left side, where half a dozen black men are talking and laughing, including a tall, heavyset man who tells me his family moved to New Jersey after the schools closed. He had returned to Farmville seven years earlier.

"I swore I would never ever come back to this prejudiced place," he tells me. "But it changed."

How so? I wonder.

"I'm sitting here talking to you," he says.

Farmville is not the same place it used to be, he tells me. When he was looking for a house, his real estate agent showed him every available property. There's nowhere in town that he doesn't feel welcome. He can eat or shop anywhere he likes. And he doesn't have to worry about the negative sides of city life—being robbed or mugged. "It's a nice little town," he tells me.

He said town leaders want the school closings to be forgotten so they can transform Farmville into an upscale community. "They're just waiting for all of us to die so they can pretend it never happened," he tells me.

With black former students around, white leaders are reminded of the stain on this town. That history won't disappear until the generation of children that was locked out is dead and gone, until residents stop gathering at Moton to rehash the past.

I think about the deaths of Robert Taylor and other segregationists who took their beliefs to the grave. Maybe my own grandfather did, too. This man is on to something. If Farmville is ever going to progress, it won't happen until they're all gone.

It is an exceedingly slow evolution, growing from a racist place to one that is not. It can't be forced. It is an unlearning process that takes generations, a natural progression that still has not been completed, and may not be in my lifetime.

AN INTERVIEW WITH THE CHAIR of the county school board gets me thinking about other ways Farmville can be made whole.

Russell L. Dove can clearly pinpoint one reason that the public school system isn't better: it doesn't receive the community investment it needs from businesses and parents. He believes that business owners instead donate to Fuqua School, attended by their children or grandchildren. Many parents with resources volunteer at Fuqua, not at the public schools, he suggests.

If what Dove says is true, Fuqua's existence continues to sabotage the public schools. During my second year as a public school parent in Richmond, I've seen that parental involvement and donations can be critical to a school's success. I often think how much better Richmond's schools could be if more wealthy and middle-income parents sent their kids to public instead of private schools. Spending time on the Fuqua School campus, it's easy to see that involved parents benefit the school. And attending county school board meetings, I notice how few residents advocate for more resources for the public schools.

Dove stopped short of calling for Fuqua School to be shut down, but others have said as much. During a community dialogue in 2009, Skippy Griffin's younger brother, Eric Griffin, a pastor in Greensboro, North Carolina, suggested the school should be closed. Woodley, the *Farmville Herald* editor, told me that suggesting Fuqua School be eliminated to heal decades-old wounds just creates more wounds. Yet he acknowledges that Fuqua School's existence prevents the public schools from reaching their potential. "There's an impact on so many levels, because if we're a great big stew, there's lots of ingredients that aren't going in the public school pot," he said.

In the course of my reporting, I come to believe that Fuqua School can never leave behind its tragic legacy, no matter how much it tries to reform, no matter how many students of color it brings in or how many scholarships it offers. The presence of two school systems in a tiny county prevents either from reaching its potential. Both Fuqua School and Prince Edward County Public Schools are experiencing declining enrollment. The public schools also suffer from a lack of public support and parental engagement. It's not hard to imagine that if even half of the approximately one hundred Fuqua students who live in Prince Edward County attended the public schools, the public schools could better engage parents. Perhaps the public schools could retain more, and better, teachers. The combined schools could build a more successful athletic program. They could pool resources and work together on fund-raising efforts. They could create unity in a community that has been divided for so long.

The apologies issued to black students over the years have never been enough. It is asking too much of black residents, particularly former students shut out of school, to move past the pain caused by the school closures when vivid symbols of segregation still remain. That the former Prince Edward Academy is still open, even under a different name, suggests that white Farmville's repentance is conditional: we want to move past our history, but we still cling to the most powerful symbol of segregation.

In order for this county to unite, community leaders need to find a way to make victims whole again. Instead of working to support two separate school systems, the community could unite to transform the failing public school system into a successful one, a school system that provides a quality education for all of Prince Edward County's children.

It now seems ludicrous that county leaders in Prince Edward, or anywhere else, thought they could keep the races from mixing by preventing blacks and whites from attending school together.

Before Jason and I moved south from Boston, I worried that there wouldn't be many children in Virginia who looked like my daughters. But multiracial children are everywhere: on the playgrounds, at the frozen yogurt shops, in my daughters' classrooms. The population of people like my husband and daughters is growing rapidly, with nine million Americans now identifying as multiracial. The US Census Bureau found that the number of multiracial children increased by almost 50 percent between 2000 and 2010, making mixed-race children the fastest growing group of young people in the country. Even in the Deep South, where race mixing has been especially taboo, the multiracial population is flourishing. The 2010 census found that in the previous decade it had increased by 70 percent or more in nine states, all but one of them in the South. That population will continue to grow nationwide because of the increase in interracial marriages, which in 2010 accounted for 15 percent of new marriages.

Looking at the circle of friends Jason or I have known for ten to twenty years, I see examples of America's changing face. My white college roommate, Anne Chi, married a Chinese man. Crissy Pascual married a white man, and so did our half-Mexican, half–Puerto Rican friend, Cristina Byvik. A black friend is dating a white woman. Jason's white friend wed an Indian woman. His Korean friend married an Indian man.

Acceptance of interracial marriages has grown steadily, too. A Gallup poll found that 86 percent of people nationwide supported black-white marriages in 2011, compared with 4 percent in 1958, making it one of the largest shifts of public opinion in Gallup history.

There has also been progress in Farmville. Not long after my mother canceled her *Farmville Herald* subscription, the paper began running wedding photos of couples. And in 2014 the paper placed on its front page a photo of an interracial family celebrating the father's safe return from a military assignment.

Despite the progress, there are still uncomfortable, even heartbreaking, moments in this period of transition. Some friends' parents did not accept their marriages for years. One of Crissy's relatives used the term "slant eyes" in her presence. When she became pregnant, she felt like she had to remind her parents-in-law that the twins in her belly were mixed-race, not white, explaining how being part Asian would affect their grandchildren's lives.

Still, as the parent of multiracial children, I face fewer challenges than my in-laws did thirty years ago in the same situation. Strangers stare at our children and ask if they are mine. When I'm alone with Selma, dark-skinned and dark-haired like her father, people ask if she is adopted. They point out that she doesn't resemble me. But we don't attract much attention.

Yet from a young age, my children have been aware of the differences in our skin color and want to discuss them. When Selma makes a family portrait on a paper plate in preschool, she gives Jason, Amaya, and herself brown skin. When I inquire why my skin is orange in her artwork, she tells me she couldn't find the right color for me. One day, on the drive home from kindergarten, Amaya informs me that no two people have the same shade of skin. Another day, she describes an experiment her kindergarten teacher conducted, cracking a brown egg and a white egg into separate bowls and observing that, inside, both eggs were exactly the same. People are that way, too, she informs me—the same inside, regardless of their skin color.

I'm relieved that it is easy, natural even, to talk about race with them. Because I attended an all-white school for so many years, I was long uncomfortable around people of color. I equated being black with being poor. People of any race other than white were a curiosity, and I stared. But my daughters will view the world differently. At four and six years old, they have already been exposed to a wider spectrum of people than I had been by the time I went to college. Black and mixed-race children come for playdates at our house. In preschool, Selma hugs a black boy in the hallway and informs me that he is her boyfriend. I know my daughters will grow up having friends—and boyfriends—of every race, because this is their normal.

I realize that my children and their friends are the future of better race relations, not just in Farmville, but nationwide. President Obama acknowledged as much in a 2013 speech after George Zimmerman was acquitted in Trayvon Martin's death. "Each successive generation seems to be making progress in changing attitudes when it comes to race," he said. He told the nation that when he talks with his daughters, Malia and Sasha, and when he watches them interact with their friends, he is left with a feeling that "they're better than we were on these issues."

"We should also have confidence that kids these days . . . have more sense than we did back then, and certainly more than our parents did or our grandparents did, and that along this long, difficult journey . . . we're becoming a more perfect union—not a perfect union, but a more perfect union," the president said.

I think about how much progress has happened from my grandparents' generation to mine. On this journey to understand my hometown's past, I was at times frustrated with my mom for instructing me to stop referring to Jason as multiracial and "just let Jason be Jason." It's easy to forget that Farmville has been her world for decades and that my views have been shaped by living in other places and by having a multiracial husband and children. Over time I have decided to focus on how deeply she and my dad love Jason and the girls. I consider how sweet it was for her to cancel the newspaper subscription, how thoughtful she was to buy brown dolls for my daughters and Native American gifts for Jason. She is trying to connect, to be a good grandmother to them.

It dawns on me that my girls will one day be as irritated with me as I have been with my mother. Maybe multiracial people will become so normalized that my daughters will deem me old-fashioned, rolling their eyes when I bring up the subject of racial diversity among our friends and family. Maybe they will question the decisions Jason and I make about where to live and where to send them to school.

Imagining Amaya and Selma as high school or college students makes me wish my own grandparents were around to meet them. If Mimi had lived just six months longer, she would have confronted a new reality—a mixed-race child in her own family. In Amaya, my grandmother would have come face-to-face with this changing world: her rapidly growing family would soon include six more brown and black great-grandchildren. After her death, she and Papa's mixed-race and black great-grandchildren would briefly outnumber their white great-grandchildren.

I wish my daughters could have had the chance to know the grandparents who profoundly shaped my life. I wish Papa could take them fishing and Mimi could serve them a plate of buttery mashed potatoes. I'll never know if my grandparents could have moved beyond the commitment to segregation that drove Papa to join the Defenders. I'll never know if Mimi and Papa would have looked at my daughters' brown skin and seen something unlovable. Maybe my grandparents would have surprised themselves, surprised us all, with feelings of pure love for my beautiful girls.

It's nice to think so.

Epilogue

Over time, Mimi's relationship with Elsie changed and deepened. They ate their meals together. In the car, Elsie sat in the front seat. At my wedding, Mimi motioned for Elsie to sit beside her, and Elsie declined.

After Papa died in 1993, Mimi moved into a smaller house up the street from my parents. She didn't need help cleaning, but she still wanted "little Elsie" to come once a week, as she had for years. Mimi had stopped inviting friends over and even gave up walking the pretty tree-lined streets around her home. But she enjoyed Elsie's company.

In the last years of her life, when Elsie came to clean, Mimi often invited her to lunch at Shoney's, where they sat across from each other in a booth, talking. After the meal, they would return to Mimi's house and continue the conversation seated at her dining room table, cleaning her silver collection. Mimi rubbed each piece of silver clean and Elsie wiped it dry. Mimi started leaving out the silver, which Elsie interpreted as evidence that Mimi trusted her, after more than fifty years of service. "I'd been working for her a long time," Elsie explained. "I really had."

Weeks before Mimi died in 2007, Mom drove Elsie to the nursing home where Mimi was staying so they could say good-bye. Mimi had refused visitors for weeks, but she sat up to greet Elsie, calling her "my dear old friend." My mom, deeply moved, left the room in tears.

Elsie continued working for my parents once a week, doing light cleaning. When I visited home from Massachusetts, I stopped by her house or talked with her when she came to my parents' house on Wednesdays. Sometimes while my parents were at work, Elsie asked me what she should clean first. "You don't work for me, Elsie," I reminded her.

Still, I sensed she viewed me as her employer. But the more we talked over the years, the more comfortable she became with me. One day, seated in a chair across from me in my parents' den, she was describing what it was like to grow up in Prince Edward during segregation. She suddenly stopped herself. "Oh, I forgot you're white!" she exclaimed. Another time, as I was driving her home, she told me that my grandfather would roll in his grave if he knew I had married Jason.

When she broke her thumb in 2012, she quit working for my parents. I stopped by her house more often to drop off meals or small gifts. She invited me inside her home for the first time, and, one day, she asked me to crack a bowl of nuts for her. I offered to wash her dishes, but she wouldn't allow me into her kitchen. She thanked me for visiting and placed a roll of dimes into my hand as I left, telling me she wished she was rich so that she could give me more money. When I called her after several weeks without contact, she told me she hoped I wouldn't dial her up one day only to learn she was already dead and buried.

One day during the summer I spent in Farmville, Elsie and I went to lunch at Ruby Tuesday, her favorite spot, and then she accompanied me to pick up my daughters from day care. As we drove to her home, the girls sang from the backseat, and when we got there, they hopped out of the car and ran around her front yard. She was surprised by how comfortable they acted around her. When they were toddlers, they would cry when she held them, and she would respond, "They aren't used to being around people like me." The comment stung even though it wasn't true. But during this visit, they hugged Elsie and posed for photographs with her. They told her they loved her.

One Sunday, I put them in flowery dresses, and we drove to Elsie's church to hear her sing. Later that afternoon, Gwen, who had moved back to Farmville, mentioned to Elsie that she had seen my daughters in church. Gwen remarked how beautiful they looked. "Thank you," Elsie responded to her daughter.

Retelling the story to me the following week, Elsie laughed, saying she'd acted as if Amaya and Selma were her own children. It reminded me of the way she told me she felt being around my mom and Beverley Anne after sending Gwen to Massachusetts. Elsie was devastated by her daughter's absence but comforted by the company of other children.

Months later, when I visited Elsie at her home, we sat on the couch, flipping through her old photo albums. I came across a picture of Elsie and Gwen from the 1950s. Gwen looked to be eight or nine years old, wearing a dress and a bright smile. Pretty curls framed Elsie's young face as she smiled down at her daughter, full of love.

I was struck, suddenly, by the irreparable loss they both had endured. "I'm so sorry for what happened to your family," I told her, my eyes wet with tears. "I'm sorry white leaders closed the schools, and I'm sorry my family didn't treat you better when it happened."

She averted her eyes and didn't respond.

Now, therefore be it resolved, that we, the undersigned members of the Prince Edward County Board of Supervisors, believe that the closing of public schools in our county from 1959 to 1964 was wrong; and we grieve for the way lives were forever changed, for the pain that was caused, and for how those locked doors shuttered opportunities and barricaded the dreams our children had for their own lifetimes; and for all those wounds known and unknown; we regret those past actions.

—Excerpt of a resolution passed by the Prince Edward County Board of Supervisors, July 8, 2008

Acknowledgments

There are so many people without whom this book would not have been possible, most important, those who entrusted me with their stories. Thank you, Elsie Lancaster, for the important role you played in my life, and for telling me the story of yours. I also want to thank Betty Jean Ward Berryman, Everett Berryman, Shirby Scott Brown, Warren Ricky Brown, Mickie Pride Carrington, Eunice Ward Carwile, Peggy Cave, Joan Johns Cobbs, Dickie Cralle, the Reverend Goodwin Douglas, Russell Dove, McCarthy Eanes, Heather Edwards, James R. Ennis, James W. Garnett Jr., James E. Ghee Jr., Skip Griffin, Robert Hamlin, Oliver Hill Jr., Beverly Bass Hines, John Hines, Dorothy Lockett Holcomb, Christopher B. Howard, Marie Walton Jackson, Rebecca Butcher Kelly, Heather Lettner-Rust, Henry L. Marsh, Phyllistine Ward Mosley, Dickie Moss, Ruth Murphy, Sunny Pairet, Robert T. Redd, Craig B. Reed, Howard F. Simpson, Joy Cabarrus Speakes, Kathleen Smith, K. David Smith, Diane Stubbins, Bob Taylor, Charles Taylor, Doug Vaughan, JoAnn Vaughan, Ronnie Ward, John Watson, Charlie Williams, the Reverend J. Samuel Williams, and Ken Woodley. I am grateful to the late Robert E. Taylor for talking with me. I appreciate the people who shared their stories with me whose names do not appear in the pages of this book.

I am so appreciative of the experts who kindly shared their research and expertise with me, including J. Michael Utzinger, Brian E. Lee, Edward H. Peeples, Chris Calkins, and Edward Ayers. I want to extend a huge thank-you to the Moton Museum, especially Lacy Ward Jr. and Justin Reid, who connected me with key people and did their best to answer every question. I couldn't have done this without the two of you.

This book wouldn't be half the book it is without my generous and whip-smart readers. Thank you to Melissa Barber, an amazing line editor from start to finish who always lifts me up; Rachel Machacek, who kept me calm with her yogi ways and shared her hard-won book wisdom; Rachel Beanland, who read more versions of this than anyone should have had to; Steve Watkins, who taught me to question authority and provided wonderful guidance through the book-writing process; Larissa Smith Fergeson, who shared her research and served as a fact-checker; Skip Griffin, who answered texts and e-mails at all hours of the day; Missy Ryan, who gave the manuscript her editor's eagle eye; Mia Zuckerkandel, who believed in this project before I did; and Michael Paul Williams, who shared numerous insights and was always willing to meet for coffee.

Thanks to all the folks who have supported my writing in ways big and small: Eve Bridburg and my classmates at Grub Street Writers in Boston; to James River Writers, the fabulously supportive writing community in Richmond, especially founder Dean King; and to my writer friends Caitlin Rother, Samuel Autman, and Mary Allen, for sharing insider tips. Thank you to Alan Gustafson, Susan White, Gerry Braun, and all the editors I've had over the years who've helped improve my writing and reporting.

A big thank-you to my friends at the *Richmond Times-Dispatch*, particularly Paige Mudd, Zach Reid, Heather Moon, and Dean Hoffmeyer. Thanks to Danielle Cervantes for her research assistance and to all the other librarians who helped. Thanks to Blaire and George

Jackson for giving me shelter in Farmville, and to the lovely Trudy Hale at the Porches.

Thank you especially to the people who made this dream a reality: Laurie Abkemeier, for believing that the story of Prince Edward needed to be told and that I was the one to tell it; Gail Winston, for seeing something not only in Prince Edward's story, but in my own, and for her guidance in helping that story to emerge; Maya Ziv and Emily Cunningham for shepherding this book to publication.

Thank you to my supportive network of friends in California, particularly Crissy Pascual, for teaching me a million things, and for the beautiful video she made with her husband, Brett Millar; Cristina and Kevin Byvik for the stylish stationery; and Jenn Davies for keeping me sane with her regular check ins. Thank you to my Mary Washington crew—Kristen Barnes, Anne Chi, Flavia Jimenez, Deb Totten, and Jane Archer, who also designed the amazing book cover. Thank you to my PEA classmates and friends, particularly Hollace Dowdy, Kathy Rhodes, Jennifer Johnson, and Rene Clark.

I want to extend a huge thank-you to my family: my parents, for sharing their stories and for supporting me, even when they weren't sure what the book would say; my aunt, Beverley Anne Klein, and my uncles Steve Green, Mike Green, and Doug Green for telling me about their youth; my brothers Chaz, Ben, and Aaron, for our amazing shared childhood; my sisters-in-law Jillian and Erinn, my gorgeous nephews Myles, Jack, Tanner, and Conner, and my in-laws Ginny and Noel, John and Terri, and JB, for making my life so rich.

Lastly, I want to thank my husband Jason Hamilton for his constant faith that I could write this book, even when I lost my way, and for the many ways he ensured that I was able to complete it. Thank you to Amaya and Selma for serving as my inspiration. I'm sorry this project took so much time away from all three of you.

Notes

I conducted the first interview for this book in 2006 with Robert E. Taylor, just weeks before he died. In the subsequent years of research, I interviewed dozens of people, among them community leaders, private school officials, and students shut out of school. I went to the library of my alma mater with the long-time headmaster, Robert T. Redd, the first time he had returned to the campus; I sat in a truck cab to conduct an interview with a former Moton student.

I attended dozens of events at the Moton Museum, including the anniversaries of the school closing, the walkout, and the kneel-in. I also went to a reunion of Moton High School students in 2013. I spent time on the campuses of Fuqua School and Prince Edward County High School. I attended football games at both schools and a basketball game at which the two schools' teams met during season play. I attended meetings of the Prince Edward County School Board and Board of Supervisors.

To research the county's Civil War history, I visited the Sailor's Creek Battlefield State Park and its new visitors' center, and I interviewed the historian Chris Calkins, who manages the park. I also visited High Bridge Trail State Park. To describe Prince Edward, I drove the back roads of the county, visiting the places mentioned in the book. I walked along Main Street through historic downtown, as I had done so many times as a child, and I visited Green Front's renovated warehouses.

I pored over the *Richmond Times-Dispatch*'s clip files, which also includes articles from the *Richmond News Leader*. I reviewed *Farmville Herald* stories from the era at Longwood University's Greenwood Library and perused papers at the Library of Virginia. I spent time in the Virginia Historical Society, looking at pamphlets for the Defenders, and I researched records of the John F. Kennedy Presidential Library and Museum. I combed through Edward H. Peeples's reports and photographs in the Virginia Commonwealth University Libraries Digital Collection.

I read books about Prince Edward's decision to close the schools, as well as dozens of books about the *Brown* decision and its aftermath, segregation, and the civil rights era. *They Closed Their Schools: Prince Edward County, Virginia, 1951–1964*, written by the journalist Bob Smith, was on my bedside table for years and was most influential.

To supplement my memories of the sixteen years I lived in Farmville as a child, including the thirteen years I spent as a student at Prince Edward Academy, I interviewed my parents and talked with my brothers and classmates. I used photographs, yearbooks, and other records to fill in gaps.

For two years, I made the seventy-five-minute journey to Farmville nearly every week, sometimes multiple times each week, to conduct interviews, drive around the county, and attend events. And for two months in the summer of 2013, I moved to Farmville with my daughters to research, report, and experience life there firsthand.

PROLOGUE
This section is based on my own memories, as well as interviews with my mother, Faye Patteson Green, and Elsie Lancaster.

CHAPTER 1: A PERFECTLY CHARMING SOUTHERN TOWN
The section on Robert Taylor is based on two interviews I conducted with him in 2006. I also used "Robert Edward Taylor, 87, Farmville, Dies on Thursday," *Farmville Herald* (January 12, 2007).

I attended my grandmother's funeral in 2007. I also relied on notes from my uncle, David Klein, who spoke about her life. To write about my grandfather's roots, I turned to a family genealogy, *The Holmans of Virginia* by Harry Stuart Holman (2012). My mother told me the story of her parents' childhoods and early married life. To describe the kneel-in, I used "Protests Threaten Prince Edward Study," *Richmond News Leader* (July 29, 1963), and I relied on interviews with, or talks by, participants, including Betty Jean Ward Berryman, Ernestine "Tina" Land Harris, and the Reverend J. Samuel Williams. Gwendolyn Lancaster's arrest was documented in a Farmville Police Department arrest record, courtesy of Brian E. Lee.

For the section describing the town of Farmville, population estimates were provided by Gerry Spates, the Farmville town manager. I also used US Census Bureau QuickFact numbers for 2013. To describe the Black Belt, I used *They Closed Their Schools* by Bob Smith (Chapel Hill: University of North Carolina

Press, 1965). The background on Green Front Furniture came from a 2013 interview with Dickie Cralle and his company's website. Information about High Bridge came from the Virginia Department of Recreation and Conservation. The reference to stills of moonshine comes from "Alleged Still Seized in PE," *Farmville Herald* (February 26, 2014). Longwood University's history comes from the college's website. For the reference to churches that attempted to combine, I interviewed Beverly Bass Hines and James W. Garnett Jr. For the reference to a black family that felt accepted on First Avenue, I relied on an interview with Craig Reed. The poverty rate came from the US Census Quick-Facts on Prince Edward County.

CHAPTER 2: HOMECOMING IN BLACK AND WHITE

To write about the wedding photos, I relied on an interview with my mother. Ken Woodley, the editor of the *Farmville Herald*, confirmed the former policy not to run photographs of couples in its free wedding announcements. To write about "the Indian pony," I relied on my husband Jason Hamilton's recollections of the incident, which my father, Charles Randall Green, also witnessed.

To write the section about *Loving v. Virginia*, I used Douglas Martin, "Mildred Loving, Who Battled Ban on Mixed-Race Marriage, Dies at 68," *New York Times* (May 6, 2008). I also used "Justices Upset All Bans on Interracial Marriage," *New York Times* (June 13, 1967) and Michele Norris, "Loving Decision: 40 Years of Legal Interracial Unions," National Public Radio (June 11, 2007). I also used an undated ACLU report, *Loving v. Virginia: The Case Over Interracial Marriage.*

I also viewed *The Loving Story*, a 2011 HBO film directed by Nancy Buirski. I read other media reports about the case, including Brent Staples, "Loving v. Virginia and the Secret History of Race," *New York Times* (May 14, 2008); Isabel Wilkerson, "Black-White Marriages Rise, But Couples Still Face Scorn," *New York Times* (December 2, 1991); Jackie Gardina, "A Gay-Marriage Ban with Limits," *Washington Post* (July 25, 2013).

For the section on moving to Richmond, I used a television report on the city's history with crack cocaine and as a murder capital, see Mark Holmberg, "25 Years after the Deadliest Invasion since the Civil War," WVTR (May 24, 2012) and Scott Bass, "Body Count: A Spike in Homicide Leaves Richmond on Edge," *Style Weekly* (October 9, 2012).

To describe the opposition to the Arthur Ashe statue, I used "Storm of Opposition Postpones Groundbreaking for Ashe Memorial in Va.," *Baltimore Sun* (July 9, 1995). Also instructive were Gordon Hickey and Carrie Johnson, "David Duke Brings Campaign to Area," *Richmond Times-Dispatch* (July

16, 1999) and Mike Allen, "Rebel Flag May Wave at Ceremony," *Richmond Times-Dispatch* (August 14, 1995).

For information on the reconciliation statue, see Tammie Smith, "Benin Officials Visit Reconciliation Statue," *Richmond Times-Dispatch* (June 18, 2012). For information on the slave trail and slave jail, see Karin Kapsidelis, "Slave Trail Markers Unveiled in Richmond," *Richmond Times-Dispatch* (April 11, 2011).

CHAPTER 3: PRINCE EDWARD JOINS *BROWN V. BOARD OF EDUCATION*

To write about the Moton and Tuskegee connection, I used Daniel L. Haulman, "Tuskegee Airmen Chronology," Air Force Historical Research Agency (April 24, 2014). I also used information from the Tuskegee University website.

To describe the conditions of Prince Edward County's black schools leading up to the walkout, I relied on interviews with the former and then-students Williams, John Watson, Joy Cabarrus Speakes, and Joan Johns Cobbs, Barbara Johns's sister. I also spoke with John Stokes. I relied on *They Closed Their Schools* and the National Parks Service's website. I also used *Simple Justice: The History of Brown v. Board of Education and Black America's Struggle for Equality* by Richard Kluger (New York: Vintage, 2004) and *History of Prince Edward County, Virginia*, by Herbert Clarence Bradshaw (Richmond: Dietz Press, 1955).

Also instructive were *Finding a Way Out: An Autobiography: Moton, Robert Russa, 1867–1940*, from the University of North Carolina digitization project Documenting the American South; or, The Southern Experience in 19th-Century America.

For information on Farmville High School, see *History of Prince Edward County*, *They Closed Their Schools*, and *Simple Justice*. I also used a registration form for the town's application for a Farmville Historic District with the National Register of Historic Places.

For the section on Johns, I used her diary, provided by the Moton Museum. I conducted interviews with Watson, a strike leader, as well as the students Cabarrus Speakes, Williams, and Johns Cobbs. I also quoted from a speech Johns Cobbs gave in Farmville in 2014. I used *They Closed Their Schools* and *Students on Strike: Jim Crow, Civil Rights, Brown, and Me*, by John A. Stokes, Herman Viola, and Lois Wolfe (Washington, DC: National Geographic, 2008).

For the section about the NAACP's decision to get involved in Prince Edward, I interviewed Oliver Hill Sr.'s son, Oliver W. Hill Jr., and the senior Hill's former law firm partner, Henry L. Marsh III, then a state senator. I used the senior Hill's book, *The Big Bang, Brown v. Board of Education and Beyond: The Autobiography of Oliver W. Hill, Sr.*, edited by Jonathan K. Stubbs (Winter Park: FOUR-G Publishers, Inc., 2000).

I used an interview with Hill: Ronald E. Carrington, "Interview with Oliver W. Hill, Sr.," Special Collections and Archives, Virginia Commonwealth University Libraries, Voices of Freedom: Videotaped Oral Histories of Leaders of the Civil Rights Movement in Virginia (November 13, 2002).

I also turned to *Brown v. Board of Education: A Civil Rights Milestone and Its Troubled Legacy* by James T. Patterson (New York: Oxford University Press, 2001) and *Thurgood Marshall: American Revolutionary* by Juan Williams (New York: Times Books, 1998).

I also used the Public Broadcasting Service's website for its 2004 movie *Beyond Brown: Pursuing the Promise* (http://www.pbs.org/beyondbrown) and an obituary, "Oliver W. Hill, 100, Civil Rights Lawyer, Is Dead," *New York Times* (August 6, 2007).

Also instructive were Renee Montagne and Juan Williams, "Civil Rights Lawyer Oliver Hill Dies at 100," National Public Radio (August 6, 2007); Juan Williams, "Separate but Unequal: How a Student-Led Protest Helped Change the Nation," National Public Radio (May 13, 2004); Kara Miles Turner, "Both Victors and Victims: Prince Edward County, Virginia, the NAACP, and 'Brown,'" *Virginia Law Review* 90, no. 6 (October 2004): 1667–91.

For the NAACP's new strategy, see *Brown v. Board of Education: A Civil Rights Milestone and Its Troubled Legacy, They Closed Their Schools, Thurgood Marshall, The Big Bang*, and PBS's *Beyond Brown*.

For *Gaines* and *Sweatt v. Painter*, see *Thurgood Marshall, Brown v. Board of Education: A Civil Rights Milestone and Its Troubled Legacy*, and *The Big Bang*. Also Andrea Hsu, "'Sweatt V. Painter': Nearly Forgotten, But Landmark Texas Integration Case," National Public Radio (October 10, 2012) and Linda Greenhouse, "History Lessons," *New York Times* (October 3, 2012). Also "Oliver W. Hill, 100, Civil Rights Lawyer, Is Dead."

For Hill's taking the Prince Edward case, I used *The Big Bang* and *They Closed Their Schools*. I also used my interview with Marsh and two other interviews: Julian Bond, "Interview with Oliver W. Hill," *Virginia Quarterly Review* (Winter 2004) and George Gilliam and Mason Mills, "The Ground Beneath Our Feet: Virginia's History Since the Civil War," George H. Gilliam and the Central Virginia Educational Television Corporation, the Virginia Center for Digital History, University of Virginia, 2000.

For the suggestion that the state would intervene and use its resources to defend separate schools, I turned to *They Closed Their Schools*.

For a description of funding a new public high school for blacks, I relied on *They Closed Their Schools* and *Simple Justice*.

For Johns's moving away after threats, see "Separate but Unequal."

For the idea that some black parents thought a new black high school was enough, see Brian E. Lee and Brian J. Daugherity, "Program of Action: The Rev. L. Francis Griffin and the Struggle for Racial Equality in Farmville, 1963," *Virginia Magazine of History and Biography* 121, no. 3 (2013): 250–87.

For the section on the *Brown* cases, I used *Simple Justice, Brown v. Board of Education: A Civil Rights Milestone and Its Troubled Legacy, All Deliberate Speed* by Charles J. Ogletree Jr. (New York: W. W. Norton, 2004), *A Matter of Justice: Eisenhower and the Beginning of the Civil Rights Revolution* by David A. Nichols (New York: Simon & Schuster, 2007), and *Jim Crow's Children: The Broken Promise of the Brown Decision* by Peter Irons (New York: Penguin, 2004).

Also useful were Laura Randall, "When Schools Were Shacks," *New York Times* (January 18, 2004); Wolfgang Saxon, "Judge Collins Seitz Dies at 84; Refuted Segregation in Schools," *New York Times* (October 21, 1998); Todd S. Purdum, "Presidents, Picking Justices, Can Have Backfires," *New York Times* (July 5, 2005).

CHAPTER 4: MY FAMILY'S PART

The stories I wrote for the *Richmond Times-Dispatch* both ran in April 2012. I also relied on an article by Karin Kapsidelis, "Governor Seeks Transfer of Slave Burial Ground to City," *Richmond Times-Dispatch* (December 23, 2010).

For the section on the reaction to the *Brown* decision in Virginia and around the South, I relied on an interview with Marsh. I also used *Eyes on the Prize: America's Civil Rights Years, 1954–1965* by Juan Williams (New York: Viking, 1987), *The Race Beat: The Press, the Civil Rights Struggle, and the Awakening of a Nation* by Gene Roberts and Hank Klibanoff (New York: Vintage, 2007), and *Virginia's Massive Resistance* by Benjamin Muse (Bloomington: Indiana University Press, 1961). I also used *Thurgood Marshall, Jim Crow's Children, Simple Justice, Matter of Justice,* and *They Closed Their Schools*.

In addition, I used a Library of Congress exhibit, "*Brown v. Board* at Fifty: With an Even Hand" and *Encyclopedia Virginia*.

For Stanley's response, I also used Paul Duke, "If Only White Virginia Had Followed Its Better Instincts," *Washington Post* (May 16, 2004) and Ira M. Lechner, "Massive Resistance: Virginia's Great Leap Backward," *Virginia*

Quarterly Review (Autumn 1998). I also used *Race, Reason, and Massive Resistance: The Diary of David J. Mays, 1954–1959* by David J. Mays, edited by James R. Sweeney (Athens: University of Georgia Press, 2008).

For the "state of shock," see "Supreme Court Decision," *Farmville Herald* (May 21, 1954).

For the history of Prince Edward, I utilized *Simple Justice*, *History of Prince Edward County*, and *The Prince Edward County Virginia Story*, by John C. Steck (Farmville: *Farmville Herald*, 1960). I also used *Israel on the Appomattox: A Southern Experiment in Black Freedom from the 1790s through the Civil War* by Melvin Patrick Ely (New York: Knopf, 2004) and Ed Pompeian, "Interview with Bancroft Winner Melvin Patrick Ely," History News Network (May 23, 2005).

I also used columns by the Reverend William E. Thompson in the *Farmville Herald*, "Two Invasions of Prince Edward Courthouse" (January 28, 2004) and "The Long Hot Summers of Prince Edward History" (August 11, 2004).

For the section on the Civil War, I visited the Sailor's Creek Battlefield State Park and High Bridge. I interviewed Chris Calkins and used his books, *The Appomattox Campaign* (Lynchburg: Schroeder Publications, 2008) and *Thirty-Six Hours Before Appomattox* (Farmville: *Farmville Herald*, 2006). I also relied on *Simple Justice* and *History of Prince Edward*. Also useful was *An End to Valor: The Last Days of the Civil War* by Philip Van Doren Stern (Boston: Houghton Mifflin, 1958).

For the section on the reaction to the *Brown* decision in Prince Edward, I used "If Only White Virginia Had Followed Its Better Instincts."

I also relied on the following *Farmville Herald* op-eds: "Supreme Court Decision" (May 21, 1954); "Public Education and Public Schools" (November 9, 1954); "Majority Rights" (July 23, 1954); "Grass Roots Resistance" (September 17, 1954); "Integration and Sales Taxes" (February 5, 1960); "To Our People" (February 19, 1960).

For the section on newspaper editors and the Defenders, I read the *Farmville Herald*'s editorials after the decision was announced. I also relied on *The Southern Case for School Segregation* by James Jackson Kilpatrick (New York: Crowell-Collier Press, 1962); "The 'Impossible' Prince Edward Case: The Endurance of Resistance in a Southside County, 1959–64," by Amy E. Murrell, from *The Moderates' Dilemma: Massive Resistance to School Desegregation in Virginia*, edited by Matthew D. Lassiter and Andrew B. Lewis (Charlottesville: University Press of Virginia, 1998); *They Closed Their Schools*. I also used "Segregation Preserved," *Time* (June 15, 1959); "If Only White Virginia Had Followed Its Better Instincts"; "The NAACP and the U.S. Courts Force Prince

Edward Closings," *Richmond Times-Dispatch* (June 4, 1959); "Prince Edward Holds Two Graduations," *Richmond News Leader* (June 5, 1959).

I used letters to the editor of the *Farmville Herald*: J. Guy Lancaster, "Racial Purity: The Real Issue" (October 1, 1954) and W. W. McClintic, "Race Separation Historically Sound" (October 8, 1954).

To write about motivation to keep blacks uneducated, I used "Speaker Links School Closures to Cheap Labor," *Richmond News Leader* (October 26, 1962).

For background on Nat Turner, I used *Israel on the Appomattox* and Felicia R. Lee, "Nat Turner in History's Multiple Mirrors," *New York Times* (February 7, 2004).

To write about the Defenders' forming, I used "State Sovereignty Defenders Granted Virginia Charter," *Farmville Herald* (October 29, 1954). For information about becoming a member, I used the Defenders' "Proposal for an Organization to Defend State Sovereignty and Individual Liberties: Defenders of State Sovereignty and Individual Liberties," Special Collections, University of Virginia, Charlottesville, Virginia, (1954) via *Encyclopedia Virginia*.

For the section on my discovery of Papa's role, I used *They Closed Their Schools* and a brief from the *Richmond Times-Dispatch* on October 31, 1954.

CHAPTER 5: LOCKED OUT

For Eisenhower's response to *Brown*, I used *A Matter of Justice*, *Simple Justice*, *Brown v. Board of Education: A Civil Rights Milestone and Its Troubled Legacy*, and *Eyes on the Prize*. Also useful was the *New York Times'* "Presidents, Picking Justices, Can Have Backfires."

For the reaction in Prince Edward, see "Public Education and Public Schools," *Farmville Herald* (November 9, 1954) and *They Closed Their Schools*.

For the section on *Brown II*, see *Jim Crow's Children*, *Brown v. Board of Education: A Civil Rights Milestone and Its Troubled Legacy*, and *All Deliberate Speed*.

For the section on Prince Edward County's vote to underfund the schools in response to *Brown II*, I used *They Closed Their Schools*. I also used "Public Education and Public Schools"; "Supervisors Back Segregated Schools Here Refusal to Appropriate Operating Funds for '55–'56," *Farmville Herald* (June 3, 1955); "Budget of $150,000 Is Voted," *Richmond News Leader* (June 1, 1955).

Also useful was "Prince Edward Public Schools to Run by Month in 1955–56," *Richmond News Leader* (August 1, 1955).

For the meeting of members of the parent-teacher association, see *They*

Closed Their Schools and James Elliott, "P-TA Backs Proposal on Funds," *Richmond News Leader* (June 4, 1955).

For the meeting in Jarman Auditorium, I used *They Closed Their Schools* and "The 'Impossible' Prince Edward Case" in *The Moderates' Dilemma*. I also used L. M. Wright Jr., "Board Not Planning to Run Schools, Meeting Is Told," *Richmond Times-Dispatch* (June 8, 1955).

For the description of *Brown II*, I turned to *Brown v. Board of Education: A Civil Rights Milestone and Its Troubled Legacy*, *All Deliberate Speed*, and *They Closed Their Schools*.

For the section on funds for private schools not being needed right away, see *They Closed Their Schools* and *Brown v. Board of Education: A Civil Rights Milestone and Its Troubled Legacy*.

For the county supervisors' decision to go out of the public school business, see "Private Schools Seen As Answer to Court's Integration Order," *Farmville Herald* (May 8, 1959).

For white parents' petition to the county supervisors in May 1956, see *They Closed Their Schools* and "Plaintiff's Exhibit in Dorothy Davis, et al. v. Prince Edward Co. School Board 1956," National Archives (http://research.archives .gov/description/279122).

To write about the Gray Commission, I used "Gray Commission," Television News of the Civil Rights Era: Film & Summaries, Virginia Center for Digital History and Jo Ann Frohman, "The Gray Era Ends," *Daily Press* (July 14, 1991). I also used James W. Ely Jr., *The Crisis of Conservative Virginia: The Byrd Organization and the Politics of Massive Resistance* (Knoxville: University of Tennessee Press, 1976) and *Virginia's Massive Resistance*. For the Southern manifesto, I used *Virginia's Massive Resistance*. I also turned to "Supreme Court History: Expanding Civil Rights: Southern Manifesto on Integration," Public Broadcasting Service and "The State Responds: Massive Resistance," the Library of Virginia's *Brown v. Board* exhibition (http://www .lva.virginia.gov/exhibits/brown).

For implementing Gray Commission's recommendations, I used James H. Hershman Jr., "Massive Resistance," *Encyclopedia Virginia*. Also *They Closed Their Schools* and *Virginia's Massive Resistance*.

On the Eisenhower response, I used *A Matter of Justice*, *All Deliberate Speed*, and *Brown v. Board of Education: A Civil Rights Milestone and Its Troubled Legacy*.

For the description of what happened at Little Rock, I turned to *Warriors Don't Cry* by Melba Pattillo Beals (Simon Pulse, 2001), *Eyes on the Prize*, and

A Matter of Justice. I also used Juan Williams, "Daisy Bates and the Little Rock Nine," National Public Radio (September 21, 2007).

On Governor Almond's response, I used *Virginia's Massive Resistance* and "There Will Be No Enforced Integration in Virginia," WSB-TV (Atlanta, Georgia) clip of Almond press conference, Richmond, Virginia, (August 21, 1958) via Civil Rights Digital Library (http://dlg.galileo.usg.edu/crdl/id:ugabma_wsbn_34033). For the discussion of naval children, "The Law v. the Governor," *Time* (February 2, 1959).

For the January 19 court decisions, see "'No Surrender,' But Virginia Starts Over on Segregation," *U.S. News & World Report* (January 30, 1959).

For J. Lindsay Almond's response, see the transcription of Almond's January 20 speech, Library of Virginia (http://www.virginiamemory.com/docs/01-20-1959_trans_ck.pdf). Also, Jack V. Fox, "Almond Seeking to Rally," *Bend Bulletin* (January 21, 1959). Also see *Encyclopedia Virginia* and the *Washington Post*'s "If Only White Virginia Had Followed Its Better Instincts."

For Crawford's response, see "Prince Edward Appeal of Ruling Indicated," *Richmond Times-Dispatch* (May 5, 1959).

For the response and reaction of Prince Edward's leadership, I used *They Closed Their Schools.* For the "bombshell," see the *Farmville Herald*'s "Private Schools Seen Answer to Court's Integration Order."

I also relied on "No School Fund Voted by County," *Richmond News Leader* (June 23, 1959); William B. Foster Jr., "Schools Closing Planned," *Richmond News Leader* (June 3, 1959); "September Is Deadline, Court Says," *Richmond Times-Dispatch* (May 6, 1959); "Prince Edward Appeal of Ruling Indicated," *Richmond Times-Dispatch* (May 5, 1959); "Meeting Set to Protest Prince Edward Action," *Richmond News Leader* (June 11, 1959); James Latimer, "NAACP Action Seems Sure in School Closing," *Richmond Times-Dispatch* (June 4, 1959).

CHAPTER 6: THE SEGREGATION ACADEMY

I interviewed Steve Watkins for the section about meeting him and working with him in college.

For the founding of the academy, I relied on *They Closed Their Schools* and my interviews with Robert Redd. I also used "Schools Closing Planned," "When School Bells Ring After 4 Years' Silence . . . ," *U.S. News & World Report* (September 30, 1963) and "Farmville Private School Set," *Richmond Times-Dispatch* (September 9, 1959).

To write about the tuition grant law, I referenced "Board Adopts Two Laws to Aid Private Schools," *Farmville Herald* (July 19, 1960).

For information on Mosby, see "Private Schools Losing Makeshift, Hurried Look," *Richmond Times-Dispatch* (December 20, 1959).

For Pearson appointed to lead, see "R. R. Pearson to Direct Foundation," *Richmond Times-Dispatch* (July 17, 1959) and "Halfway Mark in Prince Edward: School Plans Advancing," *Richmond Times-Dispatch* (July 26, 1959).

For the anecdote about other localities' raising money, see "The 'Impossible' Prince Edward Case" in *The Moderates' Dilemma*. The information about the United Daughters of the Confederacy's book drive comes from "UDC Aids Prince Edward Library," *Richmond News Leader* (August 19, 1959). For other communities' sending surplus materials, see *They Closed Their Schools*.

For the section on segregation academies, I relied on *The Schools That Fear Built: Segregationist Academies in the South* by David Nevin and Robert E. Bills (Washington, DC: Acropolis Books, 1976).

I also used an Associated Press story by Kathryn Johnson, "White Private Schools Booming in South," *Sarasota Herald-Tribune* (July 12, 1971); Jack White, "Education: Segregated Academies," *Time* (December 15, 1975); Sarah Carr, "In Southern Towns, 'Segregation Academies' Are Still Going Strong," *The Atlantic* (December 13, 2012).

I also used a chart prepared by Edward H. Peeples Jr., "13 known private schools in Virginia established since 1958 to circumvent desegregation," Edward H. Peeples Prince Edward County (Va.) Public Schools, VCU Libraries Digital Collection (1965) (http://dig.library.vcu.edu/cdm/compoundobject/collection/pec/id/647/rec/1).

To write about Pearson's New Orleans visit, I used "Private Schools Only Way to Keep Segregation, New Orleans Group Told," *Farmville Herald* (July 29, 1960). I also used *They Closed Their Schools* and "We Will Move: The Kennedy Administration and Restoring Public Education to Prince Edward County, Virginia," by Brian E. Lee, from *The Educational Lockout of African Americans in Prince Edward County, Virginia (1959–1964): Personal Accounts and Reflections,* edited by Terence Hicks and Abul Pitre (Lanham: University Press of America, 2010).

For the section about my grandfather's role in the school, I relied on interviews with Robert Redd.

CHAPTER 7: WAITING AND SEEING

For the section on students blocked from school, I interviewed black students including Robert Hamlin, Marie Walton Jackson, Ronnie Ward, Phyllistine Ward Mosley, Ward Berryman, Skip Griffin, and Charles Taylor.

The background on Hill Sr. came from *They Closed Their Schools*.

For the section on Griffin's making plans for the students to attend Kittrell, I relied on "The 'Impossible' Prince Edward Case" in *The Moderates' Dilemma*. I also used "'Adopt a Child' Plan Puts Negro Pupils in School," *Farmville Herald* (September 13, 1960) and "Two Hundred Negro High School Students Enrolled out of County," *Farmville Herald* (March 29, 1960).

To write about training centers, I used "Negro Training Centers to Open November 14," *Farmville Herald* (November 1, 1960); "10 Negro 'Training Centers' to Open in Prince Edward," *Richmond Times-Dispatch* (January 22, 1960); "Little Progress Made on Training Centers," *Richmond News Leader* (February 15, 1960); Ben Bowers, "Over 400 Negro Children Enrolled in 13 'Morale Building' Centers," *Farmville Herald* (November 25, 1960).

The section on students' heading for Kittrell was based on interviews with Walton Jackson, Ward, and Ward Mosley.

The section on Taylor is based on interviews with him.

The section about going to First Baptist Church is based on a 2010 visit.

CHAPTER 8: NIGGER LOVERS
For the sections on B. Calvin Bass, I relied on an interview with his daughter Bass Hines and *They Closed Their Schools*.

For the section on Virginia gentlemen, I relied on interviews with Skip Griffin and Edward L. Ayers, the president of the University of Richmond. I also used the book *Southern Politics in State and Nation* by V. O. Key Jr. (New York: Knopf, 1949). I also relied on "Relaxed, Carefree Students: Prince Edward Schools Open in Calm," *Richmond Times-Dispatch* (September 3, 1958); "To Our People," *Farmville Herald* (April 29, 1960).

For the section on the store owner who used the slur, I witnessed the interaction and had a conversation with the owner while spending several hours in the business in February 2013.

CHAPTER 9: "YOU GO WHERE YOUR PARENTS TELL YOU TO"
For the opening of the private academy, I relied on interviews with my mother and her classmates James R. Ennis and Bass Hines. I also used "Farmville Private School Set" and *They Closed Their Schools*. For the description of the Farmville Junior Woman's Club, I viewed newspaper photographs of the exterior and conducted interviews with Ennis and my mother.

To write about my father's and his brothers' experience in Farmville, I relied on interviews with him, as well as his brothers, Stephen R. Green, T. Michael Green, and Douglas M. Green.

To write about my mother's first year in the private academy, I relied on

interviews with her and Ennis. To describe Butcher's store, I also used interviews with Skippy Griffin and my mother.

To describe Rebecca Butcher Kelly's teaching experience at the private school
in the early years, I relied on an interview with her. To describe the six-year-old
who dressed every day for school, I turned to Donald P. Baker, "Shame of a
Nation," *Washington Post* (March 4, 2001).

For the section on deciding where my daughters will go to school in Richmond, I visited the Richmond preschool center referenced. Both of my daughters attended the public preschool and I later enrolled them in the neighborhood
elementary school I described.

I also used Richmond Public Schools "report card" from the Virginia Department of Education as well as information from the school district's website
and 2010 census data to explain the racial makeup of the city.

A report on modern school segregation in Virginia was also useful: Gene-
vieve Siegel-Hawley, Jennifer Ayscue, John Kuscera, Gary Orfield, *Miles to
Go: A Report on School Segregation in Virginia, 1989–2010*, The Civil Rights
Project, University of California, Los Angeles, March 13, 2013.

CHAPTER 10: ELSIE'S OTHER LIFE

The section on Elsie Lancaster is based on conversations and interviews with
her. It is also based on interviews with my mother and my aunt, Beverley Anne
Klein, as well as my own memories of my grandparents' home.

The description of the state park with two lakes came from "Making and
Preserving History at Twin Lakes," *The Crewe-Burkeville Journal* (February
23, 1995) and Kathryn Orth, "Park Manager's Career Path Makes a Circle,"
Richmond Times-Dispatch (February 24, 1995).

The section on blacks' being banned from the library's reading room comes
from Stuart H. Loory, "$400,000 Virginia 'Monument to White Supremacy,'
Farmville, Va., Build It to By-Pass Law," *New York Herald Tribune* (August
22, 1961). I also used *The Strange Career of Jim Crow* by C. Vann Woodward
(New York: Oxford University Press, 1974) and the *Jim Crow Guide: The Way
It Was* by Stetson Kennedy (Boca Raton: Florida Atlantic University Press,
1959).

Background on the Dred Scott case came from the Library of Congress, the
National Archives and Record Administration, and Washington University's
Dred Scott case collection. For *Plessy v. Ferguson* and Jim Crow laws, see *The
Rise and Fall of Jim Crow*, Public Broadcasting Service (http://www.pbs.org/
wnet/jimcrow). Also, "Supreme Court Issues Dred Scott Decision," *New York
Times* (March 6, 1857).

The section on my grandparents' failure to acknowledge that Elsie had sent Gwen to Massachusetts is based on interviews with Elsie.

CHAPTER 11: THE HOUR IS LATE

For the section on Southside Schools, I turned to *They Closed Their Schools*. I also used "Negro Protest Pilgrimage Set," *Farmville Herald* (January 1, 1960); William P. Cheshire, "Threats of Reprisals Charged in Farmville," *Richmond News Leader* (January 11, 1960); "Boycott Seen by Negroes in Farmville," *Richmond Times-Dispatch* (December 24, 1959); "State Will Pay Full Cost of Negro Tuitions," *Farmville Herald* (January 1, 1960).

For the coverage of Martin Luther King's speech and the pilgrimage, see "Negroes Ask State Legislature to Change School Law: 'Pilgrimage' Protest of Prince Edward County Closures Made," *Farmville Herald* (January 5, 1960).

For the number of black children in school across the state, see *Crusaders in the Courts: How a Dedicated Band of Lawyers Fought for the Civil Rights Revolution* by Jack Greenberg (New York: Basic Books, 1994).

For the delays in opening the Southside schools, see "Negro School Opening Delayed Until September," *Farmville Herald* (January 19, 1960) and "Threats of Reprisals Charged in Farmville."

For Byrd's response, see "In Defense of Prince Edward County, Virginia," *Congressional Record* (May 17, 1961).

For academy officials' seeking a new building, I used "Foundation Wants to Buy High School Building," *Farmville Herald* (January 15, 1960) and "Future School Planning," *Farmville Herald* (January 19, 1960).

To write about the *Farmville Herald*'s support of the new school, I used reports in the paper: "State Will Pay Full Cost of Negro Tuitions" and "Future School Planning."

For reports of Andrews's and Bass's resignation, I used *They Closed Their Schools*.

For the *Farmville Herald*'s response, see "Private School Pattern," *Farmville Herald* (April 29, 1960). For an account of how the NAACP attempted to prevent the sale of the buildings, see "Forced Public Schools Aim of New NAACP Court Action," *Farmville Herald* (June 14, 1960).

For the academy's establishing a permanent building, see *They Closed Their Schools*. Also see "School Unit Acquires New Site," *Richmond News Leader* (February 15, 1960); "Prince Edward Private School Asks $300,000," *Richmond News Leader* (June 23, 1960); "Schools Gets Aid from Many Firms," *Richmond Times-Dispatch* (November 16, 1960).

I also relied on *The Burden of Brown: Thirty Years of School Desegregation* by Raymond Wolters (Knoxville: University of Tennessee Press, 1984).

For the response by poor white families, I relied on interviews with Eunice Ward Carwile and John Hines.

For a description of how all-white kids attended the academy, see WSB-TV news clip of interview of Roy R. Pearson, via the Civil Rights Digital Library (February 29, 1960).

For the section on the Bush League, I used *They Closed Their Schools*. I also used interviews with Bass Hines and Gordon Moss's son, Dickie Moss.

Also, for county business and community leaders' unwillingness to discuss resuming schools, see "Speaker Links School Closures to Cheap Labor," *Richmond News Leader* (October 26, 1962).

CHAPTER 12: A BUS TICKET AND A WORLD AWAY

This chapter was based on interviews of students locked out of school, including Betty Jean Ward Berryman and her siblings Ronnie Ward and Phyllistine Ward Mosley; Dorothy Lockett Holcomb; Warren Ricky Brown and his wife, Shirby Scott Brown; Doug Vaughan and his wife, JoAnn Vaughan; Mickie Pride Carrington; and John Hines. I also relied on interviews with Elsie Lancaster.

I also used Holcomb's book, *Educated in Spite of . . . A Promise Kept* (Farmville: MAKKA Productions, 2012). To describe the training centers, I used "Three Negro Training Centers Opened," *Farmville Herald* (February 19, 1960).

CHAPTER 13: THEN AND NOW

For the section on Elsie Lancaster sending her daughter to Boston, I relied on interviews with her. To write about my mother's response, I relied on interviews with my mother and Elsie.

CHAPTER 14: *BROWN* STOKES THE FLAMES

For the section on *Brown*'s aftermath, I used the Library of Congress's *Brown* aftermath exhibit, Brown v. Board at Fifty: "With an Even Hand," Library of Congress (http://www.loc.gov/exhibits/brown/brown-aftermath.html).

For Eisenhower's reaction, I turned to *A Matter of Justice*. Also, Erwin Knoll, "Desegregation's Tortuous Course: Washington: Showcase of Integration," *Commentary* (March 1959).

To write the section on Clinton High School, I used "With an Even Hand: *Brown v. Board* at Fifty," Library of Congress and Carroll Van West, "Clinton Desegregation Crisis," *Tennessee Encyclopedia of History and Culture,* (December 25, 2009).

To write about Ruby Bridges's experiences, I used her website and her book,

Through My Eyes (New York: Scholastic Press, 1999). I also used an Associated Press report by Rick Callahan, "Ruby Bridges Meets with Marshal who Escorted Her," *Indianapolis Star Tribune* (September 5, 2013).

For the section about Dorothy Counts, I used "Where Are They Now? Dorothy Counts," *Charlotte Magazine* (August 2010).

For the section on the Little Rock Nine, I used "With an Even Hand: *Brown v. Board* at Fifty," Library of Congress. For Virginia's being one of seven states, see "The Segregation Dike Is Broken," *Business Week* (February 7, 1959) and "With an Even Hand: *Brown v. Board* at Fifty."

For black children across the country attending integrated schools, see "American President: A Reference Resource: Dwight David Eisenhower," Domestic Affairs, The Miller Center, University of Virginia (http://millercenter .org/president/eisenhower/essays/biography/4).

To write about Rosa Parks, I turned to *Eyes on the Prize*.

To write about the sit-ins, I used *Eyes on the Prize* and *Thurgood Marshall*. I also used Claude Sitton, "Negro Sitdowns Stir Fear of Wider Unrest in South," *New York Times* (February 15, 1960) and Owen Edwards, "Courage at the Greensboro Lunch Counter," *Smithsonian* (February 2010). I also interviewed a participant, J. Samuel Williams.

To write about the demonstration coming to Farmville, I used *They Closed Their Schools* as well as interviews with Williams and Goodwin Douglas.

To write about how Birmingham became a turning point, I used "Program of Action."

To describe what happened in Birmingham, I used Corky Siemaszko, "Birmingham Erupted into Chaos in 1963 as Battle for Civil Rights Exploded in South," *Daily News* [New York] (May 3, 2012) and Foster Hailey, "Dogs and Hoses Repulse Negroes at Birmingham," *New York Times* (May 4, 1963).

For the section on the Michigan State researchers, I used "Catching Up in Prince Edward," *Time* (August 9, 1963). To describe what happened to the students, I used William J. vanden Heuvel, "Closing Doors, Opening Doors: Fifty Years after the School-Closing in Prince Edward County, Virginia," *The Ambassadors Review* (Spring 2009): 38–49.

To describe the AFSC's involvement, I used Betsy Brinson, "The AFSC and School Desegregation," *Friends Journal* (April 2004) and " 'Adopt A Child' Plan Puts Negro Pupils in School: Quaker Unit Takes 50; Others Go to Kittrell," *Farmville Herald* (September 13, 1960).

To describe the arrival of teachers and students to run summer programs, I turned to "Catching Up in Prince Edward" and "Lock Begins to Open," *Ebony* (November 1963).

To describe what happened in Danville, I used Tess Taylor, "The Price of

Rebellion," *New York Times* (June 1, 2013); John R. Crane, "Bloody Monday: History-Changing Day," *News and Advance* (June 2, 2013); David Bearinger, "What Is Bloody Monday, and Why Don't We Know about It?" *Parade* (August 24, 2013). I also used an August 1963 report by Dorothy Miller documenting the events. The report was published by the Student Nonviolent Coordinating Committee (http://www.crmvet.org/docs/danville63.pdf).

To write about the decision to protest in Farmville, I used "Boycotts on an 'If Necessary' Basis Organized," *Farmville Herald* (December 16, 1960). I also used *They Closed Their Schools*, "Program of Action," and "Catching Up in Prince Edward." I also interviewed Douglas, Williams, and Griffin.

To write about training for the protests, I interviewed Ward Berryman.

To write about the demonstrations and the kneel-in, I also interviewed Ward Berryman, Williams, Douglas, Griffin, and Everett Berryman. Peggy Cave provided a description of what the kneel-in sounded like inside the church. I also utilized a talk that Ernestine "Tina" Land gave at the Moton Museum. And I interviewed Sunny Pairet about the protests in front of his store.

I reviewed photographs in Virginia Commonwealth University's digital library collection, Farmville Civil Rights Protests, Protestors on Main Street, July 1963 (http://dig.library.vcu.edu/cdm/landingpage/collection/far). I also used "Program of Action" and a Farmville Police Department list of those arrested at the kneel-in provided by Lee.

I also relied on media reports, including "Protests Threaten Prince Edward Study," *Richmond News Leader* (July 29, 1963) and "Catching Up in Prince Edward." I also used "Farmville, 1963: The Long, Hot Summer," by Jill Ogline Titus, from *The Educational Lockout of African Americans in Prince Edward County* and *They Closed Their Schools*.

CHAPTER 15: TWO STEPS FORWARD, ONE STEP BACK
To write about Eisenhower's failure to intervene, I used *The Educational Lockout of African Americans in Prince Edward County* and *A Matter of Justice*.

To write about the position blacks took in the 1960 presidential campaign, I used "Presidential Candidates Queried on Schools Here," *Farmville Herald* (October 25, 1960).

For the percentage of blacks who voted for Kennedy, I used the website for the John F. Kennedy Presidential Library and Museum.

To write about Kennedy's denouncement of school closings and attempts to intervene, I used "We Will Move" in *The Educational Lockout of African Americans in Prince Edward County* and *Parting the Waters* by Taylor Branch (New York: Simon & Schuster, 1988).

To write about Watkins M. Abbitt of Appomattox, "totalitarianism," and "the naked and arrogant declaration of nine men," I used Michael Janofsky, "W. M. Abbitt, 90, Lawmaker Who Advocated Segregation," *New York Times* (July 15, 1998). For Albertis S. Harrison Jr., see *They Closed Their Schools.*

To write about the Freedom Riders, I relied on *Parting the Waters* and *Freedom Riders: 1961 and the Struggle for Racial Justice* by Raymond Arsenault (New York: Oxford University Press, 2006). Also useful was "Remembering the Freedom Riders," *New York Times* (May 15, 2011).

To write about James Meredith, I used Fred Powledge, "Mississippi Gives Meredith Degree," *New York Times* (August 20, 1963). Also useful was the website for the John F. Kennedy Presidential Library and Museum (http:// microsites.jfklibrary.org/olemiss/meredith/).

To write about Kennedy's frustration with Prince Edward's closed schools, I used "Education: Back to School," *Newsweek* (August 26, 1963).

To write about how Griffin coordinated with other agencies, I used "Program of Action."

For the section on George Wallace, I used Howell Raines, "George Wallace, Segregation Symbol, Dies at 79," *New York Times* (September 14, 1998); Debra Bell, "George Wallace Stood in a Doorway at the University of Alabama 50 Years Ago Today," *U.S. News & World Report* (June 11, 2013); "'Segregation Forever': A Fiery Pledge Forgiven, but Not Forgotten," National Public Radio (January 10, 2013).

I also relied on Robert F. Kennedy speeches on the Department of Justice website (http://www.justice.gov/ag/speeches-25). For Kennedy's special message to Congress, see "Shame of a Nation." For Kennedy's urging his brother to accomplish something, see "Classes Again Soon for Prince Edward Negroes," *U.S. News & World Report* (August 26, 1963).

For calls to mediate in Farmville, I used "Student-Teachers Pr. Edward 'Remedy' Awaits JFK's Action," *Richmond Times-Dispatch* (May 18, 1963) and "The Educators to Confer with JFK," *Richmond Times-Dispatch* (June 19, 1963). I also used a transcript of John F. Kennedy's "Report to the American People on Civil Rights," June 11, 1963, from the John F. Kennedy Presidential Library and Museum.

I also used "George Wallace Stood in a Doorway at the University of Alabama 50 Years Ago Today."

To write about Medgar Evers, I used Ashley Southall, "Paying Tribute to a Seeker of Justice, 50 Years After His Assassination," *New York Times* (June 5, 2013) and David Stout, "Byron De La Beckwith Dies; Killer of Medgar Evers Was 80," *New York Times* (January 23, 2001).

For the decision to create Free Schools, I relied on "Classes Again Soon for Prince Edward Negroes." I also used "Program of Action."

For the March on Washington, I interviewed Griffin and Ward Berryman. See also Martin Luther King Jr., "I Have A Dream Speech," National Archives (http://www.archives.gov/exhibits/featured_documents/mlk_speech).

For the Free Schools and information about its leader, I used *Bound for Freedom: An Educator's Adventures in Prince Edward County, Virginia* by Neil V. Sullivan (Boston: Little, Brown, 1965). I also used Elaine Woo, "Neil Sullivan, 90, Led Fight to Desegregate Schools in Virginia, Boston, Berkeley," *Los Angeles Times* (August 14, 2005) and "Neil V. Sullivan Dies at 90; Helped Integrate Schools," *New York Times* (August 12, 2005). I used "Dickie's Decision," *Time* (September 27, 1963); "When School Bells Ring After 4 Years' Silence"; vanden Huevel's "Closing Doors, Opening Doors."

To write about the Birmingham church bombings, see Claude Sitton, "Birmingham Bomb Kills 4 Negro Girls In Church," *New York Times* (September 16, 1963) and Tanya Ott, "Long Forgotten, 16th Street Baptist Church Bombing Survivor Speaks Out," National Public Radio (January 25, 2013). Also useful was Tim Padgett and Frank Sikora, "The Legacy of Virgil Ware," *Time* (September 22, 2003).

To write about the schools' reopening, I used *Bound for Freedom*. I also used "When School Bells Ring After 4 Years' Silence" and "Dickie's Decision." Also useful was Henry McLaughlin, "At Least One White Student Will Attend New Free School," *Richmond Times-Dispatch* (August 15, 1963).

I also interviewed the former students McCarthy Eanes, Dickie Moss, Griffin, and Ward Berryman. I spoke with George Abernathy at the Moton Museum, where he gave a talk. I also met Betty Lewis and Thomas Lewis at a Free Schools anniversary event at the Moton Museum.

For *Griffin v. Prince Edward*, see *Jim Crow's Children*.

To write about how Farmville responded to President Kennedy's death, I used *Bound for Freedom*. To write about Robert Kennedy's visiting Farmville after the president was killed, I used vanden Huevel's "Closing Doors, Opening Doors," "Shame of a Nation," and "Political Issues Played Down: Kennedy Restrained in Visits to State," *Richmond Times-Dispatch* (June 5, 1968). I also reviewed *Richmond Times-Dispatch* photos from the visit.

For reaction to *Griffin v. Prince Edward County*, I interviewed Griffin. Also "State Court Affirms County Position: Declares No Duty to Have Public Schools," *Farmville Herald* (December 3, 1963). For the quote "The time for mere 'deliberate speed' has run out," see the US Supreme Court's decision in *Griffin v. County School Board of Prince Edward County*.

For the sections on checks to academy parents, I used an August 6, 1964, photo by the *Richmond-Times Dispatch* and the *Washington Post*'s "Shame of a Nation." I also used interviews with Elsie.

To write about passage of the Civil Rights Act of 1964, I used media coverage: E. W. Kenworthy, "Civil Rights Bill Passed, 73–27," *New York Times* (June 20, 1964) and E. W. Kenworthy, "President Signs Civil Rights Bill; Bids All Back It," *New York Times* (July 3, 1964).

For the section on Peggy Cave, I talked on the phone with her. I also talked with the former Prince Edward Academy students René Hurley Clark and Suzanne Rogers Powell.

CHAPTER 16: BUILDING A LIFE WITHOUT A FOUNDATION
For stories about how students were affected, I relied on interviews with Ricky Warren Brown and his wife, Shirby Scott Brown; Doug Vaughan and his wife, JoAnn Vaughan; and Elsie.

CHAPTER 17: "WE ARE ALL GOD'S CHILDREN"
For background on my mother and her family, I relied on interviews with my mother and her sister, Beverley Anne Klein. I also utilized *The Holmans of Virginia.*

For the section on my father's childhood, I relied on interviews with my dad and his three brothers. I also utilized their father's US Navy records. Two newspaper stories about my great-grandmother were also helpful. Grace Holman, "Virginia Mother of Year: 'Helping Others' Called 'Best Part of Life,' " *Southside Virginian* (March 29, 1967) and "Mrs. Epsie Vale, 90, Virginia 1967 Mother of the Year, Dies," *Farmville Herald* (November 23, 1988).

I relied on interviews with my parents to write about their leaving Farmville, dating, and marrying. Barbara J. Payton at the Virginia Commonwealth University School of Dentistry provided statistics on black graduates. For school busing in Richmond, see the Virginia Historical Society's website (http://www.vahistorical.org/collections-and-resources/virginia-history-explorer/civil-rights-movement-virginia/school-busing). See also Clara Silverstein, "The Great Experiment," *Style Weekly* (January 1, 1980).

I relied on interviews with my parents for the section about their decision to move back to Farmville and to send my brothers and me to the academy.

For background on James Anderson, I used R. C. Smith, "Prince Edward County: Revisited and Revitalized," *Virginia Quarterly Review* (Winter 1997): 1–27. I also used *The Burden of Brown.*

For the academy's nonprofit status being pulled by the Internal Revenue

Service, see Bruce Potter, "Lone Black Responds to Academy," *Richmond News Leader* (February 20, 1986). For the story about my dad coaching a black boy on the academy's fields, I interviewed my dad. His co-coach and my twin brothers, who played on the team, confirmed the story. My dad also recounted the story about my grandfather's telling him he couldn't recommend him for the board.

For information about the academy integrating, I relied on interviews with my dad and with Redd. I also used "Lone Black Responds to Academy"; Overton McGehee, "Academy's Integration Seen as Sign of Healing," *Richmond Times-Dispatch* (June 7, 1987); "1968 Will that left $676,000 to Academy Is Subject of Suit," *Richmond Times-Dispatch* (April 4, 1987); Overton McGehee, "Compliance Costs School $1.5 Million; Retiree Home Here Gains from Ruling," *Richmond Times-Dispatch* (October 10, 1990).

To write about Prince Edward Academy's financial problems, I relied on interviews with Redd and Taylor.

To write about how the academy became Fuqua School, I used *Fuqua: A Memoir: How I Made My Fortune Using Other People's Money* by J. B. Fuqua (Atlanta: Longstreet Press, 2001). I also used Ken Belson, "J. B. Fuqua, 87, Entrepreneur Who Gave Millions to Duke U., Dies," *New York Times* (April 9, 2006); Gwen Kinkead, "Why J. B. Fuqua Loves Money Losers," *Fortune* (March 4, 1985); Mark Alpert, "Southern Fox," *Fortune* (March 13, 1989); "His Brother's Keeper," *Philanthropy* (May/June 2004).

I also relied on Kathryn Orth and Jamie Ruff, "Academy Renamed in Benefactor's Honor," *Richmond Times-Dispatch* (August 24, 1993); Kathryn Orth, "Students Celebrate First Day at Fuqua," *Richmond Times-Dispatch* (August 26, 1993); Kathryn Orth and Jamie Ruff, "Fuqua Chief Sees 'Peaceful Coexistence,'" *Richmond Times-Dispatch* (May 16, 1994); Carl T. Rowan, "$10 Million to Buy Out a Relic of Segregation," *Baltimore Sun* (August 27, 1993); Wes Allison and Kathryn Orth, "Fuqua Envisions School as Boon to County," *Richmond Times-Dispatch* (January 9, 1994); Wes Allison, "Giving Something Back," *Richmond Times-Dispatch* (January 9, 1994).

For the section about the summer in Farmville, I lived in the town for two months in 2013. I used an interview with Heather Edwards, a Longwood professor.

For the reconciliation pilgrimage, see Kathryn Orth, "Tensions Arise on the Last Day of 'Pilgrimage,'" *Richmond Times-Dispatch* (May 1, 2006).

For Hampden-Sydney College, I interviewed college president Christopher B. Howard. Also, see Guy Raz, "Black President Stands Out at Mostly White College," National Public Radio (September 26, 2009) and Steve Szkotak, "Hampden-Sydney Student Expelled for Racially Motivated Uproar after Obama Election," *Huffington Post* (December 13, 2012).

CHAPTER 18: THE SCHOOLS TODAY

For the section on funding Prince Edward County Schools, I used "Prince Edward County: Revisited and Revitalized"; Rob Chapman, "Boards Talk Schools, PE Focused On Funding," *Farmville Herald* (March 26, 2014); "Prince Edward County Needs the Facts about 50 Years Ago, Today," *Farmville Herald* (March 27, 2014).

For tax rate information, I used *Virginia Local Tax Rates, 2011 Information for All Cities and Counties and Selected Incorporated Towns*, by John L. Knapp and Stephen C. Kulp, in cooperation with the Virginia Association of Counties and the Virginia Municipal League (Charlottesville: Weldon Cooper Center for Public Service, University of Virginia, 2012).

For the section about the road, see "8News Investigates: 'Road To Nowhere,'" ABC 8 News (July 8, 2013) (http://www.wric.com/story/22784594/8news-investigates-road-to-nowhere).

To write the section about Ruth Murphy, I relied on a series of interviews with her. Also useful were Lisa Harpole, "Turning a City School Around," *Leader* [Research Triangle Park], (October 6, 1988); Steve Adams, "In Pursuit of Excellent Schools," editorial, *Leader* [Research Triangle Park] (October 6, 1988); "Excellence Creates This Problem," *Durham Morning Herald* (December 20, 1988).

Murphy provided the Fuqua School's diversity statistics. For the section on the unintended consequences of Murphy's programs, I relied on an interview with Charles Williams, as well as interviews with Ricky Brown and his wife, Shirby Scott Brown, and Doug Vaughan and his wife, JoAnn Vaughan. I also used Kevin Sieff, "Fuqua School Looks to African American Football Star to Shatter Racist Legacy," *Washington Post* (December 11, 2011).

Murphy provided enrollment numbers for Fuqua. I relied on the school's website for other information about the student body, including tuition and classes offered. The county's median household income came from the US Census Bureau's QuickFact numbers for 2013.

Murphy provided information on the school's scholarships and the number of students who receive them. She also provided information about valedictorians in 2013 and 2014. I witnessed Fuqua students march in the reenactment of Barbara Johns's walkout in 2014.

To describe Fuqua School, I shadowed a teacher, Diane Stubbins, in the spring of 2013.

The section on Chinese students was based on interviews with Murphy.

To describe John P. Wynne Campus School and the progress under Anderson's administration, I used *The Burden of Brown* and "Prince Edward

County: Revisited and Revitalized." Also useful was an article by the school's director, Dr. E. Lee Land, "John P. Wynne Campus School," *Bulletin of Long-wood College* 62, no. 2 (Winter 1972–73).

To describe how Prince Edward County became a model, I used Timothy M. Phelps's series for *Newsday* [New York], "Brown vs. Board, 40 Years Later." I used "A Model for the Nation" (May 17, 1994); "Still Separate in S. C.: Brown decision's unintended effect" (May 16, 1994); "A Bid to Resegregate? In Delaware, new inequity feared in challenge to busing" (May 19, 1994); "The Legacy of *Brown vs. Board*: Decades after the Supreme Court barred separate but equal schools, in Topeka and elsewhere the battle is still being waged" (May 15, 1994); "In Capital, An Exodus Integration led to white flight" (May 18, 1994).

I also used the *Richmond Times-Dispatch*'s "Fuqua Envisions School as Boon to County."

For the county's 2009 scores, I used the Virginia Department of Education, Prince Edward County, approved application for school improvement funds (http://www.doe.virginia.gov/support/school_improvement/title1/1003_g/div_apps/prince_edward_county.pdf). To write the section on Prince Edward County High School being named a turnaround school, I interviewed Kathleen Smith, the department's director of the Office of School Improvement, as well as Principal Craig Reed and Prince Edward County Public Schools superintendent K. David Smith. Reed also provided the Prince Edward County Public Schools' test scores. See also the Department of Education's turnaround schools information page (http://www.doe.virginia.gov/support/school_improvement/title1/1003_g/).

To describe the modern day Prince Edward County High School, I interviewed Craig Reed on campus in Spring 2013.

For the section describing the advances made at Prince Edward County High School during the three-year turnaround program, I used my interview with Kathleen Smith and interviews with Reed.

CHAPTER 19: "WE ALL WISH IT HADN'T HAPPENED"
To write about Farmville's recognition of the anniversary of the kneel-in, I attended the July 2013 event and utilized a statement by the Episcopal Church's vestry.

Also useful was an account of the kneel-in's anniversary written by J. Michael Utzinger, a Hampden-Sydney College professor, and Liz Sawyer, "Farmville Community Remembers Kneel-In," *Richmond Times-Dispatch* (July 29, 2013).

The section about black residents' reactions to the low turnout at the kneel-in event was based on a conversation I heard at the Moton Museum brown bag luncheon on July 29, 2013, the day after the kneel-in anniversary.

The section on Ward Berryman is based on interviews with her.

The section with my mother is based on a conversation we had over lunch in August 2013.

The section with Bob Taylor is based on an interaction we had on Main Street in Farmville in August 2013.

CHAPTER 20: A HEALING PLACE FOR THE COMMUNITY

The history of the Moton building's being put up for sale and bought by a community organization is based on interviews with Lacy Ward Jr. and Woodley. I also used a letter the county wrote to the state asking for a delay in adding Moton as a National Historic Landmark or to the Virginia Registry.

I also discussed with the Chairman of the Board of Supervisors Howard F. Simpson and County Manager Wade Bartlett the county's decision not to fund the museum. I used "Prince Edward County Revisited and Revitalized"; Donald P. Baker, "Support for a Va. School and Its History Lesson," *Washington Post* (March 6, 1995); "Shall We Tear Down America?" *Farmville Herald* (February 15, 1995). I referred to a time line of events on the Moton Museum's website (http://www.motonmuseum.org/about/history/timeline).

For the pushback to the museum, I relied on interviews with Ward Jr. I also used a piece I wrote for the *Richmond Times-Dispatch*, "Prince Edward's Turning Point" (April 24, 2011).

For background on the scholarship, I interviewed the *Farmville Herald*'s editor, Woodley. I also used Barbara Bedway, "Virginia Editor Crusades to Right Past Wrongs," *Editor & Publisher* (September 15, 2005).

For background on the construction of a civil rights memorial, see Jim Nolan, "Civil-Rights Memorial Dedicated at Capitol," *Richmond Times-Dispatch* (July 21, 2008) and Anita Kumar, "Paying Homage to Desegregation's Pioneers," *Washington Post* (July 22, 2008). For information about the honorary Moton graduation, I used *Educated in Spite Of . . .*

For background on the light of reconciliation, I interviewed Woodley. For Joy Cabarrus Speakes's response, I used my *Richmond Times-Dispatch* piece, "Prince Edward's Turning Point."

To write the section on Moton Museum as a healing place, I attended more than a dozen brown bag lunches. In 2013, I witnessed firsthand Everett Berryman's discussing why he had never wanted to tell his story before, and I heard Mickie Pride Carrington responding to him.

I also listened to a StoryCorps interview of Pride Carrington and Rebecca Butcher that did not air, and I relied on my own interviews with each of them. I also relied on interviews with Berryman.

For the section about my experience at Moton and with blacks who suggest I should forgive my grandfather, I relied on conversations with Lacy Ward Jr.'s wife, Ardeania Ward, and Elsie's nephews. I also conducted interviews with Marsh, Douglas, Griffin, and R. C. "Bob" Smith.

For the section on Sally Hemings, see Leef Smith, "Jeffersons Split over Hemings Descendants," *Washington Post* (May 17, 1999). To describe how whites blamed blacks for school closures, I used "Prince Edward under Attack," *Farmville Herald* (December 2, 1960).

For the section on Wall's influence, I relied on vanden Heuvel's "Closing Doors, Opening Doors." I also used "The 'Impossible' Prince Edward Case" in *The Moderates' Dilemma* and *They Closed Their Schools*.

I used an interview with Ayers to discuss why Virginians were in favor of segregation.

For the description of blame being spread around, I used *American Oracle: The Civil War in the Civil Rights Era* by David W. Blight (Cambridge: Belknap Press of Harvard University Press, 2011).

For the section on shame I turned to *I Thought It Was Just Me (But It Isn't): Making the Journey from "What Will People Think?" to "I Am Enough,"* by Brené Brown (New York: Gotham Books, 2007). I also listened to her TED talks, "The Power of Vulnerability" and "Listening to Shame" (http://www.ted.com/talks/brene_brown_on_vulnerability?; http://www.ted.com/talks/brene_brown_listening_to_shame?).

CHAPTER 21: THE NEW NORMAL

For the section about McDonald's, I had multiple informal conversations over coffee with a black man who grew up in Farmville, left when the schools closed, and returned decades later. He asked that his name not be used. During the summer I lived in Farmville, I routinely drank coffee in McDonald's and witnessed the dynamics between the white and the black regulars.

The section about Prince Edward County's having two school systems was based on an interview with the school board's chair, Russell Dove. To write about Eric Griffin's call for Fuqua to close, I used Jamie C. Ruff, "Fuqua School Remains Point of Contention in Prince Edward," *Richmond Times-Dispatch* (February 28, 2009). I also used "Prince Edward's Turning Point" and interviewed Woodley.

To write the section about mixed marriages and multiracial kids, I relied on census reports from 2010, as well as a Gallup poll about the acceptance of mixed-race marriages. See Susan Saulny, "Census Data Presents Rise in Multiracial Population of Youths," *New York Times* (March 24, 2011); Andrea Stone, "Multiracial American Population Grew Faster Than Single-Race Segment in 2010 Census," *Huffington Post* (September 27, 2012); William H. Frey, "Census Projects New 'Majority Minority' Tipping Points," Brookings Institution (December 13, 2012). I also used a story I wrote, "One Family, Many Shades," *Richmond Times-Dispatch* (May 8, 2011). I used an interview with Ken Woodley to describe how the *Farmville Herald* started running photographs of couples. A multiracial family was on the cover of the *Farmville Herald* on February 5, 2014.

The three conversations with my daughters about skin color occurred in 2013 and 2014.

To write about Obama's speech after the acquittal of George Zimmerman in the killing of Trayvon Martin, I used a transcript provided by the *Washington Post* (July 19, 2013).

EPILOGUE
I based the section about how Mimi and Elsie's relationship changed on interviews with Elsie, my mother and my aunt, Beverley Anne. Elsie and I flipped through her photo albums and talked in 2014.

Recommended Reading

All Deliberate Speed, Charles J. Ogletree Jr.
Arc of Justice, Kevin Boyle
The Big Bang, edited by Jonathan K. Stubbs
"Brown v. Board of Education": A Civil Rights Milestone and Its Troubled Legacy, James T. Patterson
Carry Me Home, Diane McWhorter
Common Ground, J. Anthony Lukas
Crusaders in the Courts, Jack Greenberg
Eyes on the Prize, Juan Williams
Freedom Riders, Raymond Arsenault
Freedom Summer, Bruce Watson
The Grace of Silence, Michele Norris
The Immortal Life of Henrietta Lacks, Rebecca Skloot
Israel on the Appomattox, Melvin Patrick Ely
Jim Crow's Children, Peter Irons
A Matter of Justice, David A. Nichols
Men We Reaped, Jesmyn Ward
The Moderates' Dilemma, edited by Matthew D. Lassiter and Andrew B. Lewis
Parting the Waters, Taylor Branch
The Race Beat, Gene Roberts and Hank Klibanoff
Simple Justice, Richard Kluger
Slavery by Another Name, Douglas A. Blackmon
Students on Strike, John A. Stokes with Lois Wolfe
Their Eyes Were Watching God, Zora Neale Hurston
There Goes My Everything, Jason Sokol
They Closed Their Schools, Bob Smith
Through My Eyes, Ruby Bridges
Thurgood Marshall, Juan Williams
Virginia's Massive Resistance, Benjamin Muse
The Warmth of Other Suns, Isabel Wilkerson

Index

About the author

About the book

Insights,
Interviews
& More . . .

Read on

Meet Kristen Green

KRISTEN GREEN has worked as a reporter for the *Boston Globe, San Diego Union-Tribune,* and *Richmond Times-Dispatch.* She holds a master's degree in public administration from the Harvard Kennedy School. This is her first book. She lives in Richmond, Virginia. ◠

About the author

A Q&A with Kristen Green

Do you consider Something Must Be Done About Prince Edward County *to be a memoir or a history book?*

It's really a hybrid. Historians can approach history with surgical detachment. I didn't have that luxury. I attended a private academy that my grandfather helped found specifically for white children. Our family's longtime housekeeper had to send her daughter out of state to get an education. I married a multiracial man, and we have multiracial children. Ultimately, the story felt too personal not to have aspects of the book be memoir.

Why did you decide to write this book?

After working for years as a journalist, I realized I had grown up in a town with this amazing, tragic history that I had never learned. I needed to explore the complex story of my hometown, the one that my classmates and I hadn't been taught at the segregated academy we attended. I also wanted to understand the role that my family played in that history.

What did you find most challenging about the project?

The time period I wanted to examine spanned more than sixty years, so I struggled to tell the entire story in ▶

A Q&A with Kristen Green *(continued)*

a succinct way. I knew that I absolutely needed to explain the school closure history, which started with the 1951 student walkout to protest the conditions of the county's black high school and ended when the public schools—shut by county leaders in 1959—were forced to reopen in 1964. I also wanted to talk in detail about the impact of that decision on the community today. This meant I had to cover a lot of ground.

I also found doing the interviews with people I had known most of my life to be challenging. I felt judged for rejecting the rationale behind the school closures and the founding of the private academy—and for taking on this project. Working on this book was at times incredibly isolating.

You write about discovering in 2008 that your grandfather had played a role in the school closures. How did it feel to learn this as an adult?

It was upsetting and confusing, especially since my grandparents were gone. Papa died while I was in college, and Mimi passed away in 2007. I would love to have talked to them about their choices and to understand their motivations. Mimi and Papa were engaged, doting grandparents who took my three brothers and me on vacations, planned cookouts and Easter egg hunts for us, and attended our basketball games and dance recitals. They were perfect in my young eyes. For a long time, it was very difficult for me to separate my love for Papa from the shame I felt about the stance he had taken on school integration. Revealing my family's hidden history of racism— America's family secret—felt like a betrayal. I wondered how I could be a devoted granddaughter, a good Southern girl, and reject the choices they made. I struggled with wanting to be loyal to Mimi and Papa yet needing to tell this story.

What was your reaction to learning the way your family's longtime housekeeper, Elsie Lancaster, was affected by the school closures?

It was heartbreaking. I was deeply saddened that Elsie had to send her only child away to get an education and that she never really got to be a mother to her daughter again. When she told me that my grandparents had failed to acknowledge that her daughter was living in Massachusetts, I was ashamed, too. I'm sorry for the pain and heartache the school closings caused Elsie's family and for the role my family played, and I'm grateful that Elsie felt comfortable sharing those stories with me.

What price have you paid for writing this book?

Many people in Prince Edward that I've known since I was a child do not accept the premise of the book or my ▶

findings. While my immediate family
has been supportive, the book's
publication has strained some close
family relationships, and that has been
painful for everyone involved. My
parents, who live in Farmville, have
been snubbed by some friends and
family members. The book's publication
has changed what home means for me.
I cannot overlook the harm done by
white leaders and the unwillingness of
some residents to acknowledge it.

Was there also some positive reaction to the book in Prince Edward County?

There are many Prince Edward residents
who have enthusiastically supported
the book and are grateful that I told
the story. The community's two colleges,
Longwood University and Hampden-
Sydney College, invited me to speak
to large audiences, and the book
has been taught in courses on both
campuses. Elsie Lancaster, our family's
longtime housekeeper, said people
regularly congratulate her on the book.
And one student featured in the book,
Charles Taylor, told me that seeing it
used as a teaching tool at universities
and schools was a dream come true.

What was a highlight of writing the book?

I developed profoundly meaningful
relationships with both white and
black residents of Prince Edward

whom I didn't know as a child. I was particularly touched by, and grateful for, the former students who invited me into their lives and shared some of their most personal, painful stories. I was saddened that I couldn't use every one of them in the book because all of their stories were moving and important.

What can be done to right the wrongs of the past in Prince Edward?

Nothing will make it right. Too much has been lost to recapture. The best way to honor those denied an education, and their families, is to create a more perfect community that gives everyone a fair chance at life. The county can show its remorse for the past by adequately funding public education today. County residents can demand more funds to hire innovative administrators who will make positive changes in the schools and can push for a publicly elected school board.

I think apologies help, too. Longwood University recently apologized for its leaders' failure to act when local officials closed the public schools rather than desegregate. What made the apology especially meaningful is that the university also partnered with the town's civil rights museum, Robert Russa Moton Museum. Those that have never admitted they were wrong for the role they played in the school closures—including *The Farmville Herald* and Fuqua School, the former segregationist academy—can issue apologies and ▶

A Q&A with Kristen Green (*continued*)

take steps to make amends. And people in the community can acknowledge the injustice and the damage it caused instead of being angry about the negative attention. That's where change has to start.

You refer to the Moton Museum as the future of the town. What makes it so important?

The museum, housed in the former black high school, is trying to tell the full story of the Prince Edward County school closures—not the black story, not the white story, but the whole community's story. The simple brick building, which explains the school closures through five exhibits, also provides residents a place to share their personal experiences in a setting where they will be accepted, not judged. It's a place where everyone can come together. It is not only sharing Prince Edward's story with visitors, it is filling a real void in the community.

You write that you were worried about moving back to the South with a multiracial family after living on the West Coast and in New England. What has the experience been like for you?

Richmond, Virginia, has proven to be a welcoming city, despite its own struggles to reconcile a history closely bound to the Civil War and to slavery. My girls go to a diverse public school, sharing classrooms with black, Latino, Asian, and multiracial students. But there is much work to be done. Not far from my house sits a monument to Robert E. Lee. The city has problems that mirror Prince Edward County's. It is still segregated in many ways, its school district is failing and underfunded, and the black residents are overwhelmingly poor.

Why didn't the school closings draw more attention nationally?

Virginia didn't have the violence that other Southern states experienced. While the school closings were certainly covered by the media, the glare of the national spotlight was not on Prince Edward but rather on people being beaten with billy clubs, attacked by police dogs, and sprayed with fire hoses in the Deep South. But the racism here was no less insidious. Virginia leaders were simply subtler in their attempts to deny equal rights to black Virginians. Closing the public schools may not have ended lives, but it profoundly changed them, stifling the hopes and dreams of generations of black residents.

How has writing Something Must Be Done About Prince Edward County changed your perception of race relations in this country?

My research showed me how far we still have to go. It's still extraordinarily difficult to have conversations about ▶

A Q&A with Kristen Green *(continued)*

race. We want to move on without the hard work, but true reconciliation is hard work. To a very large extent we haven't dealt with our complicated pasts of slavery and Jim Crow segregation. The wounds of repression are still close to the surface.

Why is it so hard to talk about our families' roles in past wrongs?

My identity was shaped, in part, by a happy childhood spent in a small town surrounded by family. It seems the South's legacy is valuing loyalty above all else. Uncomfortable topics are shelved rather than discussed. But as a journalist I want to shine a light on darkness, and I came to believe that my story is bigger than me. It is the story of our country's complicated and tragic racial history and the role whites played and continue to play. Talking about my struggles to come to terms with my town's past—and the shame I feel over my own family's role—can help move this country forward. It can contribute to a national discussion on race that has been so difficult to forge but is desperately needed. ᶜᵛ

Reading Group Guide
Discussion Questions for *Something Must Be Done About Prince Edward County*

1. What role did Elsie play in the author's life? Do you think that she ever felt that she was an equal member of the community, even after desegregation? There are many moments in the book when Elsie is silent. How do you interpret that silence?

2. Why do you think the county's white leaders criticized blacks for demanding integrated schools? What was at stake if the schools integrated? Why did so few whites speak out against the school closures?

3. How did you feel when residents of the town repeatedly expressed the sentiment that enough had already been said about Prince Edward's history?

4. Which of the black students' stories did you find most moving? What do you think are some of the lasting impacts of the school closures on them, their families, and the community?

5. The author is revealing some difficult things about her family's past. Do you think she is justified in bringing forth this information? ▶

Reading Group Guide *(continued)*

6. The author tells her story about growing up in a sheltered environment in Prince Edward County. What were the things that she learned about herself after she went away for college, and how did her experience working as a journalist help shape her new worldview? What do you think are the benefits of living outside of your comfort zone?

7. The author is thankful to be able to raise her multiracial children in a diverse community. Why is it important for her that her children know about what happened in her hometown?

8. How did you feel about the author's expression of shame and guilt for the role her town and family played in closing the schools? Why do you think she decided those feelings were important to wrestle with, especially in such a public way? Do you think any good can come from addressing them?

9. How has this story changed your perception of the history of desegregation, particularly school desegregation in the aftermath of *Brown v. Board of Education*?

10. The author writes about how her hometown, while more integrated today than it was historically, still seems divided. Is a truly racially integrated society possible in the United States?

11. It's clear why black Americans should care about this story, but why should white Americans?

12. How is the Prince Edward story related to other unpleasant truths in American history?

13. Schools in many ways are as separate and unequal today as they were sixty years ago. Why have we failed to integrate schools in this country and what can we do to make it better?

14. Discussions about the enduring nature of American racism are largely driven by blacks. Why aren't whites more engaged in this discussion? If they were, how might it benefit America?

15. When Robert T. Redd, the longtime headmaster of Prince Edward Academy, defends the actions of the proponents of school segregation, he says, "They made it on the basis of what they thought at that time was in the best interest of our country and our dearest possession—our children." Do you think that what is best for a community is shaped by the ideologies of the time, or is there always a clear distinction between what is right and wrong? ∽

"Perfectly Mixed"

Adapted from essays that ran on NPR's Code Switch *and* Racialicious.

WHEN *Something Must Be Done About Prince Edward County* was first published, a woman I didn't know approached me and told me she didn't appreciate my use of the term multiracial to refer to my husband.

"Is he black?" the white woman pointedly asked me. I responded that he was not. Empowered, she proceeded to give me unsolicited advice, firmly suggesting that I "just call him American Indian."

Many people felt it was perfectly acceptable to comment on the way I describe Jason and our children, who are a mix of American Indian and white. My mom, tired of hearing me use the term multiracial, told me to "just let Jason be Jason." One person felt my kids were "so light" their race wasn't worth mentioning in the book. Since Jason wasn't black, another wondered how his race and the race of our two daughters could be relevant to the story of my hometown.

The comments sting. People seem to think they have an understanding of Jason and the girls' lived experience, and they couldn't be more wrong.

The issue at stake is this: who gets to decide how people of color refer to themselves? For generations, whites have controlled these definitions of identity, stretching back to the one-drop rule, where anyone with a drop of "black blood"—once called "Negro blood"—was forced by law to identify as black. The rule was used to justify slavery and Jim Crow segregation. Historically, biracial children with one white parent and one black parent could not claim any identity other than black.

On the other hand, one drop of Indian blood has not made someone American Indian by federal definition. The government has methods for classifying American Indians. In some cases, if their blood is too "diluted," people of American Indian descent don't qualify for land allotments or tribal membership.

The government has utilized these definitions when it is convenient as a way of controlling people. Not that long ago mixed marriages were illegal in many states. The Supreme Court finally overthrew laws prohibiting interracial marriage in its landmark 1967 decision, *Loving v. Virginia*.

The population of multiracial Americans is now booming, and the American public will be forced to cede control of these definitions. The Pew Research Center found that in 2010, about 15 percent of new marriages in the United States were mixed. Over the next four decades, people of two or more races are expected to be the fastest growing population of Americans. This group of citizens will demand to define their identities themselves.

My husband doesn't have a cultural or tribal connection to his American Indian background. Yet his lived ▶

experience is that of a person of color; his identity is tied to how the world views him and treats him. People frequently ask, "What are you?" and aren't satisfied until he shares his racial background.

We know our two daughters will have similar experiences. Research shows that children can recognize differences in race as early as infancy, and can develop racial biases from the age of three. From the time they were toddlers, our girls have been holding their arms next to ours, comparing skin colors. They have searched for descriptive words—always landing on peach for me and variations of tan and brown for themselves. I love watching them explore this part of themselves.

Walking our neighborhood, visiting local parks, and hanging out at the swimming pool, I notice other people trying to figure out our family, too. One of the kids' classmates commented that my youngest daughter looks "nothing" like me. I want to help our daughters feel at home in a world that's still trying to figure out kids who look like them.

There is so much power in deciding how to identify oneself, and people of color rightly want to claim that power. When someone questions the way I choose to refer to my children, I think about how whites have clung to their position in society for so long. Perhaps people wonder why I would undermine the privilege associated with being white or why I would use a descriptive term like "mixed" that many still associate with its historical reference to miscegenation.

A relative suggested that I am placing a burden on my girls by referring to them as multiracial. What would she have me do instead, I wonder? Let them try to pass for white? Why shouldn't my girls proudly claim all that they are?

The definitions of mixed and multiracial no longer refer singularly to those who are a combination of white and black. The race mixing that was once considered shameful is now moving into mainstream acceptance. My husband and children are beautiful and loveable, perfect to me as they are: mixed. ✑